INDIGENOUS WOMEN AND VIOLENCE

INDIGENOUS WOMEN AND VIOLENCE

Feminist Activist Research in Heightened States of Injustice

EDITED BY

LYNN STEPHEN &
SHANNON SPEED

THE UNIVERSITY OF
ARIZONA PRESS
TUCSON

The University of Arizona Press
www.uapress.arizona.edu

ISBN-13: 978-0-8165-4262-8 (hardcover)
ISBN-13: 978-0-8165-3945-1 (paperback)

Cover design by Leigh McDonald
Typeset by Sara Thaxton in 10/14 Warnock Pro (text), Brandon Grotesque, and Iva WF (display)

Library of Congress Cataloging-in-Publication Data
Names: Stephen, Lynn, editor. | Speed, Shannon, 1964– editor.
Title: Indigenous women and violence : feminist activist research in heightened states of injustice /
    edited by Lynn Stephen and Shannon Speed.
Description: Tucson : University of Arizona Press, 2021. | Includes bibliographical references
    and index.
Identifiers: LCCN 2020036089 | ISBN 9780816542628 (hardcover) | ISBN 9780816539451
    (paperback)
Subjects: LCSH: Indigenous women—Violence against—United States. | Indigenous women—
    Violence against—Mexico. | Indigenous women—Violence against—Guatemala. | Indigenous
    women—Political activity—United States. | Indigenous women—Political activity—Mexico. |
    Indigenous women—Political activity—Guatemala.
Classification: LCC HV6250.4.W65 I5318 2021 | DDC 362.88/55082097—dc23
LC record available at https://lccn.loc.gov/2020036089

Printed in the United States of America
♾ This paper meets the requirements of ANSI/NISO Z39.48-1992 (Permanence of Paper).

CONTENTS

PREFACE

A ll the authors in this volume completed the revisions to their chapters from their homes, as we all hunkered down to wait out the global coronavirus pandemic. When we wrote our original introduction, we referred to violence against women as a global pandemic. We decided to take that out in light of the pandemic that framed the final steps in completing our book. It is time to put it back in. Today we write about the intertwined pandemics of gendered violence and coronavirus, as it becomes clear how inequalities of race, gender, ethnicity, place, and class converge to compound the vulnerabilities of so many in the pandemic and within the larger frame of settler logics. Right now, home may be the least safe place for many. The *New York Times* reports a sharp uptick in incidents of domestic violence globally, but Guatemala's *Con Criterio* reports a decrease (both articles date from April 6, 2020). Why? If the only people who are operating are police, will you report to them as an Indigenous[1] woman in Guatemala or elsewhere? If you are normally ignored because you speak an Indigenous language, why would you try to report violence in it? Who will come to help? And if you are confined to your home in a small village or an apartment in a large city, the people perpetuating violence and protecting those who do so may be even closer at hand to prevent and

---

1. By *Indigenous* we refer to people who are descendants of the original inhabitants of the Americas/Abiayala prior to European colonization.

punish you with impunity. In the United States, where immigration raids have been normalized by the U.S. government, who do you report to? In detention and on the border, men, women, and children are being shut out of health care, asylum, and basic necessities. States are complicit in these intersecting pandemics.

Embodied violences may be converging in intimate spaces, but at the same time solidarity is unfolding between relatives, neighbors, and friends. In the community of our co-authors and colleagues each and every one confronts these intertwined pandemics in her own way, up close, through distance caring and learning, with communication, and in an insistence that these twin pandemics cannot be normalized. In a spirit of solidarity and *lucha* (struggle), we put forward this book, needed now more than ever, as a way of illustrating the interconnections of our bodies, our activism, our research, and our collective resolve for change.

ACKNOWLEDGMENTS

W riting and knowledge production are always dialogic and collective endeavors, however much we labor alone at our computers. Our acknowledgments begin with the many Indigenous women whom we have worked with and learned from over the course of our careers and our lives. We are also profoundly grateful for the deep and sustained dialogue with the contributors to this volume over the course of more than two decades. One colleague and friend who has been an integral part of our group throughout the years but was unable to participate in this volume is Rachel Sieder. She has shaped our thinking in so many important ways, and her presence in the volume is real even in the absence of a chapter. Many other brilliant thinkers joined us for some of these dialogues, including, but not limited to, Maylei Blackwell, Elisa Cruz, Juan Herrera, Mercedes Pisoni, Renya Ramírez, Larisa Ortiz Quintero, Odilia Romero, and Maureen White Eagle, and we appreciate the insights they shared.

We have received significant support for our collaboration over the years, and we gratefully acknowledge a UC Mexus-CONACYT Collaborative Grant, a Faculty Initiative Grant from the Lozano Long Institute of Latin American Studies (LLILAS) at The University of Texas at Austin, a Ford-LASA Special Projects Grant, and a Radcliffe Institute for Advanced Study Seminar Grant through Harvard University. We are also fortunate to have research support from our institutions, the University of Oregon and the University of California, Los Angeles, which contributed to the preparation of this book.

We thank Annalise Gardella for copyediting assistance, and Sylvia Escárcega and Joseph Berra for translation assistance. Our appreciation also goes to Brandon Larsen, our mapmaker. We also thank Allyson Carter, our editor at University of Arizona Press, for her patience, support, and belief in this book project.

Our families have supported and sustained us throughout. Shannon has the great good fortune to be married to Joseph Berra, who provides her with lively intellectual engagement, practical daily support, and enduring love. She is also grateful for her talented and beautiful daughter, Camila de los Santos Speed; Camila's partner, Noah Coltrane Coombs; and her stepsons, Josue and Moses Berra. Lynn's marriage and decades-long relationship with Ellen Herman have provided her with daily support, ongoing love, intellectual encouragement, and nourishment of all kinds. Her two sons, José and Gabriel, have accompanied the journey of this book and grown into wonderful men with big hearts. She is so grateful to have them in her life. And she acknowledges her mother, Suzie, who has always supported and encouraged her, now in her daily life.

Finally, we are grateful to each other, for the gifts of collaboration, intellectual enrichment, mutual solidarity, and sustained friendship.

INDIGENOUS WOMEN AND VIOLENCE

INTRODUCTION

Indigenous Women and Violence

SHANNON SPEED AND LYNN STEPHEN

This volume explores Indigenous women's individual and collective struggles and those of their allies for justice and security in contexts framed by increasingly complex intersections of violence in the United States, Mexico, and Guatemala. The cases explored in each chapter illuminate how structural forms of settler power combine with recent juridical frameworks, security policies, and economic forces to structure current expressions of violence in Indigenous women's lives and the means they may use to resist them. A product of two decades of dialogue among the authors, the volume also reflects our shared efforts to understand the embodied experience of collaborative field research in contexts of violence.

As in much of the world, in the countries that are the focus of this book, gendered violence is widespread, virtually uncontrolled, and harmful to a huge swath of the population. For example, though Guatemala is a small nation, it has the fourth-highest femicide rate in the world: A woman is killed every twelve hours in Guatemala, and 7,272 femicides were recorded in the decade between November 2008 and November 2017 (Telesur 2017). In Mexico, 3,580 women were murdered in 2018 alone (Verza 2019). Indigenous women, because of the racial and gendered oppression that structures their lives, are rendered multiply vulnerable to such violence, yet they continually seek redress through the formal and informal venues that are available to them, whether at local, national, or international levels. However, the current context of erosion of collective and individual rights in these countries, combined with increasing forms of economic dispossession and the expanding role of security apparatuses, presents new challenges for Indigenous women seeking justice for intersectional violence. In short, the legal terrain for Indigenous women has been and is shifting, with a significant decrease in guarantees of collective and individual rights and potentially a decline in the available venues for legal redress.

Gendered violence has always been a part of the genocidal and assimilationist projects of settler colonialism. The racial and gender logics that underpinned Native dispossession, slavery, and successive waves of labor exploitation are structuring logics inherent to those systems. Today these structuring logics—and the forms of intersectional violence inherent to them—drive processes of criminalization and victimization of Indigenous men and women, leading to escalating levels of murder, incarceration, or transnational displacement of Indigenous people, and particularly affecting Indigenous women. In various ways, the projects discussed in this volume consider the ongoing colonial structures that generate and ideologically justify contemporary violences against Indigenous women in the Americas.

The volume brings together the ethnographic research of eight scholars who have dedicated significant parts of their careers to illuminating the ways in which Indigenous women have challenged communities, states, legal systems, and social movements to promote gender justice within a framework of collective rights. As individuals, we have also engaged our expertise in a wide range of social justice projects, acting as expert witnesses in international, national, and immigration court cases, serving as advisers to Indigenous movements and organizations, and questioning analytic frameworks that reduce Indigenous women to victims and survivors and position researchers as experts. We have learned the importance of speaking and listening in the different registers that are a part of legal processes (official testimony versus what is said in communities and shared with trusted family members), witnessed instances of violence that do not sort out neatly into perpetrators and victims, and observed how social justice is often achieved outside of formal legal systems—implying a broader understanding of "justice."

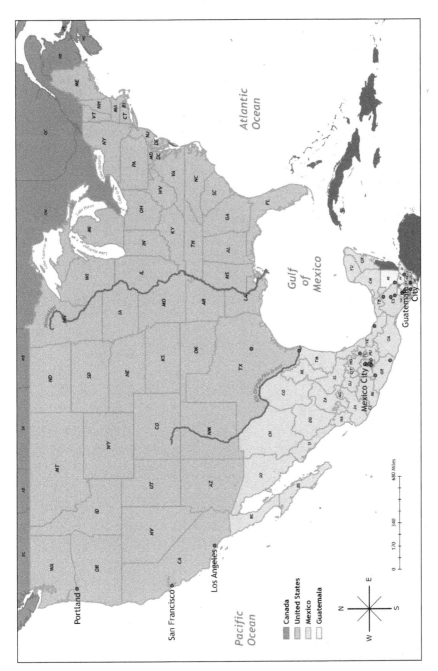

MAP 1. Locations mentioned in this book.

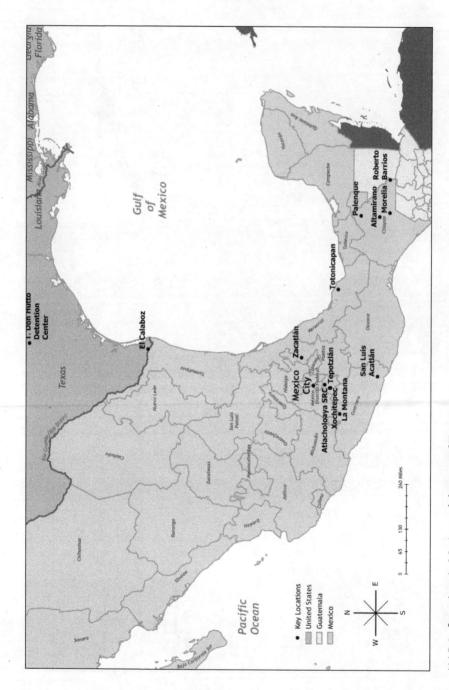

MAP 2. Locations in Mexico and the state of Texas.

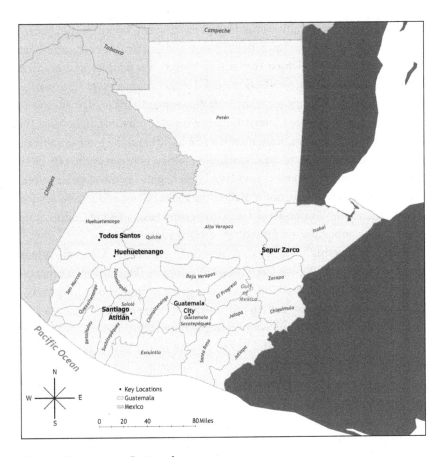

MAP 3. Locations in Guatemala.

Our Story: This Book and the Shifting Contexts of Gendered Violence

This book is about Indigenous women who survive violence, but the project did not begin that way. Rather, it began in 2008 with a group of scholars and lawyers, all activists working with Indigenous women, who came together in Tepoztlán, Morelos, to share experiences and analyses of women's strategies for gender justice in plurilegal contexts. In the two publications that emerged from that generative meeting (Speed et al. 2009; Blackwell et al. 2009), we discussed our efforts to create a shared intellectual and methodological framework for understanding women's rights and justice struggles across multiple nation-states and in particular across the U.S.-Mexico border. We considered how Indigenous women were engaging new opportunities generated through multiple avenues: the Mexican and Guatemalan constitutional reforms of the 1990s, which recognized Indigenous peoples and granted limited collective rights; new laws intended to increase access to state justice and new, nonstate (Indigenous customary law, or truth tribunal) justice venues; and recently emerged international venues for pursuing rights such as the Inter-American Commission on Human Rights and the Inter-American Court. We also considered how neoliberal multiculturalism in the U.S. context was contributing to increased tribal sovereignty, as the state devolved responsibility to Native peoples' well-being to the tribes, and to new justice spaces such as the Chickasaw Nation District and Peacemaking Courts, thus offering new opportunities for women seeking redress.

A second meeting took place in Mexico City in 2009. Maureen White Eagle, a prominent Ojibwe/Cree/Metis attorney working against domestic violence, attended this meeting, which was generative for the group's thinking on domestic violence, both in relationship to other forms of violence and as it pertains to Indigenous women throughout the Americas. Two years later, in 2011, we met in Austin, Texas, funded by the Teresa Lozano Long Institute of Latin American Studies at The University of Texas at Austin, with many of the same participants and a few new people. We discussed how the shifting of responsibilities to Indigenous communities under neoliberal multiculturalism and the slight opening to encourage women's participation in local systems of justice had permitted some women to become more active in alternative justice systems, but had also resulted in exclusions and backlash against them.

We next met in Tepoztlán, Mexico, in 2015, funded by a Ford-LASA Special Projects Grant. By this time, violence had seriously escalated in Mexico and Guatemala, and we were all feeling it in our community work and grappling with how to theorize it in our writing. The short-lived and partial gains for Indigenous women that came with the multicultural period had quickly receded as national political contexts in Mexico and Guatemala shifted, with national security becoming the dominant discourse and Indigenous and human rights increasingly being placed on a back burner. The discourse of multiculturalism had waned, and in both countries Indigenous people were increasingly being interpreted either as a politically destabilizing threat to national security or as impoverished sectors of society subject to megadevelopment projects and extractivist industries (Hernández Castillo and Speed

2012; Hernández Castillo 2013; Mora 2017). Military forces, national police, paramilitary organizations, and organized crime groups were competing for control of Indigenous territories. In response to these threats, some Indigenous communities have self-organized to protect their territories and resources. In others, national discourses criminalizing youth and hyping the threats of gangs and organized crime have resulted in the resurgence of local security committees that patrol, punish men, and discipline women (see chapters 3 and 5 in this volume). These combined dynamics are what Speed (2016) has characterized as "neoliberal multicriminalism," noting the ways these overlapping and interrelated dynamics exponentially increase the violence Indigenous women experience. Stephen (2019) has discussed similar phenomena in a transborder framework as gendered embodied structures of violence. She illustrates how historical and contemporary structures and processes of violence that normalize physical and sexual violence against Indigenous women (and often men and children) undermine efforts to strengthen Indigenous women's rights and provide access to safety and justice for them.

At our 2015 Tepoztlán meeting, finding ourselves under the shadow of cartel dominance and still managing the rage of the recent forced disappearances in Ayotzinapa of forty-three students (many Indigenous), we turned our collective attention much more directly to violence. We considered how the heightened role of state security apparatuses, increased economic precarity, and a shift of right-wing actors from the fringes to the center of political power have resulted in a dismantling of both collective and civil rights that affects not only expressions of racialized and gendered violence but also the way that Indigenous women seek redress and experience justice struggles (Brunnegger and Faulk 2016; Hernández Castillo 2016; Sieder 2019). We also pondered how the act of seeking security from multiple forms of violence has involved internal displacement or escape across international borders, in turn making women subject to new forms of violence (Speed 2016; Stephen 2019). Our discussions, perhaps inevitably, turned to the deep experiences of pain, trauma, empathy, and fear that are necessarily implicated in the type of work we do, as well as the way that each of us copes (or not) with the oftentimes conflicting emotional imprints this work leaves in us as activist and collaborative scholars. It was in Tepoztlán that we first began to discuss this volume and the possibility of sharing our ethnographic understandings, but also our profoundly personal reflections as engaged feminist scholars,

Indigenous and non-Indigenous, working with Indigenous women in contexts of violence.

The following year, we came together again, this time at an invited seminar at the Radcliffe Institute for Advanced Studies at Harvard University. There, we began a more concerted discussion of the colonial context, exploring how the permanent structures of nation-states that are engaged in ongoing occupation of Indigenous lands might illuminate how rights gained can so quickly vanish and why ongoing racialized and gendered violence is so endemic in our countries. We also discussed the ethical tensions involved in representations of violence and in the direct advocacy work in which we were engaged.[1] From there, we set out to draft these chapters, about our feminist engagements with Indigenous women across settler-imposed borders, the violences they face, and the forms of resistance they enact.

In short, this volume represents ten years of collective discussion and dialogic knowledge production. It reflects our efforts toward shared frameworks for understanding issues of violence and gendered justice for Indigenous women across settler-imposed borders, and our conversations about the ethical and emotional aspects of our work.

Racialized Gendered Violence Through Time: Logics of Colonialisms and Settler States

The racialized gendered violence that Indigenous women are subject to is a product of the colonial formations of the modern nation-state. The European colonial project brought and imposed racial and gender tropes of the uncivilized, savage, and thus disappearing Indigenous woman (Stoler 1995; Morgensen 2010). Shari M. Huhndorf and Cheryl Suzack (2010, 1) highlight the violent nature of those impositions: "For Indigenous women, colonization has involved their removal from positions of power, the replacement of traditional gender roles with Western patriarchal practices, the exertion of colonial control over Indigenous communities, through the management of women's bodies, and sexual violence." The gendered violence of colonization

---

1. Our discussions at the Radcliffe Institute were greatly enriched by the facilitation and comments of Kimberly Theidon, the Henry J. Leir Professor of International Humanitarian Studies at Tufts University; and John Willshire Carrerra, the co-managing director of the Harvard Immigration and Refugee Clinic at Greater Boston Legal Services and a senior clinical instructor at Harvard Law School.

was constitutive of the modern settler state, and the state is structured on that violence, at once generating it and normalizing it.

Thus, gendered violence has always been a part of the genocidal and assimilationist projects of settler colonialism. Writing of the contemporary settler state, Audra Simpson (2016, 10) argues that "Indian women 'disappear' because they have been deemed killable, rapeable, expendable. Their bodies have historically been rendered less valuable because of what they are taken to represent: land, reproduction, Indigenous kinship and governance, an alternative to heteropatriarchal and Victorian rules of descent." Settler ideologies of gender and race that construct Indigenous women as the inevitable subjects of sexual violence and control continue to undergird the ongoing occupation and dispossession of Native peoples of the Americas. Today these structuring logics—and the forms of intersectional violence inherent to them—drive processes of criminalization and victimization of Indigenous women, leading to escalating levels of murder, incarceration, and transnational displacement. Authors in this volume engage with theories of internal colonialism and settler colonialism in an effort to understand the ongoing nature of Indigenous occupation and dispossession, the racialized violence that maintains colonial forms of power, and the specific effects on Indigenous women. For example, R. Aída Hernández Castillo examines contemporary processes of state criminalization of Indigenous peoples as an aspect of the continuity of colonialism (chapter 2), while Irma A. Velásquez Nimatuj finds mass-scale sexual violence deployed against Indigenous women during the Guatemalan Civil War to be "an extension of the colonial relationships of dependence and exploitation" (chapter 4), and Mariana Mora highlights the permanence of colonial relations between Indigenous peoples and the Mexican state as expressed through the continual occupation of their territories through diverse means (chapter 6). Morna Macleod highlights the convergence of ideas under the terms *internal colonialism* and *settler colonialism* (the former more associated with theorizing south of the U.S.-Mexico border, the latter in the North) in her chapter 7 examination of the ethical tribunals in Guatemala. Margo Tamez considers how Ndé women have repeatedly stood up against the predations of the settler state, most recently in the fight against Indigenous dispossession in the context of Homeland Security's construction of the U.S.-Mexico border wall (chapter 8). Lynn Stephen and Shannon Speed both adopt a settler-colonial analytic for understanding the multiple violences that cause Indigenous women to migrate and that affect them in migration (chapters 1 and 5). An understanding of race and gender as logics of the settler state, and settler states as structures of ongoing colonial occupation, helps shed light on racialized gendered violence and explain its enduring nature in the lives of Indigenous women.

Spaces and Strategies of Gendered Justice: From Institutional to Autonomous

The historical structures mentioned above result in a state of legal pluralism for Indigenous women: they have access to justice in more than one legal order, and these orders have differing and sometimes opposing normative values (Merry 1988). The different arenas in which Indigenous women have attempted to access justice offer important context for the women's varied struggles and strategies for achieving that justice. Indigenous women often engage with multiple legal orders that are "superimposed, interpenetrated, and mixed," creating spaces of interlegality (see Santos 1987, 297–98). The cases discussed here often take place in official and alternative spaces of justice simultaneously.

The legal institutions with which the chapters engage include international spaces such as the Inter-American Court of Human Rights (Corte Interamericana de Derechos Humanos, Corte IDH), which was created in 1979 and is based in Costa Rica. The Inter-American Court of Human Rights is supposed to serve as an autonomous judicial system alongside the Inter-American Commission on Human Rights (IACHR) as the human rights protection system of the Organization of American States (OAS). The OAS is a regional political organization that includes all thirty-five independent states in the Americas. Founded in 1948 and becoming operational in 1951, the OAS "constitutes the main political, juridical, and social governmental forum in the hemisphere" (OAS 2019). The Inter-American Court rules on whether member states have violated individual or collective human rights, resolves contentious cases, supervises sentences, consults, and issues provisional measures (Corte Interamericana 2019, 3). States that recognize the court include Argentina, Barbados, Bolivia, Brazil, Chile, Colombia, Costa Rica, Ecuador, El Salvador, Guatemala, Haiti, Honduras, Mexico, Nicaragua, Panama, Paraguay, Peru, the Dominican Republic, Surinam, and Uruguay. The IACHR is also an autonomous organ of the OAS. Its office is in Washington, D.C. When human rights and civil rights cases are unsuccessful in national courts, people can turn to the IACHR to attempt to access justice. Such is the case, as described in chapter 8 by Margo Tamez, of Ndé women's outspoken rejection of the U.S. border wall construction on their traditional homelands.

Indigenous women also find themselves on the other side of administration of justice processes. For example, as Hernández Castillo describes in chapter 2, thousands of Indigenous women have been subjected to prosecution through state criminal justice systems and now reside in Mexico's penitentiary centers. Although official statistics tend to obscure indigeneity, calculating Indigenous women as only 5 percent of the total female prison population, Indigenous women account for 43 percent of those women serving sentences in Mexican prisons for drug-related crimes. In the United States, Indigenous women refugees from Central America or other places who have no knowledge of the possibility of asylum or the need to request a credible fear hearing can remain in detention for significant periods of time. They may be put into deportation proceedings and mass courtroom hearings of up to seventy people at a time through a policy that began in 2005 called Operation Streamline. In this process, those caught in the act of crossing the U.S. border without authorization can be detained and made subject to criminal prosecution. The first time someone is caught crossing without authorization, they can be charged with misdemeanor illegal entry and sentenced to up to six months in prison. If a person has been officially deported and is caught reentering the United States without authorization, they can be charged with felony reentry and sentenced to two years in prison. Indigenous refugee women are thus criminalized in this process and detained. Indigenous women are multiply subject to the logics of the carceral state.

As detailed in Speed's chapter on Indigenous women detained in the Hutto Residential Center and Stephen's chapter on Guatemalan Indigenous refugees seeking asylum (chapters 1 and 5, respectively), U.S. policies and practices that criminalize undocumented immigrants have particular embodied and long-term impacts on women's lives, as does the practice of racially profiling and criminalizing Indigenous women in Mexico through the "war on drugs." In the case described by Hernández Castillo, women have worked to remake the prisons they live in and transform them into spaces of autonomous justice-seeking, knowledge production, and empowerment that in some cases can result in the liberation of women from state carceral institutions. For Indigenous women caught in the U.S. detention system, liberation requires external legal support through lawyers, expert witnesses, and networks of kin that can help them get asylum and pay bail. Without these resources—which a majority of women lack—they may be detained for long periods of time or released into uncertainty.

Indigenous refugee women such as those described by Speed and Stephen have the right to seek asylum on U.S. soil. Asylum can be granted to an applicant in the United States if the applicant can demonstrate that he or she has been persecuted in the past or has a well-founded fear of persecution in his or her country of origin on one of five grounds: (1) membership in a particular social group, (2) religion, (3) race, (4) nationality, or (5) political opinion. Asylum permits those receiving it to apply for legal permanent residence and ultimately citizenship as well as to receive work authorization. The United States is bound to recognize valid claims for asylum under the United Nations' 1951 Convention Relating to the Status of Refugees and its 1967 Protocol Relating to the Status of Refugees. While international law grants refugees the right to seek asylum, they must access that right through U.S. immigration courts, which are under the jurisdiction of the attorney general of the United States.

In an unprecedented campaign to shut off avenues for asylum seekers, the U.S. government now offers prison to families who petition for asylum. This latest step follows other efforts to limit access to asylum. In 2016, U.S. Customs and Border Protection (CBP) officers along the U.S.-Mexico border began preventing asylum seekers from making claims in U.S. territory and, at points of entry along the border, they turned the asylum seekers back to Mexico. In January 2019, the Trump administration announced the Migrant Protection Protocols, popularly known as "Remain in Mexico," whereby from ten to thirty people who have been waiting in Mexico for the opportunity to request asylum are escorted into the United States, given an interview, and then returned to Mexico. The program was initiated at the San Ysidro Port of Entry in San Diego. Begun with single men, it now includes families with young children. As of March 2020, approximately sixty thousand people were waiting in various ports of entry in Mexico to be called for their interview, often in dangerous circumstances. That month, the COVID-19 pandemic hit U.S.-Mexico border regions, and the United States closed access to the border for non-U.S. citizens and residents. On March 21, 2020, the U.S. government disallowed anyone seeking asylum to enter the country

(Ahmed, Jordan, and Semple 2020). These measures have been particularly hard on Indigenous women refugees from Mexico and Central America, who often do not speak Spanish or English and do not understand explanations and instructions offered. This same problem plagues those who are already in detention awaiting an asylum hearing. Nevertheless, women persist and often help one another with translation, support, and connections inside and outside of detention.

For Indigenous women who remain in Guatemala, as described in other chapters included here, specialized national courts have been the site of their engagement with state systems of justice. Importantly, the 1996 peace accords of Guatemala and the Indigenous and women's social movements that accompanied the process of the peace accords were crucial in pushing for reformation of the justice system. As detailed by Macleod and Velásquez Nimatuj (chapters 7 and 4, respectively), earlier efforts to bring attention to the genocide and sexual violence of the Guatemalan Civil War—efforts undertaken through the IACHR, national and international tribunals, and long-term commitments by NGOs and women's organizations—were key to the process of judicial reforms. It is impossible to disentangle the establishment of specialized courts and the designation of judges focused on "high-risk" cases from the social movements that fought for them. For example, in 2008, Guatemala passed a landmark law against femicide and other forms of violence against women. This law criminalized a range of acts of violence against women in both public and private spheres and called for a number of measures to increase women's access to systems of justice, including the creation of specialized courts in 2010 to adjudicate cases of violence against women. These courts include psychologists, social workers, and daycare facilities, and all workers are trained in gender analysis and in strategies to avoid revictimizing survivors of gendered violence. This law, however is the result of a decades-long effort by a variety of women's organizations and some key legislators to establish the legal code and the courts that back it up. Further, even with the establishment and functioning of these courts, political maneuvers to under-resource them and the institutions that are supposed to support them can make them unable to function as they should. In addition, because such courts are located in departmental capitals, they are very difficult for Indigenous women to access due to distance, language barriers, poverty, and lack of information or effective accompaniment (see chapter 5).

Along with formal judicial reform in Guatemala, which resulted in specialized courts for gendered violence, the establishment of ethical tribunals in relation to genocide and human rights atrocities in Madrid in 1983—and then again in Guatemala almost thirty years later, there focused on sexual violence—highlights the importance of these forums as antecedents for more formal trials of perpetrators of sexual slavery and violence, such as the Sepur Zarco case (2011–16; see chapter 4). As Macleod describes in chapter 7, while the 1983 Permanent Peoples' Tribunal resulted in no mention of sexual violence against women despite repeated reference to rape, the year 2010 saw the establishment of the First Tribunal of Consciousness Against Sexual Violence Toward Women. This latter tribunal was organized by several women's organizations: the National Union of Guatemalan Women (UNAMG), Community Studies and Psychosocial Action (ECAP), Women Transforming the World (MTM), National Coordination of Widows of Guatemala (CONAVIGUA), and a feminist newspaper. These women's organizations and the tribunal itself were deliberate building blocks for the case of Sepur Zarco. The 2010 tribunal also built on strategies of social and psychological processes of accompaniment, which had been a part of the case of Juana Méndez, a monolingual K'iche' woman who was raped in police custody in 2005. In this context, accompaniment refers to an intensive process of working with women to prepare them for a legal process. It can involve psychological support, legal education, and intense listening and interaction. Three years after her rape, a policeman was sentenced to twenty years in prison for the crime. Those who brought the case forward pushed to have her rape acknowledged as a violation not only of individual rights but also of her rights as a member of an Indigenous pueblo (see Sieder 2019, 46–53). The strategy of accompaniment from this trial and also from the 2010 tribunal informed preparations for the Sepur Zarco case, in which fifteen Q'eqchi' women went to Guatemala's highest court in search of justice for crimes against humanity on counts of rape, murder, and slavery, and in pursuit of collective reparations for their community.

One critical way in which intersectional justice in the context of Indigenous communities differs from understandings of justice in modernist legal systems is that violence is seen as a collective harm, not as an isolated event or pattern of isolated events that happened to one individual. Outside of Indigenous contexts, even specialized courts for gendered violence treat violence as a problem to be resolved by convicting an individual perpetrator of a crime, sentencing that individual to prison time, and thus helping an individual victim receive justice and protection. In contrast, the Sepur Zarco trial resulted in not only the sentencing of two military officials to hundreds of years in prison, but also eighteen reparation measures for the women survivors and their community. "The court sentence promised to reopen the files on land claims, set up a health center, improve the infrastructure for the primary school and open a new secondary school, as well as offer scholarships for women and children" (UN Women 2018). In chapter 4, Velásquez Nimatuj makes clear that the crimes of Sepur Zarco—which included rape, sexual atrocities, sexual servitude, and involuntary detention—occurred in a larger context that included the torture, death, and disappearances of the women's husbands; the burning of property; and the destruction of crops and animals. The crimes of Sepur Zarco were crimes committed against an entire community by a state that permitted and encouraged such widespread acts of extreme violence and collective repression. The fifteen Q'eqchi' women survivors who brought the suit forward sought collective justice and reparations. It remains to be seen how many of the eighteen collective reparations can be achieved, with regularization of the community land claims being the most difficult and contentious item to resolve.

While the women survivors of Sepur Zarco brought their vision of collective rights to a state tribunal and were constrained by the legal structures of that tribunal in their search for justice, the Indigenous justice systems discussed in this book are conceptualized on the granting of reparative justice and the recognition of collective rights. In addition, through the cases of women justice promoters of the Coordinadora Regional de Autoridades Comunitarias (CRAC-PC, Regional Council of Community Authorities) and the Zapatista women who frame gendered violence as an attack on an entire community (see chapters 3 and 6), we can see how collective reparations are connected to social reintegration. Hernández Castillo also points to the importance of alternatives to the punitive models of justice that dominate Mexico's penal system and that are applied to Indigenous women.

However, systems of reeducation and reparative justice that are run according to autonomous Indigenous community legal norms can also sometimes backfire for Indigenous women. The CRAC-PC, as detailed by María Teresa Sierra here and elsewhere (see chapter 3 and Sierra 2017), operates on a model of reeducation and collective labor that is supposed to benefit the community by generating consciousness in the lawbreakers about their errors and restoring damaged communities. Sentences vary from a few weeks to eight years of community labor for crimes ranging from simple theft to murder. But the CRAC-PC model does not always work. In the municipality of San Luis Acatlán, the CRAC-PC released a man who had been accused of rape of a minor girl. Working within the structure of the CRAC-PC, women affiliated with the Casa de la Mujer Indígena (CAMI, Indigenous Women's Center) protested, on the basis that there was more than sufficient evidence of the rape. The women received threats and felt a withdrawal of protection from the CRAC-PC (see Fundar 2015). In this instance, these women—and Sierra in her description of this event and her work with CAMI—trod a fine line between supporting autonomous Indigenous structures of justice and pushing them to take seriously gendered violence. The ability for all women to maintain control of and respect for the integrity and health of their bodies must be understood as a collective right.

Collaboration, Connections, and Embodied Research

The authors of this book identify their research as engaged, feminist, collaborative, and activist. A beginning point for the invocation of these words is a refusal to bifurcate subjective and objective points of view. This refusal entails discarding the possibility of one truth or version of events and working with a consciousness about the ongoing historical and embodied structures of settler colonialism. These structures situate us as researchers just as they do the Indigenous women with whom we work. Three of us are Indigenous researchers, two of us are white researchers, and three of us are Latinx/Mestiza women. For each of us, our own history, experience, and positioning are part of how we do our research and how we relate to the Indigenous women with whom we work.

Across our differences, each of us works from the standpoint of allyship. All the projects documented here involve some shared strategic, political, and emotional stakes with our interlocutors. Hernández Castillo writes from her experience working on a variety of life history, poetry, publishing, and artistic projects with Indigenous women in Mexican prisons. Speed writes about her work visiting, listening to, and documenting the stories of Indigenous women incarcerated in the Hutto Residential Center in Texas. Sierra analyzes her experience working with Indigenous women who promote autonomous forms of justice and uphold women's collective rights to be free from violence and be respected and included in their communities. Velásquez Nimatuj documents her many-year experience with the trial of Sepur Zarco, both accompanying the fifteen Q'eqchi' women and serving as an expert witness. Stephen documents her experiences serving as an expert witness for Mam refugee women seeking asylum in the United States. Mora describes her accompaniment of Zapatista women who use the theme of gendered violence to build bridges with urban women and students in Mexico City. Macleod documents her decades of work in Guatemala with the Guatemalan Human Rights Commission and other organizations. Tamez describes her struggle to help defend Ndé people's land on the U.S.-Mexico border from U.S. government occupation and destruction. All the authors describe alliances, accompaniment, and engagement with other women. They are also deeply embedded in ongoing human and emotional relationships that are part and parcel of the research projects and products.

Writing about violence and representing struggles for justice and against violence can be challenging undertakings, and many of us have wrestled with questions of whether and how the stories we carry should be told. Many authors grapple with how much of their interlocutors' stories they should share, not wanting to sensationalize violence. At the same time, some women with whom we have worked want to share their stories so that others can learn from them and so that their struggles will be validated. There is thus an ongoing tension and double edge to every story that is shared.

In approaching the volume, we drew on Indigenous feminist writings about the value of Indigenous women's experience and its telling as both a political act and a valid form of theorization (Archuleta 2006). In the late 1980s and early 1990s, Indigenous women writers began to emphasize the significance of Native women's stories for shedding light on larger sociopolitical and historical dynamics (Brant 1995; Bird 1997; and see Burgos-Debray and Menchú Tum 1983, which also reflects this trend). In the influential essay "Felt Theory," Dian Million (2009, 54) extends this argument. She demonstrates how First Nations women in Canada, "by insisting on the inclusion of our lived experience, rich with emotional knowledges," reframed what could be known and talked about in relation to the collective experience of boarding schools. Like Mishuana Goeman (2013, 14) in *Mark My Words*, we sought to tell Indigenous women's experience "through an intersectional approach . . . choosing a feminist method of analysis that presents us with a multiple grounded 'telling' of violence and its impact on the structural, political, and representational lives of Native peoples and their communities."

Like Goeman, we were acutely aware that Indigenous women's experience of violence—and their struggle against it—is collectively lived. While formal judicial institutions, police, NGOs, and other actors who work in state-linked institutions are often trained to see violence as composed of discrete events enacted by one person against another, in the lives of Indigenous women, gendered violence often is not separate from other forms of racial, ethnic, economic, and physical violence; it is experienced as interconnected and mutually constituted. Thus, "violence against women" is not necessarily experienced or understood as such but is signaled in other registers. It may be embedded in and normalized as part of a wide range of relationships and places, from kinship and marital relations to everyday existence for Indigenous people who are seen as "out of place."

Women's resistance to interrelated violences is often expressed in ways that may be outside of how we are accustomed to seeing movements for social justice or conceptualizing resistance. To tell a story, speak up, request asylum, or ask to be heard can be seen as a revolutionary act when women do it in a context where they are supposed to be silent and are punished for asserting their presence and voice—whether in prison, with police, in community gatherings, or elsewhere. In order to represent the ways in which women assert themselves as individual and collective social actors, we must look outside of customary windows on social movements. Spending years preparing to speak in court as the women from Sepur Zarco did, resisting the construction of a wall on the U.S.-Mexico border by holding firm to small pieces of land and suing the U.S. government, or organizing a writing group and the production of books in prison are struggles for justice. These other registers of action are important contributions in the chapters that follow. Artistic and creative engagement has been an important part of numerous projects, used to channel different forms of participation and knowledge production, and to promote emotional and physical healing. Hernández Castillo describes the intimate process of collecting life histories and poetry, which then find new life as hand-produced books and in radio shows and public performances and engagements. Macleod describes the importance of healing approaches that involve herbs, energy work, and attention to the heart, mind, body, and spirit in workshops with Maya women focused on trauma and sexual violence.

A number of us comment on our own embodied histories and experiences of fieldwork, which have affected our engagement with and analysis of the topic of gendered violence. Speed and Stephen describe feelings of intense frustration, anger, and immobility as they work with detained and asylum-seeking women in a political context that has grown ever more hostile to immigrants and asylum seekers. These feelings translated in some cases into physical aches and pains requiring direct interventions such as increased exercise, yoga, meditation, and other forms of healing. Making connections between our own embodied experiences and secondary trauma with what we witnessed in the women pushed our analysis further. Macleod, Velásquez Nimatuj, Stephen, Hernández Castillo, and Mora all discuss the links between sexual violence on individual bodies and strategies of territorial control. The interlinked physical, spiritual, social, emotional, and structural nature of gendered violence is a common epistemological standpoint for most authors here. In this sense, a deliberate intersectional, embodied, and emotional engagement with gendered violence is for many of us directly reflected in our findings, in our strategies of knowledge production, and in the ways we describe our "findings" on the page.

One question we might ask is whether and how the ethnographic work we describe here is qualitatively different from what might be termed "regular" ethnography. Engaged feminist ethnography does share some characteristics of what we would call attentive ethnography. Being an excellent listener and stepping back and allowing our interlocutors' ideas and interpretations to come to the fore are practices consistent with most life history interviewing techniques. Using poetry and creative arts as strategies of participation might also be considered among a range of collaborative ethnographic techniques of engagement that have included photography, drawing, mapping exercises, and walking tours that embed history in geography (see Hale and Stephen 2013). Where the ethnography described here departs from "regular" anthropological work is perhaps best found in the kinds of relationships we have worked to build with our interlocutors and also with the unique kind of knowledge we have produced. We have made our political commitments central, and our social commitments to these women are explicit in the work. While not wanting to engage in self-focused "autoethnography," we have tried to connect our embodied and emotional experiences of research with our analytic framework and specific findings.

Connecting our embodied and emotional experiences of researching accumulated gendered violences through time also results in tensions on the page and important questions of representation. Many of us have struggled with how much of the women's stories to share, depending on their desire for how their life histories are told. But we are also conscious of the possibilities for producing texts that sensationalize and promote a kind of voyeuristic optic of violence, as is often seen in media accounts of sexual violence, femicide, and other forms of gendered violence. The challenges of representation also extend to the kind of academic publishing conventions that can act as straitjackets on our writing. Here, we have sought through various means to refuse the straitjacket and tell the women's stories and our own in the hope that they will find emotional resonance and provide intellectual insight for our readers.

Conclusions

In sum, this volume represents a collection of analyses of the violence experienced by Indigenous women in the United States, Mexico, and Central America, and the women's forms of contestation against this violence. It emerges from a shared dialogue among the contributors and brings together a number of different literatures, but most fundamentally it is a shared call to deepen collaborative ethnographies through engagement with research as embodied experience; a shared effort at understanding the interrelated nature of structural, extreme, and everyday violences across time and space; and a collective treatise demanding that violence against Indigenous women be understood as a central dimension of colonial power.

Producing embodied knowledges about the different historical and contemporary forms of gendered violence and the multiple strategies and venues that Indigenous women exploit to combat that violence has been a slow-cooking but very rich experience for each of us. Sharing this information collectively through time in different countries, languages, and locations has tied us together, perhaps like a collection of intensely colored pieces of cloth waving together on a common clothesline. By highlighting the details of our engagement, and the emotional and social impact of our research, we hope to peel back a layer of the modernist academic onion to reveal not just the humanity and connection that results from our work but also the tensions, difficulties, and challenges we face. Dialoguing about our research and experiences has enriched each of us and our writing—and we hope, as a whole, that this work will provide inspiration and insight for others who might want to engage in similar kinds of research.

Our analyses, and our lives, have been shaped by the Indigenous women with whom we have worked. Their intersectional experiences of violence and their powerful efforts to refuse that violence in the context of settler processes and settler structures speak volumes about contemporary forms of power in the world. It is our hope that this collection conveys their crucial message to the reader.

References

Ahmed, Azam, Miriam Jordan, and Kirk Semple. 2020. "A Closed Border, Dashed Hopes and a Looming Disaster." *New York Times*, March 21, 2020. https://www.nytimes.com/2020/03/21/world/americas/coronavirus-mexico-border-migrants.html.

Archuleta, Elizabeth. 2006. "'I Give You Back': Indigenous Women Writing to Survive." *Studies in American Indian Literatures* 18 (4): 88–114.

Bird, Gloria. 1997. "Breaking the Silence: Writing as 'Witness.'" In *Speaking for the Generations: Native Writers on Writing*, edited by Simon J. Ortiz, 63–74. Tucson: University of Arizona Press.

Blackwell, Maylei, Rosalva Aída Hernández Castillo, Juan Herrera, Morna Macleod, Maria Teresa Sierra, and Shannon Speed. 2009. "Cruces de Fronteras, identidades indígenas, género, y justicia en las Américas." *Desacatos* 31:13–34.

Brant, Beth. 1995. *Writing as Witness: Essay and Talk*. Toronto: Three O'Clock Press.

Brunnegger, Sandra, and Karen Ann Faulk, eds. 2016. *A Sense of Justice: Legal Knowledge and Lived Experience in Latin America*. Stanford, Calif.: Stanford University Press.

Burgos-Debray, Elisabeth, and Rigoberta Menchú Tum. 1983. *Me llamo Rigoberta Menchú y así me nació la conciencia*. Barcelona: Editorial Argos Vergara.

Corte Interamericana de Derechos Humanos. 2019. *ABC de la Corte Interamericana de Derechos Humanos: El qué, cómo, cuándo, dónde y porqué de la Corte Interamericana. Preguntas frecuentes*. San José, Costa Rica: Corte IDH. http://www.corteidh.or.cr/tablas/abccorte/abc/.

Fundar. 2015. "Agresión a la Casa de Salud de la Mujer Indígena de San Luis Acatlán." *Fundar*. October 16, 2015. http://fundar.org.mx/acoso-a-las-companeras-de-la-casa-de-la-mujer-indigena/.

Goeman, Mishuana. 2013. *Mark My Words: Native Women Mapping Out Nations*. Minneapolis: University of Minnesota Press.

Hale, Charles R., and Lynn Stephen, eds. 2013. *Otros Saberes: Collaborative Research on Indigenous and Afro-Descendant Cultural Politics*. Santa Fe, N.Mex.: School for Advanced Research Press.

Hernández Castillo, Rosalva Aída. 2013. "¿Del Estado multicultural al Estado penal? Mujeres indígenas presas y criminalización de la pobreza en México." In *Justicias indígenas y Estado: Violencias contemporáneas*, edited by María Teresa Sierra, Rosalva Aída Hernández Castillo, and Rachel Sieder, 299–338. Mexico City: CIESAS/FLACSO.

Hernández Castillo, Rosalva Aída. 2016. *Multiple InJustices: Indigenous Women, Law, and Political Struggle in Latin America*. Tucson: University of Arizona Press.

Hernández Castillo, Rosalva Aída, and Shannon Speed. 2012. "Mujeres Indígenas presas en México y Estados Unidos: Un desafío hemisférico para los estudios indígenas." *LASA Forum* 43 (1): 17–20.

Huhndorf, Shari M., and Cheryl Suzack. 2010. "Indigenous Feminism: Theorizing the Issues." In *Indigenous Women and Feminism: Politics, Activism, Culture*, edited by Cheryl Suzack, Shari M. Huhndorf, Jeanne Perreault, and Jean Barman, 1–17. Vancouver: University of British Columbia Press.

Merry, Sally Engle. 1988. "Legal Pluralism." *Law and Society* 22 (5): 869–96.

Million, Dian. 2009. "Felt Theory: An Indigenous Feminist Approach to Affect and History." *Wicazo Sa Review* 24 (2): 53–76.

Mora, Mariana. 2017. *Kuxlejal Politics: Indigenous Autonomy, Race, and Decolonizing Research in Zapatista Communities*. Austin: University of Texas Press.

Morgensen, Scott Lauria. 2010. "Settler Homonationalism: Theorizing Settler Colonialism Within Queer Modernities." *GLQ: A Journal of Lesbian and Gay Studies* 16 (1–2): 105–31.

Organization of American States (OAS). 2019. "Who We Are." http://www.oas.org/en/about/who_we_are.asp.

Santos, Boaventura de Sousa. 1987. "Law: A Map of Misreading: Towards a Postmodern Conception of Law." *Law and Society* 14 (3): 279–302.

Sieder, Rachel. 2019. *Acceso a la justicia para las mujeres indígenas en Guatemala: Casos paradigmáticos, estragegias de judicialización y jurisprudencia emergente*. Guatemala City: Serviprensa. http://www.radiotemblor.org/wp-content/uploads/2019/05/Acceso-a-la-justicia-para-las-mujeres-ind%C3%ADgenas.pdf.

Sierra, María Teresa. 2017. "Indigenous Autonomies and Gender Justice: Women Dispute Security and Rights in Guerrero México." In *Demanding Justice and Security: Indigenous Women and Legal Pluralities in Latin America*, edited by Rachel Sieder, 97–119. New Brunswick, N.J.: Rutgers University Press.

Simpson, Audra. 2016. "The State Is a Man: Theresa Spence, Loretta Saunders and the Gender of Settler Sovereignty." *Theory and Event* 19 (4). https://www.muse.jhu.edu/article/633280.

Speed, Shannon. 2016. "States of Violence: Indigenous Women Migrants in the Era of Neoliberal Multicriminalism." *Critique of Anthropology* 36 (3): 280–301.

Speed, Shannon, Maylei Blackwell, Aída Hernández, Teresa Sierra, Morna Macleod, Renya Ramírez, Rachel Sieder, and Juan Herrera. 2009. "Remapping Gender, Justice, and Rights in the Indigenous Americas: Towards a Comparative Analysis and

Collaborative Methodology." *Journal of Latin American and Caribbean Anthropology* 14 (2): 300–331.

Stephen, Lynn. 2019. "Fleeing Rural Violence: Mam Women Seeking Gendered Justice in Guatemala and the U.S." *Journal of Peasant Studies* 46 (2): 229–57. https://doi.org/10.1080/03066150.2018.1534836.

Stoler, Ann Laura. 1995. *Race and the Education of Desire: Foucault's History of Sexuality and the Colonial Order of Things.* Durham, N.C.: Duke University Press.

Telesur. 2017. "At Least 62 Women Killed Every Month in Guatemala: Report." November 3, 2017. https://www.telesurenglish.net/news/At-Least-62-Women-Killed-Every-Month-in-Guatemala-Report-20171103-0028.html.

UN Women. 2018. "Sepur Zarco Case: The Guatemalan Women Who Rose for Justice in a War-Torn Nation." October 19, 2018. http://www.unwomen.org/en/news/stories/2018/10/feature-sepur-zarco-case.

Verza, Maria. 2019. "Mexico Acknowledges Failure on Gender Violence, Unveils Plan." Associated Press, March 6, 2019. https://www.apnews.com/9ddd80f4fc5c44fea5e3f09b9f978b1c.

CHAPTER 1

Grief and an Indigenous Feminist's Rage

The Embodied Field of Knowledge Production

SHANNON SPEED

> Our written words betray our screams, which are neither audible nor appro-
> priate in the academy. Confronting violence not just as individual survivors,
> but as knowledge producers, enhances our collective struggle.
>
> —Maya J. Berry, Claudia Chávez Argüelles, Shanya Cordis, Sarah Ihmoud,
> and Elizabeth Velásquez Estrada, "Toward a Fugitive Anthropology"

T*he bright sun made me squint as I exited the detention center, eyes
unaccustomed to the daylight. Heat waves wafted up over the black
asphalt as I set out across the lot. My car's interior, having sat locked
up tight for the last several hours with all of my portable possessions inside,
gave off a convectional blast of heat as I opened the door. Leaving the door
ajar, I started the engine and cranked the air conditioning to max. Cold air
rushed mercifully toward me. I was briefly grateful to Volvo. I quickly reached
for my laptop, tucked under the passenger seat, and began typing: "Gloria
left home in June, not July. The boat trip was to avoid crossing the border
by land—unclear where boat departed or landed, where they were when the
engine died." I stopped momentarily and looked out the front windshield at the
graffitied train stopped dead on the tracks across from the detention center.
You couldn't see past it to the small, economically depressed town on the other
side. I returned to my work, noting, "The rape took place after the boat, but
before the train." I racked my brain for other details from our conversation,
other clarifications or adjustments to the story I was piecing together, smug-
gled out of the detention center in my brain.*[1]

I had been visiting the T. Don Hutto Residential Facility for more than two
years with the Hutto Visitation Program (a project of the organization Grass-

---

1. Some portions of this article are excerpted from my 2019 volume *Incarcerated Stories:
Indigenous Women Migrants and Violence in the Settler-Capitalist State.*

roots Leadership), in which volunteers worked to accompany the detained women and monitor the human rights situation inside the infamous facility. A former medium-security prison run by the private prison administrator Corrections Corporation of America (now CoreCivic), "Hutto" had formerly housed women and children, making it a symbol of increased immigration policing. After a 2007 lawsuit against the Department of Homeland Security ended family detention there, the facility had been the subject of two federal investigations into sexual abuse against women detainees, and one guard had been convicted on multiple counts of sexual assault. It needed monitoring.

My activist involvement morphed into a research project after a short time. The stories of the women I visited gave rise to this project as we sat for long hours in the sterile space of the visitation room, talking about their lives and how they had come to be caged there. Their stories were stories of violence. Multiple forms of violence, interconnected and interwoven. Often, I was astounded that they had survived at all. Almost always, their emotional trauma was palpable. Their stories spoke so lucidly, so directly to the structural violence of settler-occupied lands and capitalist depravations, to the interlocking gender and racial ideologies to which they are multiply subject. The anthropologist in me knew I had to write down these stories. And this was no small challenge, given that writing implements, indeed anything other than the clothes on one's back, were prohibited in the visitation room. So I memorized what I could, scribbling it down or typing it out in the parking lot of the detention center, asking questions to fill holes in my memory or their narrative on succeeding visits. This led me to the title of the book that would emerge from the research, *Incarcerated Stories*.

I pull out of the lot and past the tractor sales lot, onto the highway and the farm road that will take me from Taylor, Texas, back to Austin. As the Volvo rolled through the countryside, I felt the familiar feeling of unease that always accompanied me home from the detention center: anxiety, anger, pain, and sadness all welled up together in a physical reaction of vague nausea and clenched muscles. It was a feeling I knew intimately, personally. It was the feeling of trauma.

The Map We Aren't Given

More than thirty years ago, in "Grief and a Headhunter's Rage," Renato Rosaldo (1984) shocked the anthropological world by writing about—and indeed theorizing from—his personal grief and mourning at the loss of his wife, feminist anthropologist Michelle Rosaldo, in a tragic accident while she was conducting field research among the Ilongot peoples of the Philippines. Rosaldo argued that until he had experienced intense personal grief, and the rage born of it, he could not fully comprehend what his Ilongot collaborators told him about the relationship between headhunting, grief, and rage. Only through lived personal pain was he able to reach the insights that would allow him to comprehend the practices he was seeing and hearing about in his field research. What was radical about Rosaldo's argument, Ruth Behar (2012, 207) would later argue, was not his revelation of emotion in a field still dominated by the idea of positivist objectivity, but rather his argument that "he had gained a level of intellectual depth and understanding [of his field research] by drawing upon the force of emotions he'd experienced as a result of his profound grief." Indeed, in her moving homage to Rosaldo, Behar waxed poetic:

> Renato gave us a new map. It was a map of our postcolonial, nostalgia-saturated world. And it was a map of our haunted global souls. A map, too, of a different kind of academy, where diversity and inclusiveness might become real living truths and not mere slogans. An academy where our hearts didn't have to be checked at the gate as if they were a danger to institutions of higher learning. (205)

As Behar's hopeful reading indicates, such a map held the promise of charting how we might retain our humanity as part of our knowledge production, and through this, change our disciplines and the academy.

However, most of us do not get handed that map in graduate school. Nor are we encouraged to pick it up and consult it as we move through the course of our academic careers. While Behar, writing in 2012, enthusiastically suggested that "emotion, social commitment, political engagement—all the things classical anthropology taught us to suppress—are now the bedrock of our discipline as a result of Renato's work" (210), I see little evidence of the bedrock. Activist and committed collaborative work remain marginalized in the discipline, and emotion as part of researcher subjectivity and analysis even more so. Despite several decades of anthropological reflexivity—and some problematic forays into autoethnographic folly—we still do not often raise our profound and difficult emotions and give consideration to how they shape our understandings of what we encounter "in the field."[2] In this chapter, I reflect on my experience doing fieldwork with Indigenous women migrants incarcerated in the immigration detention centers of Central Texas. I offer a personal account of some aspects of field research, particularly feminist activist research, that are rarely discussed, much less openly brought into our analysis. Most importantly, I discuss the embodied experience of field research and its implications for the knowledge we produce, following on the critique of Maya J. Berry and colleagues (2017, 537) that "paradoxically, while activist research narrates the experiences of violence enacted on racialized, gendered (queer and gender nonconforming) bodies, the complexities of doing anthropology with those same bodies have tended to be erased in the politics of the research." Berry and her colleagues focus on how race, class, and gender shape research and possibilize gendered violence in the field. Here, I want to consider how intersectional violence of race, class, and gender experienced in another place and time—and irreversibly seared on our bodies and our psyches—also travels with us into the field.

When I was twelve, I was kidnapped by a stranger off a busy Los Angeles boulevard in broad daylight. My captor raped and otherwise brutalized me over the course of several hours, eventually tossing me out, mostly naked and bleeding, from his moving vehicle on the access road of what was then a relatively remote freeway north of the city. After hiding in the bushes until I felt sure he would not return, I wandered in a daze toward the only light other than those of the cars rushing by on the freeway: a car sales agency. It must have been near closing time, and I remember the startled look on the faces of the sales agents when I walked through the sliding electric doors into the harsh light of the agency. They brought me a blanket and called the police, standing about awkwardly until they came. The police drove me to the hospital, where they bandaged me up and administered a rape kit. No one talked to me. My mother picked me up from the hospital. On the approximately one-and-a-half-hour ride home, she did not talk to me. When I got home, I showered

---

2. A strong field of anthropology of emotion exists (see Lutz and White 1986 for an early review of the growing field, and see Beatty 2019 for a recent example of the genre). However, this work is about how to anthropologically understand the emotions of others, not about how the emotion of the anthropologist affects their understanding. Similarly, the lively field of affect theory intersects with emotion, seeking to understand how people engage with the world through subjectively experienced feelings, but it does not consider how those subjective feelings shape the knowledge produced. See, for example, Gregg and Seigworth (2010).

and went to bed. In a state of shock, I didn't feel pain, only embarrassment and a vague nausea I would come to know well. Not then, nor in the days and months that followed, did anyone—with the exception of police questioning and eventually trial testimony—talk with me about what had happened. I rather effectively, as humans will when the survival requires it, shut my feelings off entirely. When I felt anything, it was shame and guilt.

The Map We Are Given

It was in college that I began to first unravel and make sense of my own experience. Through studying literature, political science, and ethnic and women's studies, I encountered theory and began to formulate an understanding of the place of violence and oppression within the structures of state and capitalist power—what I would many years later understand as settler-capitalist power. It was academics that gave me the ability to relate the gendered violence that I had experienced to other violences and forms of oppression. Eventually, my feeling of embarrassment and guilt would change to something more akin to grief and rage. I began to direct my somewhat unfocused punk rock rebelliousness toward political action, and as I moved on to graduate school, activist scholarship became my passion—studying structures of power and oppression, while actively working to resist them through collaborative knowledge production. It felt at once socially productive and personally cathartic. Though my analysis of power has evolved over the years, not much else has changed. I still find theories of power and oppression to be a lifeline, tying my own experience and those of the people with whom I work to larger forces such as capitalism and patriarchy. Once rendered visible and understood, those forces can be better opposed and resisted. While this assertion undoubtedly sounds simplistic or even facile, I raise it make a point: although we aren't given Rosaldo's map of an academy where our hearts do not have to be checked at the gate, institutions of higher learning do—or can—give us a different kind of map. That map involves theory that allows us to understand our own and others' oppression in the context of larger frames of power, and, if we are lucky, it opens the possibility of collaborative, activist research methods, which have been my map and compass in the academy and outside of it for much of my life.

What I mean by *activist research* perhaps bears some discussion. In the past, I have argued for the value of research that combines critical analysis with an overt commitment to our research participants. This research must be directed toward shared social justice goals in a way that is doubly accountable, not just to furthering our theoretical understanding of social dynamics but also to advancing concrete objectives in the lives of those with whom we work. I have argued that this kind of research is ethically warranted, but also that, through the types of engagements it engenders, it produces better knowledge (Speed 2006, 2008). That is, for me, the activist engagements around pressing political issues has led to an understanding of the lives and cultures of those with whom I was working, an understanding that traditional ethnographic research simply could not have provided. It does so, importantly, by putting Indigenous knowledges on an equal footing with academic ones, creating a shared knowledge production (the "co-labor" in collaborative work) that at least attempts to address the unequal and generally colonial relations of power that inhere in most researcher/researched relationships (Leyva Solano and Speed 2008).

This attention to the power relations between researcher and "research subject" (an unfortunate, long-used term that encompasses precisely the colonial nature of the relationship, in which Indigenous peoples are subjects of the sovereign researcher) has been a hallmark of collaborative and activist research, which itself has a long trajectory in the Americas.[3] This focus also intersects with feminist scholarship, which calls on us to situate ourselves in relation to our research and our research subjects, while also debunking the myth of scientific authority (see Haraway 1988; Harding 1986). Indigenous scholars from Vine Deloria Jr. (1969) to the present have also called for attention to power relations in knowledge production, and particularly the "complex ways in which the pursuit of knowledge is deeply embedded in the multiple layers of imperial and colonial practices" (Smith 1996, 2). Without a doubt, attention to the forms of power that inhere in field research contexts is crucial to any effort toward a less colonized anthropology. However, as Berry and her colleagues (2017, 539) suggest, the focus on the researcher's power and privilege relative to the people encountered often unwittingly reinforces the presumption of a white male body entering the field, and it has left us blind to the ways in which power—and indeed

3. A review of this literature is beyond the scope of this chapter. See, for example, Freire (1970), "The Declaration of Barbados" (1973); Fals-Borda (1986, 1987), Gordon (1991), Greenwood and Levin (1998), Hale (2006a, 2006b, 2008), Kirsch (2006, 2017), Lassiter (2005), Perry (2013), Sanford and Angel-Ajani (2006), Stephen (2013, 2015), and Stuesse (2016).

violence—may be enacted by those same subjects we align our politics with in field research contexts: "Paradoxically, while activist research narrates experiences of violence enacted upon racialized, gendered (queer) bodies [of research subjects], the complexities of those same bodies doing anthropology have tended to be erased." In contrast, by drawing on ethnographic accounts of their own experiences of gendered violence in the field, activist researchers can make a powerful intervention in our understanding of the embodied experience of power and violence in field research.

Although my principal interest in this chapter is not violence in the field, but rather the ways we bring past violences to the field with us, my analysis coincides with that of Berry and colleagues (2017, 558), who assert that "centering the body in the stakes of activist research advances the path toward the project of decolonizing anthropology." Like them, I advocate for "a critical feminist activist anthropology that holds us politically accountable to our interlocutors as well as to our own embodied reality, as part of the same liberatory struggle." Acknowledging our embodied experience of field research, including the emotional and affective aspects of that embodiment, is crucial not only because it gives us a less partial view of power relations, but also because, as Rosaldo asserted long ago, it may make for more profound understandings of the lives and experiences of those we collaborate with in the field and write about in our work.

I sat with Estrella in the cold, awkward space of the visitation room in the T. Don Hutto immigration detention facility. Her jeans, provided by the facility, were folded over five or six times above her bright orange crocs, accommodated to her four-foot-eleven-inch stature. I forced myself to look back into her tear-filled eyes, which reflected fear and embarrassment as she recounted her uncle's brutal beatings and repeated rapes. "I'm so sorry that happened to you," I said. "You didn't deserve to have that happen." These were words I had learned to say, over the course of a life, to friends and even acquaintances, to my sister, my students, as they struggled to live through their own violent sexual assaults. I said them over and over to the Indigenous migrant women I met inside and outside immigration detention facilities in Texas. I said them over and over, trying to fill the vast space left when they were not said to me. The words sounded stilted, even contrived. But I knew how much they would have meant to me. As Estrella talked, tears rolled down her face and an occasional sob escaped. It was not until I felt a sob shake my own body that I realized I, too, had been crying. Later in the car, I pondered. Had

I been crying for Estrella's pain or for my own? I decided it was out of grief and rage for us all.

This was not an activist research project in the sense that I had known and elaborated them in the past. Former projects, like the one I carried out with the Zapatista community of Nicolás Ruiz in Chiapas, Mexico, a decade earlier, were conceived as aligning with an organized group in struggle on some shared or overlapping political goals. The Zapatistas and I shared goals: fighting for Indigenous autonomy and increased gender justice for Indigenous women, and challenging the settler state and capitalist power. Further, their highly organized movement made dialogic interaction relatively straightforward. The project had its challenges, tensions, and contradictions, of course, but its structure and politics were always clear. Working with Indigenous women migrants was quite different. They were not, obviously, an organized movement. I did work in alignment with advocacy organizations, and I have the highest respect for the incredible work of Grassroots Leadership, Texans United for Families, and the Hutto Visitation Program. But the people I was writing about were not the people I was aligned with in the organizations, and the possibility of dialogic collaboration was extremely low. I spoke to the women when I could, in detention and after detention. Many left the area after being released, and follow-up was impossible. In short, this was a very different kind of engagement, and it made an accountability to the community much more complicated. I asked members of the advocacy organizations to read and give feedback on the work. I got extensive feedback from the women with whom I was able to stay in touch. With the organizations, I shared the goals of accompanying and advocating for the women who are in the immigration system, especially in detention. We also, most of us, shared the goal of ending immigration detention altogether. But what were the women's goals? They organized hunger strikes for better conditions in detention and for an end to prolonged detentions, goals I shared. Yet in this project, a book based on the oral histories of their lives and their experiences of violence, what were our goals? Without a doubt, to a one, *the women wanted to tell their stories, and they wanted them to be heard.*

As a Native feminist, I wrestled considerably with the question of telling these stories, and I have written about this struggle elsewhere (Speed 2017, 2019). There was plenty to wrestle with. Could I tell these stories—particularly from the colonial field of anthropology—without recolonizing the women involved? Could I tell them without engaging in or facilitating a sort of pornography of violence? Could I tell them in such a way that it conveyed the horror of gendered violence, without construing Indigenous women as eternal victims? Would telling their painful stories bring us any closer to social justice goals? Or, were all these questions just a way of look-ing for an out, a way to ethically avoid having to actually write *Incarcerated Stories*? After all, it was not an easy book to write. Less so, given the per-sonal trauma it regularly triggered for me. Was I a masochist? With the book completed, I still cannot answer these questions. It will be up to readers to decide, and I suspect their opinions will vary. But in the end, I did write the book, because the women wanted their stories told. And the world needs to hear them.

Indigenous feminist scholars have emphasized that telling stories facil-itates an understanding of broader sociopolitical and historical dynamics. Two decades ago, Native scholars such as Beth Brant (1995) and Gloria Bird (1997) argued that telling Indigenous women's stories through writing was an act of witnessing, and they suggested that these stories are by their very nature political and contestatory to the colonial structures and legacies that silence Indigenous voices and render our collective experience invisible. Likewise, a decade later, Dian Million (2009, 54) made the case in her article "Felt Theory" that by centering their "lived experience, rich with emotional knowledges, of what pain and grief and hope meant or mean," First Nations women in Canada reframed what could be known and talked about in rela-tion to the collective experience of boarding schools in the country. Million thus showed that the emotional knowledge born of Indigenous women's experience had a lot to tell us about the larger social dynamics within which they are enmeshed. More recently, Mishuana Goeman (2013, 14) argued for taking Indigenous women's stories (in literary form) seriously, as "a multiple grounded 'telling' of violence and its impact on the structural, political, and representational lives of Native peoples and their communities." In other words, telling Indigenous women's stories is important because they make visible the social processes of colonization, and they do so from a distinct ideological perspective. Thus, telling women's stories, and bearing witness to their pain and grief, matters because it brings alternative knowledges, "felt theory," to the fore, contesting dominant discourses and laying bare often-invisible structures of power. In the book, this is my argument for why I chose to tell the stories, and it is true. But something else, a "felt theory" born of my own experience, gave the matter a certain urgency: I understood the profound importance of telling one's story and having it heard. I wrote to contextualize that hearing in an analysis of the violent structures of the settler-capitalist state for Indigenous women, but at some fundamental emotional level, I just knew that the stories needed to be heard.

The following is a vignette that opens the concluding chapter of the book: *The evening news broadcast captured the horror: small children, ripped from their parents' arms and cast into tent cities along the border or spread throughout the country in various prisonlike facilities. The children did not know where their parents were, or whether they would ever see them again. Their parents suffered the same torture. This broadcast was focused on the reunification of Guatemalan mother Buena Ventura Martín-Godinez with her seven-year-old daughter, Janne. I watched from my now entrenched position on the living-room couch, where I had spent countless hours over the year and a half since Trump's election watching the news as the United States, already enmeshed in illegality (I had argued), descended into open repudiation of any intention to remain a law-abiding state. At the front line of this widespread and open flaunting of domestic and international law were women and children refugees. I stared at the television, battling to subdue the now familiar blend of rage and grief, as the heart-wrenching scene unfolded. Janne stands still, arms around her mother's waist, not smiling. She has a glazed look on her face. In the back of my mind, I considered whether one ever recovers from such a trauma, especially one so young. Janne had been in a detention center for sixty-one days. The reporter noted that while thousands of children were separated from their parents during the spring of 2018 based on the Trump administration's "zero tolerance" policy, which explicitly used family separation as a deterrent to further refugee migration, and despite the order of a federal judge in California, such reunifications had been "few and far between." The reporter closed by adding, "This girl does not have Spanish as a first language. She is an Indigenous child from Guatemala, which no doubt increased her fear and isolation" (CNN News, July 1, 2018). Angrily brushing aside my tears, I growled uselessly at the television, "Exactly as they intended."*

In the vignette, I was trying to capture my profound rage—one I know many people shared—at the unconscionable policy and practice of family separation, disproportionately affecting Indigenous migrant families. My rage was further fed by the June 2018 policy directive issued by Attorney General Jeff Sessions that—in violation of international law—overruled the precedent-setting 2014 case that established domestic violence as a possible ground for asylum, (see chapter 5 in this volume). In the same sweeping directive, Sessions eliminated gang violence as a criterion. All I could think of was that all the women I had talked with, all the women in my book—virtually all of whom were fleeing violence and seeking political asylum—would eventually lose their cases and be deported, sent back, along with thousands of others, to certain violence and potential death. My rage was like a living thing that I carried around with me, unsure where to place it or how to live with it. Then came family separation, the cruel deaths of Indigenous children in the custody of the state, and echoes of the "stolen generations," the decades of the late nineteenth and early twentieth centuries in which Indigenous children in the United States, Canada, and Australia were torn from their families and sent to boarding schools to be forced into assimilation, or adopted into white families for the same purpose under the guise of protecting their "welfare" (Archuleta, Child, and Lomawaima 2000; Jacobs 2009; Milloy and McCallum 1999). Many people were outraged by these cruel and horrific practices, of course. My anger was fueled by the emotional connection I felt. As I had cried with Estrella (and many other women), mourning our collective vulnerability to violence, I felt the pain generated by these policies in a way that was at once intensely personal and also shared. All of it fueled my resolve to theorize from their experience, and to highlight the continuities of patriarchal and racial violence in the settler-capitalist state.

Grief, Rage, and Embodied Knowledge Production

What Indigenous feminists like Million are talking about is embodied knowledge. I want to suggest that, just as our activist engagements inform and bring greater depth to our knowledge production, so too do our embodied knowledges. These knowledges include—but are not limited to—trauma, grief, and rage. Having intimate knowledge of the experience of violence shaped how I understood both what my research collaborators experienced, and what I made of it—the knowledge I produced. Just as Rosaldo (1984) could better understand a headhunter's rage, so I could better understand the experience of gendered violence of the women I met, having experienced gendered violence myself. Thus, raising one's personal experience of violence, grief, or rage to the work is about more than just the question of positionality in research relationships, it opens the potential for a more profound human understanding of the kind that Rosaldo was evoking in his controversial work. As he would later assert in *Culture and Truth*, "The process of knowing involves the whole self" (Rosaldo 1993, 181). Similarly, Dorinne K. Kondo (1986) examined her emotions as a Japanese American woman conducting field research in Japan, particularly the fear, and ultimately knowledge, generated by a "collapse of identity" in the field. She argued for, "open[ing] anthropological understanding to a more explicit recognition of the various modes of knowing that are part of what we do as ethnographers. We must recognize that our emotions and sympathies are inevitably implicated in our foreunderstandings. These too can be legitimately productive of knowledge" (85). These foreunderstandings are what we bring with us into the field. Kondo ultimately argued that "in terms of anthropological interpretation, a recognition of the role of experience, [of] power, and of the involvement of the entire self, cognitive and emotive, in all that we do implies that context is, so to speak, of the essence. . . . [It] may lead us to other, relatively unexplored pathways to knowledge" (86).

Of course, some folks will always argue that the ethnographer's emotion is too subjective, directing thinly veiled ridicule at ethnographers who venture to discuss their own emotional experience in relation to fieldwork. As Million (2009, 64) argued, "Academia serves as a gatekeeper, challenging alternative forms of knowing. Because the emotional knowledge of our [Indigenous women's] experience is an alternative truth, it is challenged ferociously."

One vocal challenger has been anthropologist Andrew Beatty (2010, 2019). In his oddly titled article "How Did It Feel For You?," Beatty (2010, 430, 440) directly contests Rosaldo, arguing that "confessional accounts" are "unreliable" and "deeply problematic." He claims, quite remarkably, that "the anthropologist's emotions in the field are mostly to do with the trials of fieldwork: they do not (with rare exceptions) illuminate the predicaments of our hosts." Beatty's argument hinges on the incommensurable nature of individual personal experience—Rosaldo's rage is not the same as the Ilongots' rage—and thus he writes, "If personal experience is useful in understanding others, its usefulness surely depends on relevance, closeness of fit; and relevance, in turn, depends on the historical particularities" (432). Beatty finally dispenses with emotions altogether:

> however we choose to write about the field, our remembered feelings don't matter for the written account in the way they mattered at the time. They

had practical consequences for . . . forming us as fieldworkers. . . . But they were often irrelevant to what we wanted to know. And they are colored by our later, more mature judgments. Indeed, we can't write truthfully about the field until we can leave those feelings behind. (440)

Beatty's argument represents many of the implicit biases that anthropologists and others hold, the same biases that underpin the often ferocious gatekeeping that Million flagged. First, Beatty's assertions are ethnocentric. He departs from a very Western notion that all experiences and all feelings are individual. He goes on to presume that each individual experience is fundamentally incommensurable: "Rosaldo's personal story linking his own grief with rage does not convincingly translate to the Ilongot because their experiences are too different" (433). In other words, if their experiences and emotions are not fundamentally equivalent, Rosaldo's can have no meaning in his understanding of the Ilongots. Nor would my experience as a survivor of gendered violence have any bearing on my understanding of the gendered violence experienced by the women with whom I worked: our experiences, after all, were not equivalent. Needless to say, Beatty rejects the possibility of collective experience or emotional knowledge of the kind that Million suggests First Nations women in Canada might have. Further, his construction of the anthropological field reifies antiquated, masculinist ideas about "the field" as a place that is elsewhere, a site that the anthropologist penetrates and withdraws from, and within which all emotion is a product of that particular "other" space and anthropological labor. One does not bring any emotions with them to the field, and Beatty clearly instructs that any emotions felt there should remain there, as they cannot be useful to our ethnographic description later.

Perhaps the most problematic aspect of Beatty's argument is that it assumes that such a thing as leaving our emotions in the field is possible, that we can simply check our emotions at the door when landing (presumably) in the space of the Other that is the field, and then do the same at departure, dropping off any new emotions that might have arisen. This notion would seem silly if not for the lurking positivism (despite Beatty's recourse to narrative rather than objectivity as the solution). That is, if we can suspend the emotional knowledge born of our experience, do we then suspend the other aspects of our subjectivity? Our race? Our gender? Our sexuality? If not, why is it reasonable to draw on these aspects of our subjectivities, but not our emotional knowledge? Are all these things not part of our emotional knowledge? Of course, the matter is that we cannot suspend any of these at any time. They will all influence the knowledge we produce. To assert otherwise is to pretend that there is some objectivity outside of human subjectivity that we can access in our ethnography. We all draw on our emotional knowledge, indeed "our whole selves," as Kondo and Rosaldo both argued. In bringing an Indigenous/feminist of color lens to activist research, Berry and her colleagues (2017, 540), call for the same, asking us to "envision avenues for social transformation while recentering our physical, mental, and spiritual bodies in our methodological and epistemological toolkits." Indeed, they have been in our toolkits all along, because they are us.

In conclusion, my experience researching and writing a book about the multiple ways Indigenous women are subject to violence supports what Indigenous feminists have been arguing for some time: that emotional knowledge born of lived experience is a fundamental part of knowledge production. Just as I would argue of our political commitments (and the two overlap, of course), rather than attempting to somehow excise our emotion from our scholarship, we should acknowledge it as part of our process and engage it as an essential aspect of how we know what we know. Despite the current hegemony of scientistic ideas, not all knowledge comes from observation. Much of what we know about the world we know because we feel it. We cannot, and should not even if we could, check our feelings at the door when we enter graduate school, when we enter the field, or when we sit down at the computer to think and write. This does not mean that we should all just write about our feelings, of course, but rather that we must actively engage our feelings to take into account the role they play in shaping our understandings of the world. Because of our particular positionality as Indigenous feminist anthropologists—concerned with the workings of power in the world and the way that it bears down on our lives—we often research and write about social processes that make us grieve and make us angry. Rather than putting energy into pretending we do not feel this way (as academia so often asks us to do), let's put that energy to the task of building knowledge that can be used to change those very dynamics.

As a final note, I want to acknowledge both the personal pain, grief, and rage produced by working on issues of outrageous injustice and violence, which the experiences of the authors in this volume reflect, and also the potential healing aspects of tackling these issues head on. For many activist scholars, including the authors in this volume, *not* engaging these issues is far more dehumanizing and alienating than confronting them. For us, ignoring the collective pain wrought by the current levels of violence is not an option we could live with. For me personally, while working with women directly affected by gender and sexual violence was in many ways retraumatizing, grappling with their experience and theorizing the larger structures of power that permit—indeed guarantee—gendered violence was also one more step in what I consider to be a lifelong process of healing. For this, I am profoundly grateful to the women who shared their painful stories with me.

References

Archuleta, Margaret, Brenda J. Child, and K. T. Lomawaima, eds. 2000. *Away from Home: American Indian Boarding School Experiences, 1879–2000*. Phoenix, Ariz.: Heard Museum.

Beatty, Andrew. 2010. "How Did It Feel for You? Emotion, Narrative, and the Limits of Ethnography." *American Anthropologist* 112 (3): 430–43.

Beatty, Andrew. 2019. *Emotional Worlds: Beyond an Anthropology of Emotion*. Cambridge: Cambridge University Press.

Behar, Ruth. 2012. "What Renato Rosaldo Gave Us." *Aztlán: A Journal of Chicano Studies* 37 (1): 205–11.

Berry, Maya J., Claudia Chávez Argüelles, Shanya Cordis, Sarah Ihmoud, and Elizabeth Velásquez Estrada. 2017. "Toward a Fugitive Anthropology: Gender, Race, and Violence in the Field." *Cultural Anthropology* 32 (4): 537–65.

Bird, Gloria. 1997. "Breaking the Silence: Writing as 'Witness.'" In *Speaking for the Generations: Native Writers on Writing*, edited by Simon J. Ortiz, 63–74. Tucson: University of Arizona Press.

Brant, Beth. 1995. *Writing as Witness: Essay and Talk*. Toronto: Three O'Clock Press.

Deloria, Vine, Jr. 1969. *Custer Died for Your Sins*. New York: Macmillan.

"The Declaration of Barbados: For the Liberation of the Indians." 1973. *Current Anthropology* 14 (3): 267–70.

Fals-Borda, Orlando. 1986. *Conocimiento y poder popular: Lecciones con campesinos de Nicaragua, México, y Bogotá*. Bogotá: Siglo XXI.

Fals-Borda, Orlando. 1987. "The Application of Participatory Action Research in Latin America." *International Sociology* 2:329–47.

Freire, Pablo. 1970. *Pedagogía de los oprimidos*. Mexico City: Siglo XXI.

Goeman, Mishuana. 2013. *Mark My Words: Native Women Mapping Out Nations*. Minneapolis: University of Minnesota Press.

Gordon, Edmund. 1991. "Anthropology and Liberation." In *Decolonizing Anthropology: Moving Further Toward an Anthropology of Liberation*, edited by Faye V. Harrison, 149–67. Washington, D.C.: American Anthropological Association.

Greenwood, Davydd, and Morton Levin. 1998. *Introduction to Action Research*. London: Sage.

Gregg, Melissa, and Gregory Seigworth, eds. 2010. *The Affect Reader*. Durham, N.C.: Duke University Press.

Hale, Charles. 2006a. "Activist Research vs. Cultural Critique: Indigenous Land Rights and the Contradictions of Politically Engaged Anthropology." *Cultural Anthropology* 21 (1): 96–120.

Hale, Charles. 2006b. *Más que un Indio: Racial Ambivalence and Neoliberal Multiculturalism in Guatemala*. Santa Fe, N.Mex.: School of American Research.

Hale, Charles R., ed. 2008. *Engaging Contradictions: Theory, Politics, and Methods of Activist Scholarship*. Berkeley: University of California Press.

Haraway, Donna. 1988. "Situated Knowledges: The Science Question in Feminism and the Privilege of Partial Perspective." *Feminist Studies* 14:575–99.

Harding, Sandra. 1986. *The Science Question in Feminism*. Ithaca, N.Y.: Cornell University Press.

Jacobs, Margaret. 2009. *White Mother to a Dark Race: Settler Colonialism, Maternalism, and the Removal of Indigenous Children in the American West & Australia, 1880–1940*. Lincoln: University of Nebraska Press.

Kirsch, Stuart. 2006. *Reverse Anthropology: Indigenous Analysis of Social and Environmental Relations in New Guinea*. Stanford, Calif.: Stanford University Press.

Kirsch, Stuart. 2017. *Engaged Anthropology: Politics Beyond the Text*. Berkeley: University of California Press.

Kondo, Dorinne K. 1986. "Dissolution and Reconstitution of Self: Implications for Anthropological Epistemology." *Cultural Anthropology* 1 (1): 74–88.

Lassiter, Luke Eric. 2005. *The Chicago Guide to Collaborative Ethnography*. Chicago: University of Chicago Press.

Leyva Solano, Xochitl, and Shannon Speed. 2008. "Hacia la investigación descolonizada: Nuestra experiencia de co-labor." In *Gobernar (en) la diversidad: Experiencias indígenas desde América Latina. Hacia la investigación de colabor*, edited by Xochitl Leyva Solano, Araceli Burguete, and Shannon Speed, 63–105. Mexico City: CIESAS/FLACSO.

Lutz, Catherine, and Geoffrey M. White. 1986. "The Anthropology of Emotions." *Annual Review of Anthropology* 15 (1): 405–36.

Million, Dian. 2009. "Felt Theory: An Indigenous Feminist Approach to Affect and History." *Wicazo Sa Review* 24 (2): 53–76.

Milloy, John S., and Mary Jane McCallum. 1999. *A National Crime: The Canadian Government and the Residential School System*. Winnipeg: University of Manitoba Press.

Perry, Keisha-Khan. 2013. *Black Women Against the Land Grab: The Fight for Racial Justice in Brazil*. Minneapolis: University of Minnesota Press.

Rosaldo, Renato. 1984. "Grief and a Headhunter's Rage: On the Cultural Force of Emotions." In *Text, Play, and Story: The Construction and Reconstruction of Self and Society*, edited by Edward M. Bruner, 178–95. Washington, D.C.: American Ethnological Society.

Rosaldo, Renato. 1993. *Culture and Truth: The Remaking of Social Analysis.* Boston: Beacon Press.Sanford, Victoria, and Asale Angel-Ajani. 2006. *Engaged Observer: Anthropology, Advocacy, and Activism.* Rutgers, N.J.: Rutgers University Press.

Smith, Linda Tuhiwai. 1996. *Decolonizing Methodologies: Research and Indigenous Peoples.* London: Zed Books.

Speed, Shannon. 2006. "At the Crossroads of Human Rights and Anthropology: Toward a Critically Engaged Activist Research." *American Anthropologist* 108 (1): 66–77.

Speed, Shannon. 2008. "Forged in Dialogue: Toward a Critically Engaged Activist Research." In *Engaging Contradictions: Theory, Politics, and Methods of Activist Scholarship*, edited by Charles R. Hale, 213–36. Berkeley: University of California Press.

Speed, Shannon. 2017. "Representations of Violence: (Re)Telling Indigenous Women's Stories and the Politics of Knowledge Production." In *Sources and Methods in Indigenous Studies*, edited by Chris Andersen and Jean M. O'Brien, 178–84. New York: Routledge.

Speed, Shannon. 2019. *Incarcerated Stories: Indigenous Women Migrants and Violence in the Settler-Capitalist State.* Chapel Hill: University of North Carolina Press.

Stephen, Lynn. 2013. *We Are the Face of Oaxaca: Testimony and Social Movements.* Durham, N.C.: Duke University Press.

Stephen, Lynn. 2015. "Ser testigo presencial—Acompañando, presenciando, actuando: Martin Diskin Memorial Lecture. Bearing Witness: Truths, Audiences, Strategies, and Outcomes." *LASA Forum* 46 (3): 4–14.

Stuesse, Angela. 2016. *Scratching Out a Living: Latinos, Race, and Work in the Deep South.* Berkeley: University of California Press.

CHAPTER 2

Prison as a Colonial Enclave

Incarcerated Indigenous Women Resisting Multiple Violence

R. AÍDA HERNÁNDEZ CASTILLO

U nderstanding the specific forms of gendered violence in Indigenous territories implies recognizing the continuity of dispossession, displacement, and death that is inherent to the colonial project and that has characterized the history of the Native peoples of this continent.[1] The criminalization of Indigenous peoples in Mexico and their *prisonization* because of the "war on drugs" have created another form of forced dispossession and displacement, breaking ties to the community as these peoples are placed into prisons far from their families and subjecting their bodies to multiple forms of violence (both physical and symbolic) that range from torture to isolation.[2]

---

1. This continuing colonial project has been denounced by Indigenous intellectuals from distinct conceptualizations, sometimes using the discourse of internal colonialism (e.g., Segunda Declaración de Barbados 1977; Cojti Cuxil 1994) and sometimes simply naming it as colonialism (e.g., Chirix García 2013; Cumes 2012; Nahuelpan Moreno et al. 2012). In the context of the United States, theorizations about settler colonialism (Arvin and Morrill 2013; Nakano-Glenn 2015; Speed 2017) have been fundamental to analysis of the current colonial dispossession.

2. I use *prisonization* to refer to not just the process of segregating people in the prison complex, but also the political and cultural process of building a prison culture that assumes both the mores, norms, and practices of penitentiary life and a "political anatomy" intended to reform the body of the inmates (Foucault 1977; see also Clemmers 1958). For Indigenous people, prisonization implies a new, violent form of acculturation. *Criminalization* refers not only to the legal process through which Indigenous people's activities are penalized by the justice system,

Before, during, and after detention, Indigenous women are subjected to specific forms of violence, including harassment and physical violence, as well as separation from their children, families, and communal context, which for them represents another form of torture. The use of sexual violence as a strategy to occupy the bodies and territories of the colonialized has been amply documented by Indigenous feminists (see Altamirano-Jiménez 2013; Cumes 2012; Smith 2005). These strategies remain in place as part of the repressive practice of the security forces in Mexico against Indigenous people. This chapter documents this intersectional violence through the testimonies and creative writings of Indigenous women in a Mexican women's prison.

In 2006, Mazahua activist Magdalena García Durán made public accusations against the Mexican state, about this violence, having herself been imprisoned for a year and a half for supporting protests in San Salvador Atenco.[3] Her accusations were a turning point in my academic research, fostering my growing concern with institutional racism in the Mexican criminal justice system, and influencing my decision to focus my investigation on Indigenous women in prison. My experience as a social anthropologist and feminist activist had previously been centered on the analysis of spaces of Indigenous justice and the support of women's struggles to transform their community systems of justice. However, during the administrations of Felipe Calderón (2006–12) and Enrique Peña Nieto (2012–18), the multicultural state became the penal state, bringing with it a hardened penal system, as well as the criminalization of poverty and social protest (Hernández Castillo 2013).

In this chapter, I share reflections that have emerged in ten years of work with Indigenous women in prison through different projects of activist

---

but also to the social and cultural process through which structural racism constructs Indigenous men and women and racialized poor people as potential criminals in the "war on drugs."

3. Magdalena García Durán is an Indigenous Mazahua activist, street vendor, and mother of five children who was detained arbitrarily in May 2006 during the protests in San Salvador Atenco, where the People's Front in Defense of the Earth has struggled to defend residents from displacement and repression, as well as to prevent the construction of an airport on communal lands. García was accused of the crime of kidnapping six police officers and an attack on means of communication and transport. She was declared to be a prisoner of conscious by Amnesty International. During her eighteen-month detention, she and twenty-five other women were sexually abused by the security forces. This case has been taken before the Inter-American Commission on Human Rights because of the lack of justice in Mexican judicial tribunals (see Hernández Castillo 2010c).

research that emphasize the construction of dialogical spaces and sorority among incarcerated Indigenous and mestiza women. I analyze criminalization and prison violence as the continuity of the colonial patriarchal violence that has marked the lives of Indigenous women. The chapter concludes with a reflection on strategies that the women themselves have developed: the use of creative writing for resistance by the Sisters of the Shadow Editorial Collective (Colectiva Editorial Hermanas de la Sombra), and the self-care strategies that have been integral to this project. The Spanish language, a communication tool in prison for women of distinct Indigenous and mestiza communities, is likewise used in the women's creative writing as a tool to denounce the continuum of violence that has marked their lives.

Prisonization: Continuity of the Colonial Project

The fact that racialized bodies are the majority of those who reside in the prisons in the Americas has been widely denounced by Black and Chicana activists (Alexandre 2012; Davis 1981; Díaz-Cotto 1996; Gilmore 2007, 2008), critical race studies scholars (Delgado and Stefancic 2001), Afro-Brazilian feminist scholars (Alves 2017; Carneiro 1995; Flauzina 2008), decolonial feminists in Latin America (Arens 2017; Hernández Castillo 2016; Segato 2007), and some scholars in critical prison studies (Olguín 2009; Wacquant 2000, 2001, 2009). In prison studies in Latin America, however, the so-called myth of *mestizaje* (miscegenation) has made it difficult to name or denounce the racism that structures social relations, institutions, and the collective imagination.[4] Beneath the logic that Latin American nations are a product of *mestizaje* and that they do not have the racial segregation that

---

4. The nationalist myth of *mestizaje* (the Mexican version of the melting pot) has fostered a general belief that racism is impossible: *if we are part Indian, we cannot be racist.* This myth hides the whiteness ideology that has prevailed despite the fact that postrevolutionary nationalism promotes "mestizofile," vindicating the "dead Indian" and excluding living Indigenous peoples. Some critical scholars have confronted the rhetoric of denial by forming networks against racism in Mexico (see Gómez Izquierdo et al. 2008; Gall 2004; Moreno 2012; Red Integra, n.d.). That said, the academic debate about structural racism and criminalization of Brazil's Black population has been different than in other Latin American countries, and extensive literature exists (see Adorno 1995; Cerqueira and Moura 2014; Nascimiento [1978] 2016; Sinhoretto and Morais 2018; Vargas and Alves 2010). Although the Brazilian state has promoted the myth of racial democracy as a national hegemonic discourse, the antiracist movement and the civic

characterizes countries "to the north," those in prison are seen as mostly poor "citizens," whose delinquency is a result of their vulnerable economic situation. Thus, the more critical perspectives continue to consider poverty and the corruption of the judicial system as the principal problems to be confronted when analyzing penal justice and the penitentiary system in Latin America.

Rita Laura Segato (2007, 145) points at the complicity of academic research in obscuring the racist and racialized structures that characterize the prisons in Latin America:

> We must reflect on why it is difficult to speak of race, give a name to it and consider what is evident and in plain sight about the incarcerated population of the continent. . . . The intent to declare what is seen when entering a prison, to consider the faces of the people incarcerated, is not easy because it touches the sensibilities of several enthroned actors: the traditional left and academia, since it implies placing flesh and bones to the mathematics of the classes, which introduces their color, culture, ethnicity, and in summary: difference. It touches the sociological sensibility because the data on this theme is scarce, and thus the difficulty of being objectively precise with the complexity of racial classification, and it touches the sensibility of the law, bureaucrats, and legal forces because it suggests a state racism.

What Segato calls "the complexity of racial classification" can be seen in the Mexican case, where linguistic criteria are utilized in the penitentiary census to document the number of Indigenous prisoners. In 2015 the National Security Commission of the Ministry of the Interior found that Indigenous people accounted for 8,412 of the 247,000 people interned in the country's penitentiary centers. Of these Indigenous people, 286 were women, and 8,126 were men. This same source tallies people according to Indigenous language spoken: 1,849 Nahuatl, 639 Zapotec, 527 Mixtec, 499 Tsotsil, 491 Tseltal, 412 Otomí, 403 Maya, 361 Mazateco, 356 Totonac, 334 Tarahumara, 219 Ch'ol, 216 Tepehuano, 212 Chinanteco, 196 Cora, 179 Huastec, 173 Mixe, 172 Mayo-Yoreme, 158 Tlapaneco, 152 Mazahua, and 116 Huichol (Comisión Nacional 2017a). The remaining 748 Indigenous peoples

---

organizations that confront police brutality against Black communities have influenced the research agenda of antiracist scholars in Brazil.

were not identified by their mother tongue, probably because they did not speak an Indigenous language but identified themselves as Indigenous.

However, based on my ten years of experience working in the Morelos prisons and visiting and giving workshops in Mexico City and the states of Chiapas, Puebla, Yucatán, and Oaxaca, I have found that much of the population from Indigenous communities tends to be considered not in terms of their ethnic identity but rather exclusively as poor individuals from the peasantry, thus meaning that their true numbers are higher than recorded in the penitentiary census. This nonidentification is even more common for people who have lost their mother tongue, a consequence of violent acculturation campaigns that imposed Spanish as a national language through public education institutions.

Although quantitative registration of Indigenous populations is difficult (and inaccurate); racial hierarchies are reproduced within the prisons. Few imprisoned women are from the middle class, and these few tend to be white and occupy privileged spaces within the penitentiary structure. Julia Sudbury (2005, xiv) comments on this point: "From Mexico to South Africa, exploding prison populations have resulted in the construction of private, U.S.-style megaprisons. Statistics that look at gender but not race and class underrepresent the impact of the prison explosion on women of color and indigenous women. In [countries across the globe], oppressed racialized groups are disproportionately targeted by the criminal justice system." Among the few scholars who have written about women prisoners and their ethnicity in Mexico is Ana Paula Hernández (2011), who demonstrates that Indigenous women represent 5 percent of the total female penitentiary population but account for 43 percent of women in confinement for drug-related crimes. Elsewhere, I have argued that Indigenous women are captives of the narcotrafficking war, "prisoners of statistics." The Mexican government has incarcerated the most vulnerable sectors of the drug market pyramid: poor peasant women, most of them Indigenous (Hernández Castillo 2016).

In the context of the human rights crisis of the so-called war against the narcos, which has left more than 250,000 dead and 61,637 disappeared according to official sources (RNPED 2020), the militarization of the country and the penitentiary infrastructure's growth have become part of the problem rather than a solution. The imprisonment of Indigenous women has left their underage children abandoned and vulnerable to being brought into organized crime. When these adolescent Indigenous children end up in juvenile detention centers, they are uprooted by prisonization. Their links to organized crime remain, but the prison system destroys the cultural referents that could have helped them navigate the multiple forms of violence that surround them.[5]

Despite the underrepresentation of the Indigenous population in the official census, the ethnography of the penitentiary spaces shows us that these facilities are primarily inhabited by poor and racialized men and women of Indigenous origin. Multiple racisms—both exogenous and endogenous— permeate the Mexican judicial system. *Exogenous racism* here refers to a systemic racism that places certain bodies in certain geographies where the investment in social welfare is much lower than the investment in security policies. Thus, criminalization and the consequent prisonization both tend to be more prevalent (Hernández Castillo 2017). *Endogenous racism*—or what legal anthropologist Yuri Escalante (2015) calls *judicial racism*—means that the racist ideologies of those who dispense justice permeate the treatment given to populations of Indigenous origin and affect the terms of their sentences. U.S. critical race theory can help us understand these processes, although (unlike the U.S. Black population) the Indigenous population in Mexico faces the added problem of the violation of collective rights and Indigenous jurisdictions. Each time a member of an Indigenous people is imprisoned without jurisdictional coordination with their Indigenous justice system, the state penal system violates national and international legislations, which recognize the right of Indigenous peoples to their own normative systems. Given this problem, the literature on settler colonialism and

---

5. A recent report presented by the National Commission of Human Rights lists the principal problems found in the Indigenous population in prison and detention centers as:

- discrimination by the rest of the inmate population for belonging to an Indigenous community
- lack of information on human rights
- rare family visits received because of the distance of their communities from the detention centers, added to by a lack of economic resources
- deficient medical attention received in the detention centers
- insufficient opportunities to develop labor activities that support their eventual social reinsertion
- lack of translators or interpreters
- lack of public defenders who speak their language. (Comisión Nacional 2017b)

prisonization of Native American and First Nations peoples in the United States and Canada could be more useful here, allowing us to understand prisons as colonial enclaves.[6]

In a historical sense, the imprisonment of Indigenous men and women represents a continuity of colonial practices that impose the law of the colonizer over the normative and judicial practices of the Indigenous population. Thus, not only are poor and racialized bodies incarcerated at higher rates than other populations, but the punitive system does not respond to the forms of conflict resolution developed historically by the Indigenous people of Mexico. Political theorist Robert Nichols (2014, 440) describes this continuity of colonial strategies in imprisonment:

> Indigenous peoples do not merely represent racialized bodies produced by a biopolitics of population management. Rather . . . they constitute alternative political, economic, ecological and spiritual systems of ordering, governing and relating. In the context of ongoing occupation, usurpation, dispossession and ecological devastation, *no* level of representation in one of the central apparatuses of state control and formalized violence would be proportionate. Instead, indigenous sovereignty itself calls forth an alternative normativity that challenges the very *existence* of the carceral system, let alone its internal organization and operation.

The racism, sexism, impunity, and violence that characterize the state system of justice have influenced an important sector of Indigenous women, who are defending their Indigenous autonomy while at the same time struggling to modify those practices and norms that exclude them from their own

---

6. In 2002, in response to demands for autonomy from the Ejército Zapatista de Liberación Nacional (EZLN, Zapatista National Liberation Army) and the Mexican Indigenous movement, the Mexican Congress approved the Law of Indigenous Rights and Culture, which recognizes the right of Indigenous communities and people to self-determination and to their own systems of justice. These same rights are also recognized by Convention 169 of the International Labour Organization, signed by Mexico in 1989, and the UN Declaration on the Rights of Indigenous Peoples, adopted by Mexico in 2007. In the case of the United States and Canada, where tribal agreements recognize Indigenous sovereignty, the imprisonment of the Indigenous population is both a matter of overrepresentation (with Indigenous populations being incarcerated at higher rates than other populations) and also a violation of Indigenous sovereignty. For an analysis of the Native American populations in prison, see Monture-Angus (2000), Nichols (2014), and Ross (1998).

(Indigenous) justice systems. The reeducation of youth through community service and conciliatory processes has resulted in more effective outcomes than the punitive state system, where the prisons tend to be under the control of organized crime.[7]

Constructing Community in Prison

In order to analyze the impact of the colonial legacy on the lives of Indigenous women in prison, I would like to share the experience of a co-participatory research project that documents the racialized violence of the penal state. My work with these women has confronted penal violence through writing and has become one of the most important and transformative research experiences in my academic career.

I first arrived at the Atlacholoaya Social Readaptation Center in the Mexican state of Morelos at the beginning of 2008, working within the framework of an academic investigation that proposed to document judicial racism based on life histories and prison files of women Indigenous prisoners.[8] Because these prison files cannot be accessed without prisoners' signed authorization, I accessed the prisoners through an existing poetry workshop. This venue offered me an open door to get to know them and begin a process that has since transformed into a lifelong project.

Having begun to meet imprisoned women, I created a writing workshop titled "Life Histories" to systematize the gathering of their stories. The methodology for this workshop was dialogic, beginning even with the invitations to participate. Inmates who had participated in the earlier poetry workshop invited inmates of Indigenous origin to our workshop to share their life histories through face-to-face interviews. Most Indigenous women in the prison did not how to read or write, thus these interviews were an attempt to place the "pen" of those who knew how to read and write at the service of those who were illiterate. Each week we would review the writings, and once a month they were read aloud to the protagonists. These oral readings

---

7. For an analysis of the Indigenous normative systems in contexts of multiple violence, see Hernández Castillo and Sierra (2005), Sierra, Hernández Castillo, and Sieder (2013), Hernández Castillo (2016), and Sieder (2017). See also chapters 3 and 7 in this volume.

8. This collective project, "Globalization, Justice, and Rights from a Gender Perspective in Indigenous Territories," was coordinated with María Teresa Sierra; its final product was the book *Justicias Indígenas y Estado* (Sierra, Hernández Castillo, and Sieder 2013).

resulted in reflections on the intersection of the exclusions and multiple violences that have marked their lives and, directly or indirectly, influenced their incarceration.

At a personal level, my decision to accompany Indigenous and peasant women in prison through the process of writing their life histories was based on three methodological arguments: First, these histories would give a more profound account than penitentiary statistics of the complex experiences of exclusion that women prisoners face. Second, historical memory could fill the silences that the official history of justice in Mexico has left. And third, the process of sharing and reflecting on their life trajectories could contribute to healing the women's bodies and minds through the construction of new feminine identities and prison spaces of solidarity. The political power of testimonies in the struggle for justice and their importance in the construction of emotional communities are themes that several contributors to this book have addressed, recovering feminist methodologies (see Macleod and De Marinis 2018; Stephen 2011, 2016; chapters 1, 5, and 7 in this book).

For my part, I arrived to Atlacholoaya with the conviction that I had a privileged knowledge to share with the inmates, but during the last ten years I have been transformed by these prison dialogues, learning more than I could teach and recognizing my epistemological arrogance. Many women with whom I have worked in prison have long confronted and survive systems of classist, sexist, and racist domination. Their knowledge, sometimes captured through art or literature, is a window into the contradictions and the violence of contemporary Mexico.

My work during these years has evolved in two realms: the external world of the academy and society, and the internal community of women. At a critical, textual level, I have worked to document, analyze, and denounce the violence and impunity that women experience in prison. These efforts have influenced my academic writing, and I have also participated as a public intellectual in the national debates about the penitentiary system. I have used my national newspaper column, documentaries, and radio to denounce human rights violations and share testimonies (see Hernández Castillo 2016, 2017, n.d.). At the same time, the political, pedagogical, and artistic project has developed among the women, with these moments of knowledge exchange fostering community in institutions that promote violence, disconnection, and a lack of trust among inmates. The workshop space is described by the inmates in these terms:

This workshop, I feel, helps me know my fellow inmates better, knowing one another's ideas. It also teaches us to express ourselves better, and I hope also to be sisters. I believe that the workshop is helping me to be a better person, to express my ideas and feelings, and to be open with my fellow inmates. For the Indigenous women who cannot read or write, our work is a way of offering to know her life history and at the same time our own, a form of mutual help. (May 2010 reflection)

The workshop is one of few meeting spaces between Indigenous and non-Indigenous women within the prison. The coproduction of life histories, written by those who know how to read and write and narrated by those who are illiterate, has created new bonds among the inmates. It was with the intent to accompany the women through this self-representation process that the workshop "Life Histories" (2008–10) was initiated, beginning a long journey that has led to other workshops and provoked the development of a penitentiary editorial project in which inmates not only write but also design, edit, and publish books. Their first book, *Bajo la sombra del guamúchil. Historias de vida de mujeres indígenas y campesinas en prisión* (Under the shadow of the guamuchil. Life histories of Indigenous and peasant women in prison, Hernández Castillo 2010a), began its life under the shade of the guamuchil (pink tamarind) tree, the only tree that allows the inmates to get close to nature, in the middle of the cement sea that forms the prison. There, Indigenous and peasant women sit to weave, and they have made this outdoor space their shelter, leaving the classrooms and workshop spaces to the urban women, most of them mestizas. As with Mexican society at large, Atlacholoaya is marked by racial and class hierarchies, and these are reflected in the physical distribution of penitentiary spaces. The cultural workshops were traditionally for those who "knew more" and had more resources to acquire the new knowledge arriving from outside the prison. In our workshop we proposed to break with these hierarchies and become close to the women who wove and sewed silently beneath the guamuchil's shadow. One woman described the importance of this privileged space: "the greenness of the guamuchil, the birds that nest in it and the laughter of the children that arrive from the nearby playground, makes us feel that we aren't closed off" (Cadena and Zavaleta 2010, 35).

In November 2011 the inmates decided to give a name to this effort, calling it the Sisters of the Shadow Editorial Collective (Colectiva Editorial

Hermanas de la Sombra). Our numbers of external volunteers continued to grow over the next few years under the coordination of feminist poet Elena de Hoyos, editor and performance artist Marina Ruiz, visual anthropologist and documentarian Carolina Corral, writer María Vinos, and myself. Our distinct work trajectories, politics, and personalities, as well as our generational differences, challenged us to transform our differences into strengths and to learn how to work collectively from this platform. We developed a new workshop called "Life Histories, Artisan Books, and Construction of Identities Through Literature." We proposed to continue working from autobiographic reflections, exploring distinct literary styles such as poetry, short stories, and essays. At the same time, we appropriated the editorial process initiated in Ruiz's earlier "Artisan Books" workshop, with the women utilizing a variety of artistic and practical techniques to develop their own books.

The group's composition substantially changed with the liberation from prison of all the Indigenous and peasant women who had participated in *Under the Shadow of the Guamuchil*. The diffusion of a documentary by the same name on the university television channel applied political pressure to review their judicial files (Hernández Castillo 2010b). Four of these women—Leo Zavaleta, Rosa Salazar, Alejandra Reynoso Alarcón, and Martha Elena Hernández Bermúdez—now freed from prison, continued participating in the collective. Their trajectories, to be analyzed later, demonstrate the consequences of prisonization for Indigenous women, but also their capacity of resistance, something that developed from their sorority.

Despite our interest from the beginning to overcome the divide between Indigenous and mestiza, rural and urban, schooled and illiterate women, it has been difficult to confront the perception that the workshops are for those who "know more." One way that we have slowly drawn in peasant women is through the introduction of the Japanese painting technique Sumi-e, as led in the workshops by local artist Pilar Hinojosa.[9] As of 2020, the collective has published fifteen poetry books, life histories, narratives, and chronicles in distinct formats that range from artisanal books to the trilogy *Intermural Revelations* (Colectiva Editorial Hermanas en la Sombra 2013). This

---

9. Sumi-e is a technique of monochromatic painting, developed in China during the Song Dynasty (960–1279) and introduced into Japan by Zen monks. Its popularity in Japan grew rapidly because, as with Zen practice, it involves expressing reality by reducing it to its pure, bare form. Local artist and project collaborator Pilar Hinojosa has promoted this art in Mexico, not only as an artistic technique but also as a tool for physical and spiritual healing.

last involves three volumes of short stories and narrative essays that were published through a grant from the National Institute of Fine Arts. Every prison in the country received a copy, with more than three thousand sets distributed.

Hierarchies still exist: despite the sisterhood shared by those external volunteers and imprisoned women, our dialogues have been marked by our differences of ethnicity and class. However, keeping a dialogue open about the reasons for writing has allowed for evolving textual strategies to help mitigate these structural inequalities. Collective forms of knowledge building become part of a larger struggle for self-representation. Rather than narrating the life histories of other women, the writers and anthropologists accompany women through the process of telling their own stories, including developing their own editorial projects.

Documenting the Continuum of Violence and the Intersection of Exclusions

When we initiated the "Life Histories" workshop in 2008, my principal interest was to document judicial racism and Indigenous women's experiences with penal justice. However, the process of historical reconstruction—of their lives in their regions of origin, the causes that forced several of them to migrate, and the complexities of their love relationships—converted the life histories into stories of exclusion, where to be an Indigenous and poor woman means having survived multiple colonial violences.

The criminalization of these women did not begin when they arrived in prison, nor did it end upon their being freed. Many of them are natives of regions where militarization has been a constant: first because of the counterinsurgency operations of the so-called Dirty War, and more recently because of the "war against the narcos."[10] Several of them were detained at military checkpoints and sent to prison without an arrest warrant, in many cases not even knowing the accusations against them.

10. The Mexican Dirty War (*Guerra sucia*) refers to the Mexican theater of the Cold War, an internal conflict in the 1960s and 1970s between the Mexican government (led by the Institutional Revolutionary Party, PRI, and backed by the United States) and left-wing student and guerrilla groups. Across the presidencies of Gustavo Díaz Ordaz, Luis Echeverría, and José López Portillo, government forces carried out an estimated twelve hundred disappearances as well as systematic torture and extrajudicial executions.

Torture is a daily practice used in arbitrary detentions to obtain confessions, and the women's descriptions of torture has been one of the most difficult and emotional phases of writing the life histories. Six women who participated in the first book were tortured, and one of them almost died in a diabetic coma as a result of the torture (see Hernández Castillo 2010c).

In her book *Los sueños de una cisne en el pantano* (Dreams of a swan in a swamp), Leo Zavaleta (2016, 93–94), describes a torture session during her illegal and arbitrary detention:

> —You have to cooperate with us, if you don't, we'll give you more Tehuacán.[11]
> —I have told you a thousand and one times that I don't know them.
>
> I continued saying nothing, I heard my husband's screams. When they tortured him, they put a plastic bag over his head to smother him. Everything passed so fast that I could not even explain it. Both of us were beaten nonstop; two guys arrived, who had been arrested two hours before us. They asked if I knew them, and when I denied it, they continued hitting me. So many hours passed. About three o'clock in the afternoon they took us out of the house to the deputy attorney general for Special Investigations on Organized Crime (SIEDO).

Zavaleta, a Me'phaa woman who did not know how to write when we started with the "Life Histories" workshop, has written and published her own life history since her release. Her book is a successful example of the ways in which creative writing is being used as a decolonizing tool by Indigenous women to confront the erasure of their voices and experiences from the national discourse. It is also a public denouncement of the use of torture as a common strategy in the criminalization of poor racialized men and women.

A 2017 report from the UN Subcommittee on Prevention of Torture and Other Cruel, Inhuman, or Degrading Penalties (SPT), denounced torture in Mexico: "torture is commonly applied during the arrest, transfer, entrance to places of detention and interrogation with the goal that the victims make self-incriminating declarations or obligate them to sign blank pieces of

---

11. Tehuacán is a brand of Mexican carbonated water that is used for torture, poured into detainees' respiratory channels. The term *tehuacanazo* is commonly used in Mexico to refer to the torture that uses this soda water.

papers." The report indicated that torture was widespread, practiced by federal, state, and municipal police agents, as well as by immigration agents and members of the armed forces (Naciones Unidas 2017). In the case of Indigenous women, this torture has included sexual violence. To control the bodies of women through sexual violence and imprisonment is, for security forces, a way to manifest control of the territories of the colonized (see Arvin, Tuck, and Morrill 2013).

As I have indicated elsewhere (Hernández Castillo 2017), these women come from racialized geographies that have been deeply affected by militarization, paramilitarization, and organized crime. Even if the violence of the security forces of the state or organized crime does not have a racial character or even if it does not only affect the Indigenous population, the violence has "racialized effects," disproportionately affecting these populations and marginalizing them (Wade 2011: 17).

The experiences of five Indigenous members of the Sisters of the Shadow Editorial Collective reveal how the intersection of exclusions marked their life trajectories, leading them to prison and, in the case of two of them, to their deaths. Even though a tendency exists in criminological studies and among some social researchers to use autobiographical narratives for criminal profiling (tracing "delinquent" personalities to "dysfunctional" family contexts),[12] I view these life histories as a window through which systems of class, race, and gender oppression mutually constitute and mark the criminalization process of poor Indigenous women in Mexico. I have further developed this analysis in other writings, where I have treated the experience of Indigenous women in relation to penal justice (Hernández Castillo 2016). Here, I want to emphasize how colonial violence manifests in the criminalization of these women and how they have developed resistance strategies to confront this violence.

The experiences of Rosa Salazar, Honoria Morelos, and Alejandra Reynoso (Indigenous Nahua women from Morelos, Guerrero, and Puebla); of Leo Zavaleta (a Me'phaa woman from the mountains of Guerrero); and Martha Elena Hernández Bermudez (a Tsotsil woman from Chiapas)—are a memorial of grievances, but also of resistances. Rosita Salazar, a Nahua woman

---

12. Such conservative criminological studies include, for example, Cavazos Ortiz (2005), Cuevas-Sosa, Mendieta Dima, and Salazar Cruz (1992), and Garrido Genovés and Sobral (2008). These studies psychologize the origin of crime instead of contextualizing the framework of social processes. For my analysis, I use the intersectional perspective developed by Kimberlé Williams Crenshaw (1991) to question such tendencies.

from Xoxocotla, Morelos, was sent to the Atlacholoaya women's state prison for not being able to repay 40,000 pesos (around US$2,000) to a creditor who had loaned her this money to support her son who immigrated to the United States looking for a better life. She signed papers that she could not read, and with the bad faith of the loan provider she was taken to the Atlacholoaya prison. Salazar's parents were peasants, but she did not inherit any land because she was a woman, and so she had to do construction work with her husband, who did not own land either. Xoxocotla is next to the community of Atlacholoaya in the municipality of Xochitepec, where both men and women's prisons were established. The peasants from this region have had to migrate to other urban zones because of a lack of land and a lack of government support for agricultural production—even as the government funded the prison and public housing construction in the "judicial city." These projects have completely changed the rural surroundings, leading to a great urban sprawl in the center of the countryside. Not only does the prisonization force out the Indigenous populations, but, many times, the prisons are built in regions previously occupied by Indigenous peoples.

During the four years that she was in prison, Salazar was given the wrong dose of insulin for her diabetes; when she left prison, she was almost blind. The years in prison deeply affected her health, eventually causing her death. During the years that Salazar survived in prison, she continued to write, and her texts denounced the injustices and the racism of the judicial system. They show her love toward nature and her closeness to the earth:

We are
We are beautiful women, rare ones
Workers, intelligent students
We are responsible mothers,
We are free birds singing each instant that passes . . .
We are captives of this prison
But our heart is free
Many of us are innocent
Judges have refused to hear our words
Justice does not exist for us
There is no human justice for poor Indigenous women
That's why we ask God for justice
That he hears our Testimony that has been silenced . . .
(translation of "Somos," Salazar 2012)

Like Zavaleta, Salazar learned to write in our workshop. Her poetry is a denunciation of the judicial racism that characterizes the penal system in Mexico. She also writes about her pride at being a Nahua woman and about the multiple violences that affect Indigenous women.

Honoria Morelos, a Nahua woman from the mountains of Guerrero, was seventy years old and had been in prison for seven years when she arrived at our workshop. She had been imprisoned without being informed that she had the right to a public defender. Her children, like Salazar's, had migrated in search of a better life, and her two grandchildren were left in her custody. One grandchild was gravely ill, and when her children stopped sending money, Morelos decided to leave them in the care of a neighbor and travel to Mexico City for the first time in her life, seeking the support of some relatives. On the highway she was detained at a military checkpoint and accused of transporting drugs. Without a translator or an understanding of why she was detained, she was transferred to Atlacholoaya, where she lived for seven years and ten months, and learned Spanish. The agony of having abandoned her grandchildren in the mountains provoked a gastric ulcer, which would lead to her death six months after she was freed from prison. Morelos told her life history to her cellmate Susuki Lee Camacho, who transcribed this history in the first stage of the workshop, describing the arbitrary detention and the racism that characterizes the security and justice system in Mexico:

It was approximately 11:00 or 12:00 at night, I don't remember well, the driver woke us up and told us to get off the bus. I was very scared to do this. There in front of me were many soldiers. They suddenly surrounded us. So, in a corner of the bus they found some suitcases, and because I was standing beside them, they said: "this yours, right?" I answered them that I only have a bag of seeds, beans, plums, a little bit of Chinese beans that were a gift for my relatives. That's how I answered. But they said: "what do you mean, granny, don't be funny, you traveled right beside the bags, do not deny that they belong to you." Even though I explained they were not mine, it was my word against theirs. Later they took me to a separate revision area, and the supposed package did not appear, but they insisted that the package was mine. In three days, they transported me to the prison, where someone read me a supposed declaration that I supposedly made but I didn't say anything since I could barely speak Spanish. I made many attempts to tell them that I didn't say most things that were written there; they didn't believe me and sentenced me to eleven years and eight or nine months. (Lee Camacho 2010, 46–47)

Part of this testimony was included in the documentary film *Under the Guamuchil's Shadow*, which denounced Morelos's arbitrary detention as well as the miscarriage of justice and the structural racism that mark many such criminal cases of Indigenous women (Hernández Castillo 2010b). Political pressure following the film's airing led to the state prosecutor reviewing Morelos's case and releasing her for lack of evidence.

Alejandra Reynoso's story is perhaps the most painful of those documented in the workshop. It shows very clearly how patriarchal violence, poverty, and racism intersect to mark the lifetime and bodies of these women. Reynoso was born in Zacatlán, a Nahua community in the state of Puebla, and was orphaned. A mestiza family took her in but treated her badly, and when she was seven years old her foster father raped her. After two years of sexual abuse, she told her foster mother, who then threw Reynoso out onto the street. Her life in the streets was marked by several incidents of sexual violence and rape, and she gave birth to twins when she was only ten years old. For six years she lived with a violent man and had four more children. At seventeen years of age, she had seven children, had suffered two rapes, and bore multiple marks on her body from domestic violence. She was imprisoned after her youngest child was kidnapped, taken from the hospital by a middle-class man and woman. When she asked for help, this couple accused her of kidnapping the child. Describing the incident to us, she emphasized that it was about "good people" whose socioeconomic class meant that their words were given more weight than hers. Reynoso was in prison seven years, without the couple ever retracting the accusation or returning her kidnapped baby.

Reynoso learned to write in our workshop, and she wrote her own life history (see Reynoso 2015). After she was liberated, she participated in the radio series *Songs from the Guamuchil* (Colectiva Editorial Hermanas en la Sombra 2016) and in a second documentary film, *Seeds of the Guamuchil: Now in Freedom* (Corral 2016). Now that she is free, she denounces the violence and injustices of which she has been a victim, and she has given several talks against gendered violence in high schools and middle schools. She continues to look for her son.

Leo Zavaleta landed in prison after some problems with alcohol, which led to her being found unconscious in the wrong place at the wrong time.

She was detained and sexually tortured by agents of the Federal Investigation Agency (AFI) until the torture put her in a diabetic coma that almost killed her. Paying for an expensive private defense attorney by selling her house, Zavaleta was declared innocent after a legal process that lasted four years. Although she could not write when she entered prison, she became one of the most prolific writers in the collective. Now liberated, she has stopped consuming alcohol, and she published her 2016 autobiography with the help of the collective. In it, she describes the importance of writing in her life:

> I discovered in writing that now I am someone else. And this I owe to my "Chompis" [Friends] of the Collective. I love them because in school I should have learned to read and write, and I wouldn't have dared to write my own book. The work in the collective has served to express and get out my feelings. To discover that I am worthy, what I can do and continue doing. If a door closes on me, I have to look for a way of opening another. To not be struck. (98)

Zavaleta has represented the Sisters of the Shadow Editorial Collective in several cultural events and participated in the radio series. While working on her second book, she tragically died in May 2020 of COVID-19, likely due to her torture, weakened body, and lack of access to appropriate medical care.

Finally, Martha Elena Hernández Bermudez is a petite Tsotsil woman who served a sentence of fourteen years for her alleged complicity in a kidnapping. Marthita, as she is known by all in Atlacholoaya, was always available with a sweet smile to help her fellow inmates with whatever they need. Her long stay in the prison, as well as her solidarity with fellow inmates and hard work in the penitentiary industry, earned her respect and affection from all her fellow inmates.

Hernández Bermudez was born in the jungle of Las Margaritas, where her parents had migrated from the highlands of Chiapas in search of a piece of land. Like many Indigenous girls, she was delivered to mestizos—in her case two mestiza women from the city of Comitán—so that she could go to elementary school. These *madrinas* (godmothers) were in charge of her education, and they prohibited her from speaking Tsotsil or using her traditional Indigenous dress. But no punishment was enough to make her forget her language and cultural roots, a theme that occupies her writings. When she was a teenager, she was delivered to nuns, who took her to Mexico City where she helped in caring for orphaned children.

Hernández Bermudez's life reveals the continuity of colonial structures in Chiapas society, the racism that marks the relationships among Indigenous and mestiza women, and the penal system's aberrations. It is also a testimony to the solidarity networks that accompanied her from outside jail during those fourteen years she was incarcerated, and to the unconditional love and support of her husband during this time. The solidarity networks associated with the Catholic Church—and her own personal strength—allowed her children to achieve university studies. The youngest is a violinist, has traveled the world in a mariachi group, and is about to finish studies in robotic engineering. Her oldest child is finishing a master's in public administration. The people who falsely accused her of kidnapping never imagined that she would be capable of maintaining her family from inside the prison, or that she would be able to offer opportunities for higher education to her children with her penitentiary work—let alone that she would learn to write or publicly denounce the injustices of which she was a victim (see Tonella 2015).

Now that she is free, Hernández Bermudez returned with her family to the jungle of Las Margaritas in order to visit her parents for the first time in twenty years and proudly present to them the accomplishments of her educated children:

> To return to Nuevo Huixtán and see my parents after so many years was a great happiness. They knew that I was in prison, but they asked me nothing about it. They received me with much love, and I felt much pride when presenting them my children, who are professionals, responsible women, educated, and talented. The fourteen years during which I was separated from them were very hard, but I tried to maintain communication and tried to educate them from a distance. No prison could destroy the ties that unite my children. It's like living a long nightmare, but also there were many things learned; in the writing workshop I found myself and recuperated the confidence to tell my story. My children listen to the radio programs, they watch the documentary film and read my writings, and they feel proud of me. They know that the prison could not break me, I came out strengthened to continue forward. (pers. comm., August 18, 2018)

Like Zavaleta, Hernández Bermudez has participated in *Songs from the Guamuchil* and represented the collective in multiple cultural activities in favor of prisoners' rights since her release.

The radio programs, stories, and poems written by these five women have been tools of decolonialization in their lives and histories, helping them confront the disciplinary and subjective power of the penitentiary apparatus and making their voices heard. They have stopped being one more statistic of the penal state and have become social critics, narrators of their own history, and activists for the rights of other women in prison.

Although the colonial violence of the penitentiary apparatus interrupted the lives of Rosa Salazar and Honoria Morelos, their documented testimonies in their writings and those of their fellow inmates keep them alive in the memory of this community of survivors. Their poetry is read aloud in cultural events in the prison, and their names are invoked in the writings of their fellow inmates. They continue to be a fundamental part of an *emotional community* that we have constructed inside and outside of prison.

Punitive Cultures That Cross Borders

This chapter—like the others in this volume—is not a unique case study of a local, isolated reality. The patriarchal and colonial violence that marks the lives of Indigenous women is related to a global culture of violence and death, one whose punitive models, militarist cultures, forms of torture, and control of racialized bodies are all transnational (see Speed 2017). In the Mexican penitentiary system, these cultures of death have been accompanied by U.S. military investment masked as "security help" in the so-called Mérida Initiative (also known as Plan México for its similarities to Plan Colombia).

Despite complaints about the impact that incarceration has on the social network of Indigenous communities and the other poor and marginalized sectors of the Mexican population, the administrations of Felipe Calderón (2006–12) and Enrique Peña Nieto (2012–18) prioritized a hardened system of penal justice and the construction of new prisons under a policy of "pacification." Across these two six-year administrations, fifteen new prisons were built. They were constructed in part through private financing through contracts service lending (*contratos de prestación de servicios*), which has begun transforming the prison model within the parameters dictated by the American Correctional Association (ACA) (México Evalúa 2016).

The new forms of colonialism are related to new forms of global capitalism (Hardt and Negri 2000), which in the Mexican context means the promotion of the arms market and the development of the penitentiary infrastructure through the Mérida Initiative. This initiative, which dates to December 2008, established the basis for a program of collaboration between the U.S. and Mexican governments that began by strengthening the justice and penal institutions. For example, the United States contributed US$14 million in support of the Mexican federal and state penitentiary systems during the Peña Nieto administration (Dávila 2016, Hernández Castillo 2014). This "program of cooperation" has been questioned for its interventionist character, for its prioritization of punitive methods to counteract the production, traffic, and consumption of drugs, and for its disregard of prevention strategies. Its implementation has strengthened the state penal model, increasing the penitentiary industry's infrastructure while creating a legal framework that criminalizes poverty and political dissidence. This process has meant territorial displacement and dispossession for the criminalized Indigenous population.

Mexico's imported prison model has been widely criticized for its dehumanization and racism. The literature that corresponds to the growth of the U.S. prison industrial complex is abundant and speaks to the dangers of a penitentiary system focused on economic profit and not social reintegration (see Gilmore 2007, 2008). Imprisonment is a lucrative business, and carceral punishment has become the U.S. government's principal solution to social problems. This is the model that is being imported into Mexico through the Mérida Initiative and the ACA, which in 2017 certified fifty-six Mexican prisons.

During the ten years that I have worked in penitentiary spaces, I have documented the impact of this transformed model on the quality of life of women inmates. The standardization of food and the subcontracting of private businesses for the preparation of food have meant the elimination of communal spaces that existed within the prisons to prepare food and share culinary knowledge and tradition. In the regions where the Indigenous population previously wore traditional clothes, prisons have converted to uniforms, which in many cases must be bought with the prisoners' own money. Women inmates are now prohibited from having their own books, but a promise of building libraries for common use remains unfulfilled. Of the 138 standards established by the ACA, only the disciplinary measures have been implemented: modernization of prison infrastructure, training for personnel, and establishment of control measures and disciplinary restrictions. "Lack of resources" is purportedly responsible for the dearth of measures that might improve prisoners' lives.

The certified prisons are the new colonial enclaves; in the name of "institutional modernization," governments are dehumanizing the penitentiary space (see Arens 2017). Eight years after the Mérida Initiative was introduced, a human rights NGO evaluated the certified prisons in Mexico and noted:

> The proposed standards by the ACA are not adequate for penitentiary certification from a human rights perspective. It is an accreditation on paper that leaves the needs of the inmates out of the process and allows the prison system to pay for media accreditation, without having to change its institutional practices. But, beyond the limitations and costs implied, this process of certification must be analyzed as a step in a process of funneling economic resources from the international cooperation toward a private-sector model that has been extensively criticized for encouraging violations of human rights. (México Evalúa 2016, 37)

This hardening of prison norms and new forms of penitentiary violence were rejected by the inmates of the Atlacholoaya Social Readaptation Center through a hunger strike in August 2014. Several of the women who led this strike were moved to high-security prisons as punishment for their protest. After this repression the inmates fell in line with the new standards in a depressing environment and organizational demobilization that took several years to overcome. Despite this institutional violence and punitive policies that returned to the practice of isolation, a group of Indigenous and mestiza women continue rebuilding a sense of community in the prison, using creative writing as a tool to denounce the multiple forms of violence that have marked their lives.

Emotional Communities in the Penitentiary Space

Reading aloud is a common practice in our writing workshops; the participants read their writings to their fellow inmates, and the rest comment in detail. They appropriate, repeat, and borrow some metaphor used by their *chompis* (friends). We have rituals of reading. For example, we read a part of our own poem or someone else's while walking in a circle as if we are repeating a mantra that penetrates our bodies and causes emotion; more than once we have cried in these moments. For some of them, this space is the first time they have heard their poetic voice, and for many this is the first time they feel listened to. These readings are a form of giving testimony, facing others, and—once liberated—facing a public distant to or ignorant of the grievances that they have suffered and continue to suffer.

In dialogue with the Colombian anthropologist Myriam Jimeno (2010), we can affirm that these testimonies presented in diverse textual strategies create emotional bonds of empathy among the participants of the collective, who then become political actors. The concept of *emotional communities*, proposed by Jimeno and considered by various feminist academics who work on the context of violence, is described as a process through which shared pain transcends indignation and feeds collective mobilization (see Macleod and De Marinis 2018; Stephen 2018). In the penitentiary space, this mobilization is limited by the punitive power of the state but takes creative forms, such as the hunger strike against certification or collective complaints sent to human rights organizations. Those who have not experienced imprisonment and have arrived as creative writing instructors are also transformed through the emotional bonds of empathy.

In my case, the initial academic research is now part of a longer process that includes the collective construction of texts, radio programs, and videos, which document and denounce the penal system's injustices. This collective work has at the same time consolidated and strengthened our heterogenous community, formed by women both within and without prison. During these ten years of accompaniment, I have cried with the inmates many times from indignation, impotence, or the bittersweet feelings that emerge when someone leaves into freedom. These emotions have been a source of solidarity between the outside and the inside, and have allowed the construction of a safe place in a context marked by mistrust and violence.

Even though my belonging to this emotional community can be used to disqualify the "objectivity" of my academic work by those who defend neutrality in the social sciences, for me it has been a privileged space to be close to the violence of the penitentiary system and to hear the voices and witness the experiences of those who suffer it in their own flesh. And it allows me to live in my own flesh the new violence that the process of certification has brought. Several times we have been humiliated, denied access to the prison because we did not comply with a new requisite established by the prison director, who has his own interpretations of the ACA norms. Creating the trust required to speak about certification's repercussions, about the daily violence experienced in prison and the transgressions and resistances that develop collectively, requires time and participation in an emotional community that positivist and distant research could not achieve. However, participation in this emotional community implies many methodological and political challenges, especially in relation to the reproduction and analysis of these experiences in the academic environment. The writings of members of the collective speak to us in two voices. The first voice expresses the pain and sadness of those who have suffered violence not only in the penitentiary system but at times from their own families or from romantic relationships. This voice is a screaming complaint, and—when joined by a chorus of similar abuses—it speaks of the distinct exclusions that women experience. But a second voice joins in as well, a nonvictimized voice that speaks from the joy for life of those who consider themselves to be survivors of a system that intended to but could not destroy them. This is the voice of those who have survived the pain and who try to turn the experience of suffering into a fortification of life.

I, as an anthropologist, have taken on the challenge of drawing from these two voices, of writing about their pain for academia without trivializing it and at the same time acknowledging the resistance spaces that have opened here, where the state's power seems to be absolute. In documenting and analyzing their testimonies and presenting them in a wider academic context, as a complaint of patriarchal violence, I confront a dilemma of what to include in or exclude from their narratives. How do I take into account their painful experiences of violence without trivializing them? As I wrote this chapter, I left out many stories of extreme violence, fragmenting their narratives and taking their experiences out of context. My strategy has been to refer at length to the women's own publications, many of which are accessible online, and thus invite the reader to get closer to their analytic voices.

The Colombian psychologist and social researcher Juan Pablo Aranguren Romero (2010, 25) describes the contradictory aspects of social research with testimonies of violence:

> With the idea of capturing the memory of pain and its diffusion exists the conception that we are near achieving solidarity and respect for the other: to give voice to those who do not have one. What authorizes one to give voice to the victim? Isn't there something of an epistemological violence and subalternatization in this process? . . . What is lost in the translation of the victims' testimonies into the language of human rights? In wider contexts:

what is lost in this process is, in principle, the same journey that goes from one experience to a writing, and thus is about the same journey that goes from the interview to the book, or the oral history to the research monograph. In both cases the fact can be alluded to that what is lost in the transit from the encounter with the Other to the written document, is the body and presence of this Other in the text.

Reconsidering the so-called anthropology of suffering, Veena Das (2008) has gone deeply into these dilemmas, stating that the conceptual structures of our disciplines translate suffering into a distinct language that takes away the victim's voice and distances the immediacy of their experience. I have attempted in my writings to take into account this pain, which is reproduced fully in the Indigenous women's own writings. But above all, the approach of the Sisters of the Shadow Editorial Collective is to accompany the self-representation process of the inmates as they write their own books and experiment with textual strategies such as poetry, narrative, and essay.

After ten years of going forward together, we have learned to work with our own and others' pain, creating listening spaces and referring to forms of traditional healing such as the *temazcal* (Mesoamerican steam bath), which Elena de Hoyos promotes under the spiritual guidance of her shaman, Marta Solé.[13] We know that the emotions carried in the body can mobilize us, but that they can also paralyze us and make us ill. We need to work with this pain, outside of academic theorizations, from a caring language that allows us to heal and continue constructing community in prison.

Final Reflections

As a scholar committed to social justice, I have the responsibility to analytically reconstruct the relationships between the many types of violence suffered by the Indigenous women in prison and the colonial regimes of sexual violence and torture that relate territorial occupation with prisonization. In the current context, our investigative work must unravel the violence that manifests in Indigenous peoples' lives from the penal state. We must acknowledge the multiple systems of inequality that structure the violence

---

13. Marta Solé is a traditional healer and Aztec dancer who is also an Indigenous and women's rights activist; she does healing *temazcal* rituals for women and feminist activists.

from a patriarchal and racist semantic, and that convert Indigenous women's bodies into markers in order to delimit the colonized territories.

The construction of prisons in communal territories and the criminalization of Indigenous men and women are new forms of dispossession and displacement that continue the colonial violence that characterizes the modern states of the Americas. By building analytic bridges to comprehend these continuities, in distinct national contexts, we acknowledge the new forms that the empire takes in the moment of globalized neoliberal capitalism. The capital that constructs the detention centers (described by Shannon Speed, chapter 1), or the border infrastructure that impedes the crossing of the Indigenous migrants with whom Lynn Stephen works, is the same capital that invests in the penitentiary industry and that constructs certified prisons in Mexico. At the same time, the militarization and paramilitarization that manifest forms of torture and use sexual violence as a counterinsurgency weapon have centers of transnational production in military bases. This culture of violence crosses borders in a way that the poor and racialized bodies of the Indigenous migrants cannot.

Standing before these transnational cultures of death, the Indigenous women of the Americas have developed creative strategies of resistance that range from the creation of their own security and justice systems, such as those described by María Teresa Sierra (chapter 3), to the use of creative writing to denounce the multiple violences of the empire. Even in a space of apparent isolation and total state control, the women of the Sisters of the Shadow Editorial Collective have constructed an emotional community and developed a politics of solidarity that allows them to confront the institutional violence that daily devalues their lives.

We hope that this book serves to echo Indigenous women's accusations, constructing transnational alliances from academia to activism and allowing us, the authors and the readership, to confront the politics of dispossession, confinement, and death that affect the lives of thousands of Indigenous men and women on the continent.

References

Adorno, Sérgio. 1995. "Discriminação racial e justiça criminal." *Novos Estudos* 43:45–63.
Alexandre, Michelle. 2012. *The New Jim Crow: Mass Incarceration in the Age of Colorblindness.* New York: New Press.

Altamirano-Jiménez, Isabel. 2013. *Indigenous Encounters with Neoliberalism: Place, Women, and the Environment in Canada and Mexico.* Vancouver: University of British Columbia Press.

Alves, Dina. 2017. "Rés negras, juízes brancos: Uma análise da interseccionalidade de gênero, raça e classe na produção da punição em uma prisão paulistana." *Revista CS* 21: 97–120.

Aranguren Romero, Juan Pablo. 2010. "De un dolor a un saber: Cuerpo, sufrimiento y memoria en los límites de la escritura." *Papeles del CEIC* 2 (September): 1–27.

Arens, Juliana. 2017. "Interseccionalidad de opresiones, género, clase y raza: Experiencias de Mujeres que recuperaron la libertad y Privadas de su libertad en San Francisco Tanviet, Oaxaca." Master's thesis, Centro de Investigaciones y Estudios Superiores en Antropología Social.

Arvin, Maile, Eve Tuck, and Angie Morrill. 2013. "Decolonizing Feminism: Challenging Connections Between Settler Colonialism and Heteropatriarchy." *Feminist Formations* 25 (1): 8–34.

Cadena, Carlota, and Leo Zavaleta. 2010. "Leo: ¿Quién te dijo que las mujeres tienen derecho a enamorarse?" In *Bajo la sombra del guamúchil. Historias de vida de mujeres indígenas y campesina en prisión*, edited by Rosalva Aída Hernández Castillo, 51–79. Mexico City: CIESAS.

Carneiro, Sueli. 1995. "Gênero, raça e ascensão social." *Estudos Feministas* 3 (2): 544–52.

Cavazos Ortiz, Irma. 2005. *Mujer, etiqueta y cárcel.* Mexico City: UAM / Instituto Nacional de Ciencias Penales.

Cerqueira, Daniel R. C., and Rodrigo Leandro de Moura. 2014. "Vidas perdidas e racismo no Brasil." *Instituto de Pesquisa Económica Aplicada* 22 (1): 73–90.

Chirix García, Emma Delfina. 2013. *Ch'akulal, chuq'aib'il chuqa b'anobäl: Mayab' ixoqui' chi ru pam jun kaxlan tz'apatäl tijonïk. Cuerpos, poderes, y políticas: Mujeres mayas en un internado católico.* Guatemala City: Ediciones Maya' Na'oj.

Clemmers, Donald. 1958. *The Prison Community.* New York: Holt Reinhart and Winston.

Cojti Cuxil, Demetrio. 1994. *Políticas para la reivindicación de los Mayas de hoy.* Guatemala City: SPEM.

Colectiva Editorial Hermanas en la Sombra. 2013. *Colección Revelaciones Intramuros.* Mexico City: INBA-CONACULTA-Colectiva Hermanas en la Sombra.

Colectiva Editorial Hermanas en la Sombra. 2016. *Cantos desde el Guamúchil. Historias de Vida de Mujeres Indígenas y Campesinas en Reclusión.* Cuernavaca: IMRyT-Colectiva Editorial Hermanas en la Sombra. Radio series. Accessed October 15, 2020. https://imryt.org/radio/cantos-desde-el-guamuchil.

Comisión Nacional de los Derechos Humanos. 2017a. *Diagnóstico Nacional de Supervisión Penitenciaria.* Mexico City: CNDH.

Comisión Nacional de los Derechos Humanos. 2017b. "Personas Indígenas en Reclusión." *Informe Anual de Actividades 2017.* Accessed September 10, 2020. http://informe.cndh.org.mx/menu.aspx?id=121.

Corral, Carolina. 2016. *Semillas de Guamuchil. Ahora en Libertad*. Mexico City: IMCINE-Colectiva Hermanas en la Sombra. Documentary Film.

Crenshaw, Kimberlé Williams. 1991. "Mapping the Margins: Intersectionality, Identity Politics, and Violence Against Women of Color." *Stanford Law Review* 43 (6): 1241–99.

Cuevas-Sosa, Andrés Alejandro, Rosario Mendieta Dimas, and Elvia Salazar Cruz. 1992. *La mujer delincuente bajo la ley del hombre*. Mexico City: Editorial Pax.

Cumes, Aura Estela. 2012. "Mujeres Indígenas, patriarcado y colonialismo: Un desafío a la segregación comprensiva de las formas de dominio." *Anuario Hojas de Warmi* 17. https://revistas.um.es/hojasdewarmi.

Das, Veena. 2008. *Sujetos del dolor, agentes de dignidad*. Bogotá: Editorial Pontificia-Universidad Javeriana.

Dávila, Patricia. 2016. "El gran fracaso de la certificación penitenciaria." *Revista Proceso*, March 16, 2016.

Davis, Angela Y. 1981. *Women, Race and Class*. New York: Random House.

Delgado, Richard, and Jean Stefancic. 2001. *Critical Race Theory: An Introduction*. New York: New York University Press.

Díaz-Cotto, Juanita. 1996. *Gender, Ethnicity and the State: Latina and Latino Prison Politics*. Albany: State University of New York Press.

Escalante, Yuri. 2015. *Racismo Judicial en Mexico. Análisis de sentencias y representación de la diversidad*. Mexico City: Juan Pablos Editor.

Flauzina, Ana Luiza Pinheiro. 2008. *Corpo negro caído no chão: O sistema penal e o projeto genocida do Estado brasileiro*. Brasília: Universidad de Brasília.

Foucault, Michel. 1977. *Discipline and Punish: The Birth of the Prison*. New York: Random House.

Gall, Olivia. 2004. "Identidad, exclusión y racismo: Reflexiones teóricas y sobre México." *Revista Mexicana de Sociología* 66 (2): 221–59.

Garrido Genovés, Vicente, and Jorge Sobral. 2008. *La investigación criminal: La psicología aplicada al descubrimiento, captura y condena de los criminales* Madrid: Editorial Nabla.

Gilmore, Ruth Wilson. 2007. *Golden Gulag: Prisons, Surplus, Crisis, and Opposition in Globalizing California*. Berkeley: University of California Press.

Gilmore, Ruth Wilson. 2008. "Forgotten Places and the Seed of Grassroots Planning." In *Engaging Contradictions: Theory, Politics, and Methods of Activist Scholarship*, edited by Charles R. Hale, 31–62. Berkeley: University of California Press.

Gómez Izquierdo, José Jorge, Guy Rozart Dupeyron, Fernanda Nuñez Becerra, and Alicia Castellanos Guerrero. 2008. *Los Caminos del Racismo en México*. Mexico City: Plaza y Valdez Editores.

Hardt, Michael, and Antonio Negri. 2000. *Empire*. Cambridge, Mass.: Harvard University Press.

Hernández, Ana Paula. 2011. "Drug Legislation and Prison Situation in Mexico." In *Systems Overload: Drug Laws and Prisons in Latin America*, edited by Pien Metaal and Coletta Youngers, 60–70. Washington, D.C.: Washington Office on Latin America.

Hernández Castillo, Rosalva Aída, ed. 2010a. *Bajo la sombra del guamúchil. Historias de vida de mujeres indígenas y campesina en prisión.* Mexico City: CIESAS.

Hernández Castillo, Rosalva Aída, ed. 2010b. *Bajo la sombra del guamúchil.* Uploaded December 13, 2010, by Mediatika. Vimeo video, 41:03. https://vimeo .com/17755550.

Hernández Castillo, Rosalva Aída. 2010c. "Violencia de Estado y violencia de género: Las paradojas en torno a los derechos humanos de las Mujeres en México." *Revista TRACE* 57:86–98.

Hernández Castillo, Rosalva Aída. 2013. "¿Del Estado multicultural al Estado penal? Mujeres indígenas presas y criminalización de la pobreza en México." In *Justicias Indígenas y Estado. Violencias Contemporáneas,* edited by María Teresa Sierra, Rosalva Aída Hernández Castillo, and Rachel Sieder, 299–338. Mexico City: FLACSO/CIESAS.

Hernández Castillo, Rosalva Aída. 2014. "La certificación carcelaria: ¿Nuevo embate del intervencionismo estadounidense?" *La Jornada,* September 15, 2014.

Hernández Castillo, Rosalva Aída. 2016. *Multiple InJustices: Indigenous Women, Law, and Political Struggle in Latin America.* Tucson: University of Arizona Press.

Hernández Castillo, Rosalva Aída. 2017. "La guerra contra el narco: Violencia de Género, militarización y criminalización de los Pueblos Indígenas." In *Pueblos Indígenas y Estado en México. La disputa por la justicia y los derechos,* edited by Santiago Bastos and María Teresa Sierra, 244–67. Mexico City: CIESAS.

Hernández Castillo, Rosalva Aída. n.d. "Artículos Periodísticos." *Rosalva Aída Hernández* (website). Accessed September 10, 2020. http://www.rosalvaaidahernandez .com/es/publicaciones/articulos-periodisticos/.

Hernández Castillo, Rosalva Aída, and María Teresa Sierra. 2005. "Repensar los derechos colectivos desde el género: Aportes de las mujeres indígenas al debate de la autonomía." In *La Doble Mirada: Luchas y Experiencias de las Mujeres Indígenas de América Latina,* edited by Martha Sánchez, 105–20. Mexico City: UNIFEM/ILSB.

Jimeno, Myriam. 2010. "Emociones y política: La 'víctima' y la construcción de comunidades emocionales." *Mana: Estudios de Antropología Social* 16:99–177.

Lee Camacho, Susuki. 2010. "Flor de Nochebuena: Nacieron mujeres, ahora se aguantan." In *Bajo la sombra del guamúchil: Historias de vida de mujeres indígenas y campesinas en prisión,* edited by Rosalva Aída Hernández Castillo, 19–28. Mexico City: Colectiva Editorial Hermanas en la Sombra.

Macleod, Morna, and Natalia De Marinis. 2018. *Resisting Violence: Emotional Communities in Latin America.* New York: Palgrave Macmillan.

México Evalúa. 2016. *Privatización del Sistema Penitenciario en México.* Mexico City: Documenta-Análisis y Acción para la Justicia A.C.

Monture-Angus, Patricia. 2000. "Aboriginal Women and Correctional Practice: Reflections on the Task Force on Federally Sentenced Women." In *An Ideal Prison? Critical Essays on Women's Imprisonment in Canada,* edited by Kelly Hannah-Moffat and Margaret Shaw, 52–60. Halifax: Fernwood.

Moreno, Monica. 2012. "Yo nunca he tenido la necesidad de nombrarme: Recono-
ciendo el racismo y el mestizaje en México." In *Racismos y otras formas de intol-
erancia: De norte a sur en América Latina,* edited by Alicia Castellanos Guerrero and Gisela Landázuri Benítez, 15–49. Mexico City: Universidad Autónoma
Metropolitana.

Naciones Unidas Subcomité para la Prevención de la Tortura y Otros Tratos o Penas
Crueles, Inhumanos o Degradantes (ONU SPT). 2017. *Visita a México del 12 al 21
de diciembre de 2016 observaciones y recomendaciones dirigidas al Estado.* December 15, 2017. http://cmdpdh.org/wp-content/uploads/2018/04/anexo-informe-del
-subcomite-sobre-su-visita-a-mexico-del-12-al-21-de-diciembre-de-2016.pdf.

Nahuelpan Moreno, Héctor, Herson Huinca Piutrin, Pablo Marimán Quemenado,
Luis Cárcamo-Huechante, Maribel Mora Curriao, José Quidel Lincoleo, Enrique
Antileo Baeza, Felipe Curivil Bravo, Susana Huenul Colicoy, José Millalén Paillal,
Margarita Calfío Montalva, Jimena Pichinao Huenchuleo, Elías Paillan Coñoepan,
and Andrés Cuyul Soto. 2012. *Tai ñ fijke xipa rakizuameluwün: Historia, Colo-
nialismo y Resistencias desde el País Mapuche.* Santiago: Ediciones de Historia
Mapuche.

Nakano-Glenn, Evelyn. 2015. "Settler Colonialism as Structure: A Framework for
Comparative Studies of US Race and Gender Formation." *Sociology of Race and
Ethnicity* 1 (1): 54–74.

Nascimiento, Abdias. (1978) 2016. *O Genocidio do Negro Brasileiro: Processo de um
racismo mascarado.* Saõ Paulo: Perspectiva.

Nichols, Robert. 2014. "The Colonialism of Incarceration." *Radical Philosophy Review*
17 (2): 435–55.

Olguín, Ben. 2009. *La Pinta: Chicana/o Prisoner Literature, Culture, and Politics.*
Austin: University of Texas Press.

Red Integra. n.d. Consejo Nacional de Ciencia y Tecnología. Accessed September 10,
2020. https://redintegra.org/.

Registro Nacional de Personas Extraviadas o Desaparecidas (RNPED). 2020. *Informe
de fosas clandestinas y registro nacional de personas desaparecidas o no localiza-
das.* Mexico City: Secretaría de Gobernación.

Reynoso, Alejandra. 2015. "El sueño de agua sucia." In *Bitácora del destierro: Nar-
rativa de mujeres en prisión,* edited by Elena de Hoyos, Rosalva Aída Hernández
Castillo, and Marina Ruiz, 99. Vol. 2 of *Colección Revelación Intramuros.* Mexico
City: Colectiva Editorial Hermanas en la Sombra.

Ross, Luana. 1998. *Inventing the Savage: The Social Construction of Native American
Criminality.* Austin: University of Texas Press.

Salazar, Rosita. 2012. "Somos." In *Mareas cautivas: Navegando las letras de mujeres
en prisión,* edited by Rosalva Aída Hernández Castillo, Elena de Hoyos, and
Marina Ruiz, 90. Mexico City: Colectiva Editorial de Mujeres en Prisión.

Segato, Rita Laura. 2007. "El color de la cárcel en América Latina: Apuntes sobre la
colonialidad de la justicia en un continente en deconstrucción." *Nueva Sociedad*
208:142–60.

Segunda Declaración de Barbados. 1977. Servindi. Accessed September 10, 2020. http://servindi.org/pdf/Dec_Barbados_2.pdf.

Sieder, Rachel, ed. 2017. *Demanding Justice and Security: Indigenous Women and Legal Pluralities in Latin America*. New Brunswick, N.J.: Rutgers University Press.

Sierra, María Teresa, Rosalva Aída Hernández Castillo, and Rachel Sieder, ed. 2013. *Justicias Indígenas y Estado: Violencias Contemporáneas*. Mexico City: FLACSO/CIESAS.

Sinhoretto, Jacqueline, and Danilo de Souza Morais. 2018. "Violência e racismo: Novas faces de uma afinidade reiterada." *Revista de Estudios Sociales* 64:15–26.

Smith, Andrea. 2005. "Native American Feminism, Sovereignty, and Social Change." *Feminist Studies* 31 (1): 116–32.

Speed, Shannon. 2017. "Structures of Settler Capitalism in Abya Yala." *American Quarterly* 69 (4): 783–90.

Stephen, Lynn. 2011. "Testimony and Human Rights Violations in Oaxaca." *Latin American Perspectives* 38 (6): 52–68.

Stephen, Lynn. 2016. *Somos la cara de Oaxaca: Testimonios y movimientos sociales*. Mexico City: Ediciones de la Casa Chata.

Stephen, Lynn. 2018. "Testimony, Social Memory, and Strategic Emotional/Political Communities in Elena Poniatowska's *Crónicas*." In *Resisting Violence: Emotional Communities in Latin America*, edited by Morna Macleod and Natalia De Marinis, 53–76. New York: Palgrave Macmillan.

Sudbury, Julia, ed. 2005. *Global Lockdown: Race, Gender, and the Prison Industrial Complex*. New York: Routledge.

Tonella, Galia. 2015. "Capítulo Tonella." In *Bajo la sombra del guamúchil: Historias de vida de mujeres indígenas y campesinas en prisión*, 2nd ed., edited by Rosalva Aída Hernández Castillo, 161–86. Mexico City: CIESAS.

Vargas, João Helion Costa, and Jaime Amparo Alves. 2010. "Geographies of Death: An Intersectional Analysis of Police Lethality and the Racialized Regimes of Citizenship in São Paulo." *Ethnic and Racial Studies* 33 (4): 611–36.

Wacquant, Loïc. 2000. *Las Cárceles de la Miseria*. Buenos Aires: Editorial Manantial.

Wacquant, Loïc. 2001. "The Advent of the Penal State Is Not a Destiny." *Social Justice* 28 (3): 81–98.

Wacquant, Loïc. 2009. *Punishing the Poor: The Neoliberal Government of Social Insecurity*. Durham, N.C.: Duke University Press.

Wade, Peter. 2011. "Multiculturalismo y racismo." *Revista Colombiana de Antropología* 47 (2): 15–35.

Zavaleta, Leo. 2016. *Los sueños de una cisne en el pantano*. Mexico City: Colectiva Editorial Hermanas en la Sombra.

CHAPTER 3

Women Defenders and the Fight for Gender Justice in Indigenous Territories

MARÍA TERESA SIERRA

U sing the framework of collaborative research with Indigenous women defenders, members of the Policía Comunitaria (Community Police) in the state of Guerrero, in the southwest of Mexico, I analyze the advances and setbacks in the construction of a gender justice agenda in contexts of neoliberal violence and macro-criminality. I highlight the recurring dilemmas faced by organized Indigenous women to defend other women that have been victims of multiple violence; while confronting ethnic and gender discrimination, they also maintain strong ties to their communities. Based on the testimonies of Indigenous women defenders, I analyze the following aspects: (1) how these women bridge gaps to advance gender justice, and (2) how different layers of structural and everyday violence overlap in the lives of Indigenous women. These layers condense historical traces of multiple subordinations involving colonial legacies of dispossession, structural racism, and social inequality, increasing gender harm. Finally, I reflect on how engaged collaborative research has strengthened the subversive potential of these Indigenous women defenders, which outlines the cultural and political struggles they carry out.

The Policía Comunitaria is an emblematic autonomous Indigenous institution in Mexico known for its achievements in building a system of security and justice in a large portion of Guerrero (Sierra 2017b). Indigenous women have played a leading role in this institution since its beginning, in 1995, although they were often marginalized and made invisible in its official narrative. This was the case until 2005, when they organized themselves as a committee of women and decided to fight for public recognition within the system. I am fortunate to be able to collaborate with Indigenous women defenders, since 2007, with the aim of supporting their organizing processes within the Coordinadora Regional de Autoridades Comunitarias (Regional Council of Community Authorities) of the Community Police (CRAC-PC) (Sierra 2017c). This collaboration has been very productive both academically and personally, allowing me to contribute to a key process for Indigenous women: one that seeks to redefine Indigenous autonomy from a gender perspective. This work has meant confronting both a deeply rooted patriarchal system involved in cultural grammars of customs and the structural racism embedded in social relations in Indigenous regions.

Political narratives about the Community Police did not recognize women's contributions to its building. Nonetheless, a perspective that recovers women's memories and agency reveals their committed collaboration in various tasks since the institution's foundation in 1995. Indigenous women are disputing their place in the politico-cultural project of the CRAC-PC, redefining their own gender agenda in light of their collective identities. They connect their fight to the struggles of many other Indigenous women throughout Latin America, who defend an intersectional perspective on gendered violence to fight against the different systems of oppression that interfere in their lives (Alemán 2006; Muñoz Cabrera 2010; Sieder 2017; Speed, Hernández Castillo, and Stephen 2006; Hernández Castillo 2016).

These *promotoras de justicia* (justice defenders) have made visible Indigenous women's demands, but also their own roles in the construction of an institution that has brought them dignity and peace in a highly racialized context with profound historical inequalities. I analyze the meanings of being a human rights defender and the different types of overlapping violence that structure Indigenous women's lives. I call attention to how women located in the margins of the state are able to advance a gender agenda while also aligning themselves with their people's fight for collective rights. Indigenous women defenders name gendered violence and question its naturalization, making relevant the cultural logics of harm and the sense of justice involved in women's claims. In this process, they translate their grievances into local semantics and develop strategies to make them intelligible in the language of rights; that is, Indigenous women defenders play what I call the role of "hinges" in plurilegal fields.

I discuss the productive role of collaborative research in supporting Indigenous women's organizing and making visible their contributions to a gender justice agenda. In methodological terms, collaboration contributed to increase the subversive dimension of women's demands by dismantling naturalized visions of gender roles in Indigenous communities and by questioning the coloniality of power against women (Lugones 2008). The collaborative work comprised two main analytic phases, aligning with stages in the Community Police's struggle for autonomy. The first phase coincided with the consolidation of the Indigenous institution (2007–9). At the request of CRAC-PC authorities, I accompanied women justice defenders in their organizing process. A second phase occurred when the Community Police suffered a split, at a time of increased criminality and institutional harassment (2013–15). This fracture weakened women's participation but stimulated the growth of an alternate space called Casa de la Mujer Indígena (CAMI, Indigenous Women's House) in the city of San Luis Acatlán. CAMI emerged to deal with women's health issues and later expanded to address gender-based violence.

In this text, I highlight two main issues: I document the committed work of Indigenous women to open up Indigenous justice to their participation, and I provide a critical reflection on the scope and limits of academic collaboration in these processes. Throughout, I stress the subjective and affective dimensions of social relations for fostering social agency (Jimeno, Varela, and Castillo 2018; Macleod and De Marinis 2018) and for building a dialogue-based collaborative anthropology (Hale 2008; Hernández Castillo 2015).

In the first part, I present an analytic framework to explore the continuum of structural and everyday violence that shapes Indigenous women's agency, as well as to comprehend local understandings of gendered violence. From there, I develop my argument that collaborative research is a key tool of knowledge production for the defense of human rights and decolonizing gender ideologies. First, I analyze the historical schemes of dispossession, violence, and insecurity that fostered the emergence of the Community Police of Guerrero, and particularly the role of women in the process. Next, I feature the voices of the justice defenders who dared to name silenced grievances, making their struggles relevant for the community justice process of CRAC-PC. The tensions between the collective and the particular dimensions of gender rights become evident, as does the need to overcome these dichotomies. Following this discussion, I turn to the definition of gendered violence emerging from the experiences of women defenders in the alternate space of CAMI, and the challenges they face in highly polarized and violent contexts. Here, my interest is the maturation of a gender agenda that emphasizes women's subjectivities and rights as political tools vis-à-vis male authority. Finally, I explore the ethical and academic challenges of my collaboration aimed at promoting the rights of Indigenous women, in contexts marked by multiple forms of violence and structural racism.

Collaboration, the Continuum of Violence, and Gender Justice

> Women come here to find help, because they get there without attorneys, without any advice; the Office of the Public Prosecutor does not pay attention to them, and filing the report is not easy. This is why many women who live in situations of violence do not file reports. They live with no resources, experiencing sexual abuse and rape as well. Yet, they don't say anything because they are scared, scared of reporting it, because, "if I file a report, they could kill my son, they could kill my husband, it could spark a chain reaction and would finish off my family." There is a lot of fear. Several things are hidden in the community, and not only in the community, but also in governmental institutions. (Apolonia Plácido, pers. comm., April 20, 2017)

This testimony by Apolonia Plácido, a Na'savi woman and CAMI coordinator in San Luis Acatlán, illustrates the many obstacles faced by Indigenous women inside and outside of their communities in their search for justice and their fight against racism, impunity, and inequality. It also reveals how significant it is for women to support one another in their search for justice. Plácido's narrative summarizes the challenges that Indigenous women face in contexts of cultural diversity, legal pluralism, and racialized geographies, where long-standing violence operates. We cannot analyze the gendered violence affecting Indigenous women without considering the intersection of complex systems of oppression in their lives. I concur with Nancy Scheper-Hughes and Phillippe Bourgois (2004) that structural and everyday violence form a *continuum of violence* that must be documented in light of the moral and cultural ethos that contributes to its normalization. Indigenous women's perspectives hold the potential to defy male authority, which in turn tends to silence female voices and justify their continued subordination as a matter of *costumbre* (custom or habit). An anthropological analysis can provide new meanings for women's grievances and deepen our understanding of gendered violence by placing the experiences of actors and their governance institutions at the center (Muñoz Cabrera 2010; Sieder 2017; Macleod and De Marinis 2018; Figueroa Romero and Sierra 2020).

Indigenous women verbalize the harms in their daily life when they seek justice; these harms are related to health issues, domestic violence, property-related violence, sexual attacks, and discrimination, among others. These forms of violence reproduce histories of exclusion and dispossession that crisscross women's lives and those of their families and relegate them to highly vulnerable social positions. They also reveal everyday moral routines that justify women's subordination to male authority.

Analyses regarding the cultural conflict reveal the multiple obstacles faced by Indigenous women when they seek justice. When Indigenous women present their testimony during penal trials, they not only have to speak Spanish or use translators but they are forced to talk about gendered violence in terms that could be offensive to them and to use legal categories that distance them from their suffering (Terven 2017). Human rights narratives offer little space to understand women's claims because these narratives usually highlight legal frameworks that emphasize extreme types of violence (Mora 2017). In fact, power relations embedded in the law reproduce gender subordination and inequality, imposing norms and procedures. Indigenous women's own narratives clash with legal discourses and their underlying webs of power, with the effect of silencing their testimony. In order to avoid this ethnocentric vision of law, it is salient to consider cultural diversity and local knowledge in naming gendered violence and acting on it.

In this context it becomes relevant to analyze the role of women defenders in Indigenous communities, as well as their capacity to articulate grievances, hear claims, and file reports, among many other activities, to support women experiencing violence. Having lived through gendered violence themselves, they use their experience to generate culturally sensitive alternatives and to negotiate the language of rights in accordance with their realities. Abstract legal categories such as gendered violence acquire meaning when they are embodied in women's concrete experiences (Sieder 2017; Sieder and Barrera Vivero 2017; Stephen 2019). Local understandings of gendered violence are a powerful force to advance an intercultural gender agenda for Indigenous women that considers the horizon of possibilities anchored to their collective identities.

How, then, do Indigenous women act and express themselves in the face of the different types of violence that affect their lives? How do they connect their individual and collective identities to dispute their place in the Community Police? How do they manage to create a space for the defense of women's rights while building their own subjectivity as Indigenous women?

Layers of Violence and Community Resistance

The criminals were everywhere, around our animals, goats, beasts, coffee. We weren't free to go on roads or pathways; people weren't free to walk. This led to the creation of the Community Police. (Caritita Flores Mejía, interview by Felicitas Martínez, March 10, 2009)

They would rape women here; this is why we felt the need to talk to the comisario [community authority] . . . we could no longer bear so many assaults; we were just working for the mañosos [criminals]. The comisario told us "So, then, would you women help us out?" "Yes," we said, "we'll go house by house asking for help," and we did it. (Elsa, interview by Paula Silva, July 20, 2009)

These two testimonies of women involved in the creation of the Community Police reveal the lack of security in the La Montaña region of Guerrero in the early 1990s, when people were unable to move freely and faced harassment, robberies, and aggression from *mañosos*.[1] Above anything else, the testimonies reveal a notorious and ever-present reality: women's bodies had become the vehicle through which criminals sowed terror in the population, to the point of even "raping a woman in front of her husband and on top of a small passenger bus," according to the testimony of Gelasio Barrera, one of CRAC-PC's founders. The last straw was the raping of a minor, which triggered a collective response to the many grievances experienced by Indigenous women and men in the region. They decided to confront criminality

---

1. Both statements were gathered by justice defenders in the municipality of San Luis Acatlán. Caritita Flores Mejía was the wife of the former regional commander in the town of Espino Blanco, and Elsa was a resident of Cuanacaxtitlan (Hernández and Sierra 2009).

and guarantee public safety, a heroic act of dignity that meant not only exercising the right to protect themselves and defend their communities (Article 39 of the Mexican Constitution) but also transforming themselves into political actors willing to limit abuse, discrimination, and violence that were all endorsed (if not perpetrated) by the state. Community members and local authorities took up arms in order to defend themselves against the violence of caciques (political bosses) and criminals, but not to challenge the state authorities directly. This action thus departed from decades-long guerrilla traditions in the Montaña region (Bartra 1996).

The women's testimonies quoted here were published in a booklet that was the first product of my collaboration with justice defenders, and it had the purpose of making visible women's participation in the construction of the Community Police (Hernández and Sierra 2009). The booklet disseminated women's narratives in simple words. This text legitimated the agency of women and empowered them; as justice defenders, they interviewed CRAC-PC founders, both men and women, to talk about their experiences and the role of women in building the institution. This collective initiative increased women's awareness of their role in a heroic institution and had the pedagogical effect of encouraging them to listen to and recognize themselves in the moral justifications that motivated the community-led self-defense. The women defenders identified with the Community Police founders' testimonies, which strengthened their pride at belonging to the institution. Finally, the new narrative had the important effect of disputing the prevalent story that men had been paramount in the organization's founding, making visible the commitment of women (Sierra 2011; Sierra 2017c).

The territory in which the Community Police operate today represents a wide network of communities and diverse organizations, a multitude that stems from an unexpected expansion after 2011.[2] It is marked by histories of colonization and dispossession across temporalities, histories that weave together long-term memories of subordination, racism, highly explosive geographies, and social unrest, often faced by forceful resistance of peasants and armed organizations. These processes have all brought political and

2. The territory of the Community Police has grown exponentially since 2013. Today, the CRAC-PC has five Houses of Justice (headquarters) in the mountain and coastal regions of Guerrero, involving thirty-one municipalities and thirty-one Indigenous, mestizo, and Afro communities under its jurisdiction. See Sierra (2018).

military violence to this region, as well as widespread experiences of repression and serious violations of human rights (Bartra 1996; Tlachinollan 2018).

What is unique to this region is the high level of community organization so fundamental to a resistance based on local knowledge and legitimacy. Many factors enable the Community Police to withstand the predatory pressure of capital and the *caciquil* structures buttressed in municipal and regional power.[3] These factors include Indigenous and peasant knowledge of the territory, their care for their sacred mountains, their respect for their deities through ceremonies and festivities, the rational use of natural resources, and the legitimacy of agrarian and communal structures. For quite some time, the Community Police were able to stop the insecurity and violence in the larger mountain regions of Guerrero. It was a successful counterweight to the extractive transnational enterprises, especially in mining and forestry, that exploit the natural resources in Guerrero (Tlachinollan 2018; Sierra 2017a).

The current context of extreme violence and inequality—as well as the insidious presence of organized crime since 2013—has affected the territory under the jurisdiction of the Community Police, restricting social practices and increasing the risk for women. Despite the fact that the Community Police were able to stop the insecurity and impunity for some time, this is no longer the case. Dispossession has intensified through extractive projects, and organized crime exerts its influence and pressure in the region, at times in connivance with state and local political actors. In addition, the Community Police have experienced internal fragmentation, with polarizing effects. These circumstances have hampered the prospects of protecting the population and of making women feel safe. Moreover, gendered violence has increased: again, it is the women's bodies that constitute the footprint of the communities' subordination to criminal powers (Segato 2013). This situation is exemplified by the 2010 case of the Me'phaa women of La Montaña—raped by soldiers—whose voices and claims were taken all the way to the Inter-American Court of Human Rights (Hernández Castillo 2017), as well as by the exponential increase of crimes against humanity such as forced disappearances, the displacement of entire communities, and femicides. The case of the forty-three students who disappeared from the Ayotzinapa Rural Teachers' College on September 26, 2014—a case still unsolved as of

---

3. *Caciquismo* is the territorial and political control exercised by a "strong man" or cacique in a region.

2020—offers vivid evidence of the chain of impunity existing in the state of Guerrero (Tlachinollan 2018).

Against these grids of structural violence, the women and men of the Community Police carry out their lives and try to address the extreme vulnerability of this region, which has the highest rate of poverty in the country, together with a high level of insecurity (see IEP 2019). These conditions directly affect the social reproduction of communities. In Guerrero, migration is the principal recourse for economic survival. Given such a bleak context, the Community Police is the reference for many Indigenous and mestizo communities that intend to recover their collective strength. For instance, Carmen, a Me'phaa woman who has experienced overwhelming material poverty, abandonment by her partners, dramatic family experiences, and continuous uncertainty in her future, has found in the Community Police a locus of resistance and an important sense of identity that has sustained her through very difficult phases of her life. This is why she has never withdrawn her commitment to this institution and, as she says, will never do so.

In sum, the territory of the Community Police is marked by a long-standing history of dispossession, criminality, and *caciquil* and racist violence, which led to the organized response of Indigenous communities in building alternatives for social peace. Women's participation in the Community Police must be situated against this history, even if patriarchal frameworks prevail in the organization. For these reasons, the tough efforts made by the women of CRAC-PC to enlarge community justice from a gender perspective are particularly salient.

Constructing a Gender Agenda in the Community Police

On September 20, 2010, I met with CRAC-PC justice defenders in my small fieldwork home, in the center of San Luis Acatlán. It was a welcoming place with a small terrace where we could sit and enjoy the refreshing evening air. The objective was to evaluate the collaborative work we had done over the past two years in fostering women's organizing within the Community Police. Eight women were present: six justice defenders, Úrsula Hernández (a research assistant), and I. We had created a relaxed space of trust that would help us in the elaboration of a work plan that was to be followed over the next few years. The first two years had been very productive, and we were able to advance the content of a gender agenda within CRAC-PC.

We came up with a participatory diagnosis of violence and access to justice for women through workshops in different communities (Sierra 2017c). This study gave us the opportunity to visualize the problems experienced by women in their domestic spaces and access to justice. We presented our findings to CRAC-PC regional authorities, with great recognition for our work. It was in fact the first effort into organizing Indigenous women at CRAC-PC. A summary of our study was recorded in a widely distributed testimonial video, itself the result of this collaborative project (Sierra 2011). The "Diagnosis," as women promoters named it, became an important tool for making visible women's demands and discussing women's rights (Sierra 2017c). A second achievement was the strengthening of women's participation as authorities within CRAC-PC, which meant allowing differentiated styles for doing justice in the Community Police (Arteaga Börth 2013).

Since 2007, women have been elected as authorities of CRAC-PC; they were at the "Table of Justice" sharing responsibility with the male authorities. This has had important consequences for women by opening alternatives to their complaints. Felicitas, the first woman coordinator, introduced an amendment to CRAC-PC's internal rules that called for cases of rape to be punished, rather than settled through the customary agreements between parties. She also proposed that in cases of pension disputes, the women coordinators should worry not only about determining the amount of money to be paid by men, but also about mitigating the emotional effects on children. Asunción, a respectable woman elected as coordinator of CRAC-PC in 2009, introduced the practice that women victims of violence should first be treated at the health center before starting a trial. These were important decisions that opened new horizons for implementing community justice from a gender perspective. In addition, female coordinators initiated workshops on the topic of masculinity for the male members of the Community Police (Arteaga Börth 2013).

My collaboration with the *promotoras de justicia* contributed to this process. Through workshops, shared analysis, and activities, the *promotoras* became aware of their rights as Indigenous women. It was clear to them that they were not only defending CRAC-PC as their autonomous institution, but also daring to question machismo, a patriarchal ideology rooted in their communities.

The assessment that we performed at the September 2010 meeting, at my place, was intended to facilitate a work plan to be presented by the *promotoras* to CRAC-PC's new authorities. The aim was to legitimize women's participation and secure their representation on CRAC-PC's board. With a great sense of humor and enthusiasm, Carmen—whose life history overlaps considerably with the history of the Community Police—spoke about reeducation, the final phase of CRAC-PC's justice, in which people who are found guilty of crimes, after being processed, have to perform community service supervised by the Community Police. Carmen stated: "for me, women's participation within CRAC-PC is very important, as well as the way the reeducation process happens, as a male policeman should not supervise a female detainee, since the trust is not the same . . . it is important that women participate in the detention, [in] the reeducation process, and in determining how people will be punished. This is what is missing" (Sierra 2011, 11:40). Carmen emphasized the risk of abuse that women faced at the hands of the Community Police, as in fact happened to a detained woman who ended up pregnant. She spoke from her own experience to make women's demands visible within CRAC-PC, wanting to guarantee the creation of adequate spaces for female detainees in order to protect their integrity. This shows the positive effect that a gender discourse can have on the definition of community justice, especially in the reeducation phase.

Paula, another justice defender, shyly expressed that her dream was to have more policewomen and female commanders, as well as to prove that women can take on the responsibility of being in charge of security, which is culturally defined as a men's task: "For me, being a *promotora* is a commitment that we have toward other women. It is also difficult having to go to meetings when we are single mothers. As a defender, I want to know, to learn more. I would like the bylaws to state that there should be community policewomen, so that my dream can come true" (Sierra 2011, 20:28).

Paula served as the treasurer of the Community Police for several years. She did well in this role, which made her feel proud of herself. At the time, she was the mother of four children: a small girl with whom she basically lived at the CRAC-PC House of Justice, and three other children who were taken care of by their grandmother in Buena Vista, her community. Later on, in 2013, Paula was elected regional commander of the Community Police at a general electoral assembly. She was the first woman to occupy that high-level position, doing so at a time when CRAC-PC was experiencing a serious internal crisis. Acting as a regional commander implies supervising Community Police groups and participating in security and detention strategies. On several occasions, Paula showed her courage and proved that she was able to "do it just as well as any other man or better, because some of them are cowards," as she told me in a conversation. Since Paula took office during the height of the conflict within factions of CRAC-PC, she was regional commander for only three months and was forced to abandon her post. Nonetheless, it was enough time for her to demonstrate that women were able to make their dreams happen. Paula believed that women have rights and should not allow men to push them around. Her pragmatism was directed at reinforcing women's place in the Community Police.

Among all the *promotoras de justicia*, Felicitas Martínez most insisted on bringing up the language of gendered violence and women's rights, a focus that reflects her own trajectory within Indigenous women's organizations and her training as a lawyer. She stressed that women must be guaranteed a seat on the Community Police board of justice: "There have been *compañeras* [in the community justice system], but they were invisible, they did not administer [any] justice. Decisions are made by the board of justice" (Sierra 2011, 15:10). Martínez held the office of CRAC-PC coordinator on several occasions, as well as that of *consejera* (counselor), the most prestigious position in the institution. As coordinator at the board of justice, she had decision-making power and the ability to administer justice. Her work at CRAC-PC has been key for introducing other ways of doing justice that focus on women's perspectives and seek to understand gender-based claims. Through her experience, Martínez acquired knowledge in different political spaces that continues to shape her commitment to gender rights today.

These testimonies reveal the close ties that the women justice defenders have with the community institution, as well as the significance of gender rights to them. Collaborative processes have helped expand their political horizons as women within the Community Police. Women's voices reveal a history of marginalization in Indigenous communities, as well as the recognition of being part of an institution that has given them dignity. In the face of insecurity and violence, justice defenders find new meanings for their lives and the opportunity to contribute to a collective project they define as their own. While the fight for gender equality is not their principal demand, they consistently articulate that women have rights and the strength to defend these rights. Their organizing efforts are aimed at promoting solid participation of women in the Community Police and at building a community justice system that respects women's rights. These reflections were the outcome of an intense collaborative process that gave me the strength and the energy to build personal and academic relations with these powerful women that continue today in 2020. My involvement with these women has allowed me to promote gender rights in an emblematic institution of Indigenous people in Mexico.

Connecting Knots: Everyday Forms of Gendered Violence and the Role of Community Justice Defenders

I turn now to the testimonies of CAMI *promotoras* (community human rights defenders) in the city of San Luis Acatlán, collected as part of a new ethnographic project on gendered violence in Guerrero.[4] These testimonies reveal a persistent web of violence experienced by Indigenous women in the form of beatings, threats, false accusations, rapes, and abandonment, but also in the obstacles they confront to access justice; all of these are grievances that women bring to CAMI. This quotidian web of violence in the domestic and community spheres reflects an underlying structural vulnerability. Indigenous women's stories reveal the state of dispossession in which they live, a product of marginalization and neoliberal logics of inequality (Speed 2017).

CAMI defenders' testimonies about gendered violence refer to grievances that Indigenous women face in their daily life, concerns that women defenders process and explain through their own notions of morality and justice. In the practice of listening to and accompanying women victims of violence, the justice defenders have developed a greater consciousness of their own work. Taking on the role of human rights defender means accepting personal risk, both in confronting the traditional patriarchal order and in supporting women who are being victimized. Our dialogues with CAMI defenders are intended to help them visualize and critically reflect on the challenges inherent in defending gender rights in polarized and insecure contexts, as well as strategies to protect themselves.

Justice defenders translate women's experiences of violence in an attempt to seek remedies for Indigenous women who normally do not have access to justice. They do so by generating bonds and trust to help female victims of violence feel secure and well treated while also accompanying them to the community authority in search of mediation or legal action.

---

4. For reference to this project, see Figueroa Romero and Sierra (2020).

Life Under Threat: Risks and Vulnerabilities
Faced by Women Justice Defenders

In the context of increasing insecurity, organized crime has provoked a spiral of violence in large regions of Guerrero, with the aim to control the population and impose a regime of fear. This situation has increased the vulnerability of Indigenous women and had negative consequences for their work as human rights defenders. Apolonia Plácido, a Na'savi woman and CAMI coordinator, received threats that tested the work that *promotoras* had been doing and brought to light both their own vulnerability and the lack of security measures surrounding their work. When the *promotoras* focused on maternal health, nothing was questioned, but everything changed once they started working on cases related to gendered violence. One such case, in 2015, was especially complicated because it meant confronting CRAC-PC authorities, who had decided to protect a person accused of raping a fourteen-year-old girl. Since the accused man was a teacher with local political influence, CRAC-PC authorities dismissed the accusation and determined that it was a case of "dishonest abuse" rather than rape as had been claimed by the victim. This girl was in turn accused of lying. The relatives of the young woman came to San Luis Acatlán from the Indigenous community of Yoloxóchitl in order to seek the support of CAMI. For its part, CAMI assumed the role of defender and demanded that CRAC-PC administer justice. This demand created high levels of tension between CRAC-PC and CAMI, increasing CAMI's vulnerability. As an institution integrated into the Community Police system, CAMI should have protection from CRAC-PC. This relationship had previously been strained by internal conflicts within CRAC-PC, which coincided with threats directed at Apolonia, CAMI's coordinator. In the following section I describe Apolonia's testimony in order to illustrate the level of vulnerability and fear she experienced in a moment when the pressure of organized crime implied a real threat to Indigenous women's activities, and when the Community Police did not provide the expected support.

Support for the "Aggrieved": Victims of Gendered Violence

Apolonia, my *comadre* (godmother), has been threatened. Her anguish and concern are noticeable, but rather than staying still, she finds the strength to continue her work and support "the aggrieved," as she calls them, those women who experience violence. I decided to visit her in Chilpancingo, where she has gone to attend some workshops on gendered violence organized by the Commission for the Development of Indigenous Peoples (CDI).[5] She tells me that she is not feeling well; her head hurts, and she sometimes feels that she cannot go on anymore. She feels the pressures of her commitments to CAMI, but also the continuous pressure of her husband, a Na'savi peasant who questions her engagement. Apolonia continually refers to having body aches and pain in her spine, head, and legs, the places where her worries and fears are lodged. As she often says, "It is not easy to be a coordinator of CAMI and have to carry all the weight." She often gets massages and *limpias* (cleanses) to get rid of the bad vibes, something in which her *compañeras* (midwives) are experts. CAMI's women are attentive to their own bodies and heal them with medicinal plants, the *temazcal* (Mesoamerican steam bath), rituals, and other natural remedies. Their bodies are the receptacles of tensions caused by the important work they perform; it is in their bodies that the violence is manifested and that pain and distress are experienced (Segato 2013). Incarnated violence is the core dimension of the multiple layers of violence that scale women's everyday lives.

Apolonia tells me that she received threats, including phone calls with detailed information about her. Days after the phone threats, people were seen hanging around and taking pictures outside of the CAMI house, in the center of San Luis Acatlán, not far from the CRAC-PC headquarters, and later on, shots were fired into the air in front of the house at night. People have also seen strangers near the entrance to CAMI. These events reveal a constant deterioration of life in San Luis Acatlán, in contrast with the good times of just a few years prior, when the presence of the Community Police guaranteed justice and security. The incidents are disturbing signs of harassment directed at CAMI, especially toward Apolonia and the *promotoras*, with the purpose of intimidating them. Apolonia did not hesitate to connect the incident to her participation in reporting rapes and demanding justice for women. The phone threats came from Los Rojos, one of the most powerful organized crime cartels in Guerrero. The faction supposedly wanted to intimidate her and get her to pay *derecho de piso*, a protection fee (a practice that has been imposed by the mafia). This is how Apolonia remembers what she was told by phone on April 10, 2016:

---

5. The CDI was the official entity of *indigenista* policies between 2003 and 2018. Its contemporary counterpart is the Instituto Nacional de los Pueblos Indígenas, established in 2018.

Good afternoon Mrs. Apolonia, I come from the state of [Guerrero], my name is xxxx, we have come to protect you, to bring peace to San Luis Acatlán, and I am calling to tell you to give us an economic contribution; if you do, we will protect you very well. . . . I want you to know that we belong to Los Rojos cartel, and do not hang up, ma'am, we want you to support us in protecting you; think about it, but on this day, today, we want you to contribute 1,500 pesos.

These threats were serious, given the context of impunity and high rates of violence toward women in the state of Guerrero.[6] The threat was evaluated by national women's organizations that support CAMI. These organizations suggested specific actions for Apolonia's protection, and an international campaign for her support was promoted.

These facts made Apolonia fear for her security. Community Police were expected to protect CAMI but did not do so. During the critical moment of the threats, CAMI was left alone and had to ask the municipal police and other self-defense groups in the region for support. While these groups did respond, they could not guarantee continuous protection because it was not their territory of action.[7] For the first time, it was evident that women justice defenders were not simply threatening male power, but were also the target of powerful actors (such as Los Rojos) who wanted to intimidate women and extort them.

Generating Alternatives in Precarious Circumstances

It is in this context that we, Dolores and I, organized a workshop on security protocols in order to define criteria for the protection and self-care of CAMI's women. The workshop took place over two days at CAMI in San Luis Acatlán, May 21–22, 2016. About twenty people attended, most of them CAMI's *promotoras* and women coming from different institutions,

---

6. Since 2006, the rates of violent deaths of women in Guerrero have increased exponentially (OVICOM 2015). For this reason, the Mexican government declared a Gender Alert (official program aimed at addressing gendered violence) for some municipalities of the state on June 22, 2017.

7. Self-defense groups emerged in municipalities near San Luis Acatlán to confront organized crime and impunity. For example, the Union of Peoples and Popular Organizations of Guerrero is a huge citizens' self-defense group in the coastal region of Guerrero (Warnholtz 2016).

including former justice coordinators from CRAC-PC. This workshop was an opportunity to reflect on the conditions in which defenders perform their work, as well as the risks and dilemmas they face in accompanying victims of violence. The topic of security triggered an in-depth discussion of how to ground concrete and viable proposals in the context of strong deficiencies and economic needs aggravated by racism and ethnic discrimination.

During the workshop, I was struck by the clarity of women's narratives regarding their practice and the problems faced by those who seek their help. It was an opportunity to put into work their own relevant expertise and to enhance their knowledge. They expressed what it means to accompany women who are reporting crimes before the state's public prosecutor or before the community authority, but principally they referred to the shifting conditions they face in their duty due to the increase of insecurity in their daily life. In their narratives, they manifested empathy toward the women who experience violence and come to them for advice, and, significantly, they explored how these encounters connect to their own life experiences. They were able to contextualize what happens to women and refer to the set of accumulated grievances Indigenous women experience, making them understandable to local authorities. In fact, these women defenders act as *hinges*, translating cultural notions of harm and repair into demands and legal terms.

Inés, a *promotora*, talked about a woman who had requested CAMI's support to denounce her husband to the local authority, the *comisario*, in Pueblo Hidalgo, a Me'phaa community (Inés own community). She stressed that the *comisario* had to be approached cautiously as he was not a trustworthy person; Inés knew him personally and knew that he did not treat his wife well. The woman was accompanied by CAMI's attorney—a community female lawyer—and some *promotoras*. Inés talked eloquently about the encounter she had with the local authority, revealing that she had reached her own conclusions about the case: "My *comadre* [the attorney] told [the *comisario*]: 'No, mister, calm down, allow the young woman to talk.' Poor girl, it seems that she is suffering a lot," said Inés. "I think this is where violence begins, and it is being 'dragged' from way back. I saw that the situation was very difficult because the young woman no longer wanted to go back to her husband. The man did not want the separation; he disqualified the young woman, stating that she was crazy."

Inés theorized about the motives and forms of domestic violence, in this case, a violence coming from the past, an accumulation of harms. She understood why the young woman wanted to split from her husband, despite knowing how difficult it would be to get a divorce. The young woman ended up being labeled "crazy" by her husband, and she received a series of epithets from her father-in-law and her own father, disqualifying her for daring to make a claim and for not agreeing to wait for her husband while he went to work as a migrant in the agricultural fields. It did not matter that she had suffered a miscarriage, that she was being mistreated, and that she had experienced a number of aggressions on the part of her in-laws—and even from her own father, who sided with her husband against her because she wanted a separation—it seemed that the young woman was going to be revictimized. CAMI's support was critical for convincing the community authority, the *comisario*, that the best outcome would be the couple's separation, as well as a mandate that the husband pay support for the children, which was finally obtained. Inés was right when she stated that violence is being "dragged in" from the past; violence does not occur in a vacuum. With her statement, Inés made it clear that gendered violence can be traced.

In this workshop, conversation arose about the constant criticism that women justice defenders face from their neighbors, who call them "meddlesome" for assuming a role that "does not correspond to them." As *promotoras*, women continually confront gender ideologies that justify the subordination of women. Such was the case of the fourteen-year-old girl who was raped. CAMI's decision to defend her provoked a strong confrontation with CRAC-PC authorities, who did not want to charge or punish the perpetrator. The local newspaper *El Faro de la Costa Chica* used a loudspeaker in the community's public space to question CAMI's role. In Apolonia's words, "*El Faro* said: What is CAMI doing supporting the rape case? [CAMI's] work has to do with sexual health; it is about midwives, not about supporting cases."

Male voices at different levels of authority—CRAC-PC, the municipal president, and the local news—came together in order to question women's agency and advocacy. Using authoritarian, patriarchal language, they reminded the *promotoras* that CAMI's sphere of influence was supposed to be confined to maternal health. The women defenders were warned not to accompany women who experience violence. Gender ideologies feminizing the health field and midwifery came to light. These ideologies were also used to threaten women who confronted male authority; this, in consequence, created new risks and insecurities for them. Despite it all, the women stood firm and did not allow themselves to be intimidated. Making inroads in the public space to defend women's rights has been, without a doubt, one of the main achievements of the women defenders, which has in turn nourished and strengthened their own self-understanding as women living in precarious and racialized contexts. This understanding informs their subjectivities as Indigenous women.

Throughout our dialogues, CAMI's promoters confirmed that they would challenge community authorities and would not subordinate themselves. This is why, despite the threats, the women continued denouncing human rights violations and organizing public actions to express themselves. Women justice defenders have matured sufficiently to create a solid discourse and to position themselves against gendered violence, even if doing so means confronting community authorities; at the same time, however, they continue to express their desire to remain engaged with the CRAC-PC, an institution they helped build. In the next section, I consider the ethical and political dimensions of my collaboration in Indigenous women's organizing efforts, and the way in which this work has contributed to advancing gender justice.

Gender Justice and the Ethical and Political Dilemmas of Collaboration

The collaborative work that I undertook with the women defenders fulfilled one of its main objectives: to make women's demands visible, advancing a gender agenda within the Community Police. In addition to promoting the organization of women within the Policía Comunitaria, we help ensure their participation in the CRAC-PC board of justice and their involvement in regional assemblies, where public issues are discussed.

A cultural climate that legitimizes discourses on gender rights at the international and national level as well as the recognition of Indigenous people's rights to self-determination has strengthened Indigenous women's agency and their initiatives to fight against multiple forms of violence in contexts of racism and dispossession. The International Indigenous Women's Forum (FIMI) and the Continental Meeting of Indigenous Women of the Americas (ECMIA)[8] have been particularly active in promoting an agenda that interconnects Indigenous women's rights with the collective rights of their

8. FIMI is a network of Indigenous women leaders from Asia, Africa, and the Americas that coordinates agendas, builds capacity, and develops leadership roles. ECMIA has brought together Indigenous women's organizations of the Americas since 1995. See Channel Foundation (n.d.), Alemán (2006), and Muñoz Cabrera (2010).

people. Indigenous women activists have been especially sensitive to developing an intersectional perspective regarding violence against women as well as to insisting on the effects of the colonial legacy on Indigenous women's life (Lugones 2008). For this reason, in my collaboration with justice defenders, I followed an intersectional perspective to understand gendered violence and the way that different layers of violence (class, race, ethnicity) intertwine and accumulate in Indigenous women's lives and bodies: multiple oppressions are interconnected with naturalized gender roles that justify their subordination. Violence gets "dragged in" from the past, as Inés said, increasing women's vulnerability in highly precarious contexts. By understanding the connections among all these layers of violence in concrete cases, we can assess the role that women justice defenders play in promoting advocacy and self-care strategies.

Beyond ethnographically documenting situations at the crossroads of violence and insecurities, where women build their lives, my collaboration had a concrete but powerful goal: opening spaces to Indigenous women at the CRAC-PC, the main institution of this pluri-ethnic system of security and justice. We were successful in generating recognition of women and their important contribution to the building of this community institution. The public meeting on October 15, 2009, where we—the justice promoters and me—presented the results of our study regarding gendered violence and access to justice meant a crucial moment to promote a gender agenda within CRAC-PC. This meeting helped legitimize Indigenous women's rights and, critically, facilitated our work in the communities.

The two phases of my collaboration discussed in this text responded to key junctures in the community process. They reveal fissures, modalities, and circumstances in the internal gender dynamics of the Policía Comunitaria. During the first phase, I helped open spaces for women in the community board of justice, coinciding with the consolidation of the CRAC-PC as a regional system (Sierra 2015). In the second phase, a time of increasing tensions and macro-criminality provoked a hypermasculine response from the Community Police and an emphasis on security over justice (Sierra 2018). My solidarity with the women defenders led to tension in my relationship with the male CRAC-PC authorities at that time. This was, in fact, a bad moment that relocated me to the "right place"—as external actor—and obliged me to take some distance so as to not contribute to internal polarization. It was a practical pedagogy demonstrating the limits of collaborative research.

As Charles R. Hale (2008) points out, the tensions that arise in collaborative research are productive to analyzing the social field. Tensions between women defenders and CRAC-PC authorities revealed men's power struggles for control of the institution. The mounting divisions within CRAC-PC affected women as well. These divisions almost caused a confrontation between CRAC-PC women counselors and CAMI *promotoras* due to the active role that the latter played in defending women's rights, particularly those of the fourteen-year-old girl who was raped. This painful situation affected me personally, as I had developed a close relationship with members of both groups. Indeed, ethical and human dilemmas emerged that cannot be separated from the internal power struggles in the community system, the place that women occupy in it, and my own position as researcher.

Although emotions were not at the center of my research, they have emerged as powerful analytic keys for collaborative work and the building of bridges of mutual understanding. Emotions were the subjective element necessary to understand why justice defenders put so much stock in listening to women victims of violence, even if it was frequently difficult to solve their problem. Emotions were also the cement that linked our collaboration and my growing respect for these Indigenous justice defenders. I recognized their ability to prioritize women's voices and concerns and their capacity to generate empathy and hope. Women's fight for gender rights in precarious contexts becomes an odyssey; it is hard to overcome structural and everyday obstacles of gendered violence, especially when they are entrenched in traditional patriarchal orders. Nevertheless, these women listen to victims of violence and develop strategies to respond to their demands. A sense of fairness and unfairness emerges in the questioning of the fixed construction of gender order. Women's strength, produced by their personal commitment, allows them to take advantage of these efforts and defend what has been conquered, as well as to seek alternatives to continue their struggles.

My collaboration with women justice defenders provided the seed for advancing long-term processes that can reposition women in their communities. This solidarity and affective niche allowed me to share experiences with these courageous women and legitimized my participation as an academic in the community system. However, positioning myself also meant dealing with ethical and political challenges that even today underscore my relationship with the Community Police, as I took the side of defending women who, like Apolonia, had challenged male authority within CRAC-PC.

Let me highlight three main dilemmas of collaborative research with Indigenous women in contexts of insecurity and violence:

1. It is increasingly difficult to accompany women's organizing processes in contexts of intensified threats and vulnerabilities. This difficulty forces us to respect their accomplishments, silences, and expectations in their search for justice. An intersectional perspective is fundamental not only for the analysis of gendered violence but also for collaborative work because it helps situate the multiple layers of violence and the context in which the research is undertaken.

2. The question arises as to whether internal contradictions in community processes should be documented and made public, especially when they involve women's subordination and silencing. This is an ethical dilemma created by the tension between the defense of Indigenous autonomies and the defense of women's rights. Between these two poles—collective rights and gender rights—emerges a gender cultural policy promoted by Indigenous women that in practice challenges cultural essentialisms as well as Western concepts of womanhood. Indigenous women are not willing to stay quiet in the face of injustices; they thus appeal to the ethics of dignity involved in their fight for collective rights. The dynamics of collaborative research placed me in the position of accompanying these women in their fight for justice without imposing an external agenda.

3. Women defenders assume a fraught role in their effort to translate women's claims (from lists of grievances to a language of rights), considering their own cultural logics in differentiated, plurilegal settings. When listening to victims' testimonies of pain, the *promotoras* put into practice a central principle of anthropological research: they privilege a sensitive approach to context and seek to understand women's suffering in their own language and cosmovision. This practice is fundamental when seeking reparation and legal remedies.

Conclusions

At the very margins of the state, Indigenous women construct alternatives to help other women confront insecurity, violence, and gender inequality within an emblematic autonomous institution of Mexico, the Community Police of Guerrero (CRAC-PC). Sharing individual and collective daily grievances has allowed them to name gendered violence and articulate their own project as justice defenders. At the intersection of structural vulnerabilities and precarity, women justice defenders construct a life project and generate alternatives to defend women's integrity and shake patriarchal authority. In the end, their own condition as Indigenous women anchored in their local communities is what allows them to place themselves on the same level of interlocution as women victims, understanding their pain and finding alternatives to cope with it; at the same time, they make visible their own grievances as activists defending women's rights. What is at stake are women defenders' subjectivities, which help build a new, comprehensive, and inclusive project of justice in which the defense of women's rights becomes fundamental. As Lugones (2008) states, colonial legacies of dispossession are gendered and have differentiated effects on women lives; it is important to stress Indigenous women's own narratives of suffering and hope. The intersectional perspective therefore becomes a fundamental tool to understand the interwoven oppressions in the lives of Indigenous women and their naturalizing effects in everyday life.

This work reveals the subversive potential of a gender agenda that challenges routinized patriarchal orders within collective Indigenous institutions. Similar experiences—albeit with their own particularities—occur in other contexts and latitudes as Indigenous women build new emancipatory projects that integrate sociological, cultural, and intersectional variables "for unpacking the complex structural causes underlying the continuum of VAW [violence against Indigenous women]" (Muñoz Cabrera 2010, 7). Indigenous women are using their agency—and drawing from their own cultural rationalities and dignity—to defend a sense of gender equity, open paths for women, and destabilize male regulatory regimes. They are building new senses of subjectivity and social agency that respond to structural racism and gender inequalities. They do this by bringing together their identities and life experiences as Indigenous women, firmly committed to the struggles of their people (Alemán 2006).

With this text, my intention is to do justice to the endless labor of the Indigenous women justice defenders, who have made inroads in hypermasculinized spaces to dispute what is traditionally understood as justice without breaking their bonds with their communities. My collaboration, aligning myself with their project, helped maximize the critical and subversive dimension of women's claims and translate them into concrete demands, without imposing categories or previous definitions of gendered harm. The challenges are many, and increasing violence and insecurity in the region do not favor these women; this is why it is important to assess their achievements and consider the diverse strengths they develop in their own contexts. In the end, despite all the grievances and violence (both structural and everyday), the women justice defenders consolidate their social agency and empower themselves with a collective vision of their lives and future horizons of gender emancipation.

References

Alemán, Mónica, ed. 2006. *Mairin Iwanka Raya. Indigenous Women Stand Against Violence. A Companion Report to the United Nations Secretary-General's Study on Violence Against Women.* New York: FIMI (International Indigenous Women's Forum).

Arteaga Börth, Ana Cecilia. 2013. "'Todas somos la semilla': Ser mujer en la policía comunitaria de Guerrero." Master's thesis, Centro de Investigaciones y Estudios Superiores en Antropología Social.

Bartra, Armando. 1996. *Guerrero Bronco: Campesinos, ciudadanos y guerrilleros en la Costa Grande.* Mexico City: Editorial Era.

Channel Foundation. n.d. "International Indigenous Women's Forum (FIMI)." Accessed September 10, 2020. https://www.channelfoundation.org/grants/fimi/.

Figueroa Romero, Dolores, and María Teresa Sierra. 2020. "Alertas de género y mujeres Indígenas: Interpelando las políticas públicas desde los contextos comunitarios en Guerrero, México." *Canadian Journal of Latin American and Caribbean Studies* 45 (1): 26–44.

Hale, Charles R., ed. 2008. *Engaging Contradictions: Theory, Politics, and Methods of Activist Research.* Berkeley: University of California Press.

Hernández, Úrsula, and María Teresa Sierra. 2009. *Mirada desde las mujeres. Historia y participación de las mujeres en la Comunitaria.* Brochure.

Hernández Castillo, Rosalva Aída. 2015. "Hacia una antropología socialmente comprometida desde una perspectiva dialógica y feminista." In *Conocimiento, poder y prácticas políticas de autoría colectiva*, edited by Xóchitl Leyva, 82–106. Mexico City: CIESAS/FLACSO/UNICACH.

Hernández Castillo, Rosalva Aída. 2016. *Multiple InJustices: Indigenous Women, Law, and Political Struggle in Latin America.* Tucson: University of Arizona Press.

Hernández Castillo, Rosalva Aída. 2017. "Between Community Justice and International Litigation: The Case of Inés Fernández Before the Inter-American Court." In *Demanding Justice and Security: Indigenous Women and Legal Pluralities in Latin America*, edited by Rachel Sieder, 29–50. New Brunswick, N.J.: Rutgers University Press.

Institute for Economics and Peace (IEP). 2019. *Índice de Paz México 2019*. Sydney: IEP. http://visionofhumanity.org/app/uploads/2019/06/Mexico-Peace-Index-2019 -Spanish.pdf.

Jimeno, Myriam, Daniel Varela, and Angela Castillo. 2018. "Violence, Emotional Communities, and Political Action in Colombia." In *Resisting Violence: Emotional Communities in Latin America*, edited by Morna Macleod and Natalia De Marinis, 23–52. New York: Palgrave Macmillan.

Lugones, María. 2008. "Colonialidad y género." *Tabula Rasa* 9:73–101.

Macleod Morna, and Natalia De Marinis, eds. 2018. *Resisting Violence: Emotional Communities in Latin America*. New York, Palgrave Macmillan.

Mora, Mariana. 2017. "Voices Within Silences: Indigenous Women, Security, and Rights in the Mountain Region of Guerrero." In *Demanding Justice and Security: Indigenous Women and Legal Pluralities in Latin America*, edited by Rachel Sieder, 197–219. New Brunswick, N.J.: Rutgers University Press.

Muñoz Cabrera, Patricia. 2010. *Intersecting Violences: A Review of Feminist Theories and Debates on Violence Against Women and Poverty in Latin America*. London: Central America Women's Network.

Observatorio de Violencia Contra las Mujeres "Hannah Arendt" (OVICOM). 2015. *Informe de Homicidios Dolores de Mujeres del Estado de Guerrero (2005–2015)*. Guerrero: OVICOM.

Scheper-Hughes, Nancy, and Phillippe Bourgois, eds. 2004. *Violence in War and Peace: An Anthology*. Oxford: Blackwell.

Segato, Rita Laura. 2013. *Las nuevas formas de la guerra y el cuerpo de las mujeres*. Mexico City: Pez en el árbol/Tinta Limón.

Sieder, Rachel, ed. 2017. *Demanding Justice and Security: Indigenous Women and Legal Pluralities in Latin America*. New Brunswick, N.J.: Rutgers University Press.

Sieder, Rachel, and Anna Barrera Vivero. 2017. "Women and Legal Pluralism: Lessons from Indigenous Governance Systems in the Andres." *Journal of Latin American Studies* 49:633–58.

Sierra, María Teresa. 2011. "Abriendo brecha: Las mujeres de la policía comunitaria de Guerrero." Uploaded October 30, 2017, by CIESAS. YouTube video, 29:11. https://www.youtube.com/watch?v=vDk7hFFMWAU.

Sierra, María Teresa. 2015. "Pueblos indígenas y usos contrahegemónicos de la ley en la disputa por la justicia." *Journal of Latin American Studies and Caribbean Anthropology* 20 (1): 133–55.

Sierra, María Teresa. 2017a. "El pueblo me'phaa confronta el extractivismo minero: Ecología de saberes en la lucha jurídica." In *E-Cadernos CES* 28:165–85. https://doi.org/10.4000/eces.2553.

Sierra, María Teresa. 2017b. "Guerrero Community Police Confront Macro-Violences." *NACLA Report of the Americas* 49 (3): 366–69.

Sierra, María Teresa. 2017c. "Indigenous Autonomies and Gender Justice: Women Dispute Security and Rights in Guerrero, Mexico." In *Demanding Justice and Secu-*

rity: Indigenous Women and Legal Pluralities in Latin America, edited by Rachel Sieder, 97–119. New Brunswick, N.J.: Rutgers University Press.

Sierra, María Teresa. 2018. "Policías comunitarias y campos sociales minados en México: Construyendo seguridad en contextos de violencia extrema." *Abya-yala: Revista sobre acesso a justiça e direitos nas Américas* 2 (2): 325–51.

Speed, Shannon. 2017. "States of Violence: Indigenous Women Migrants and Human Rights in the Era of Neoliberal Multicriminalism." *Critique of Anthropology* 36 (3): 280–301.

Speed, Shannon, Rosalva Aída Hernández Castillo, and Lynn Stephen. 2006. *Dissident Women: Gender and Cultural Politics in Chiapas.* Austin: University of Texas Press.

Stephen, Lynn. 2019. "Fleeing Rural Violence: Mam Women Seeking Gendered Justice in Guatemala and the U.S." *Journal of Peasant Studies* 46 (2): 229–57.

Terven, Adriana. 2017. "Domestic Violence and Access to Justice: The Political Dilemma of the Cuetzalan Indigenous Women's Home." In *Demanding Justice and Security: Indigenous Women and Legal Pluralities in Latin America*, edited by Rachel Sieder, 51–71. New Brunswick, N.J.: Rutgers University Press.

Tlachinollan (Centro de Derechos Humanos de la Montaña). 2018. *Montaña: Manantial de la Resistencia y torbellino de esperanza. XXIV Informe, Julio 2017–Agosto 2018.* Tlapa de Comonfort, Guerrero: Tlachinollan.

Warnholtz, Margarita. 2016. *Recuperar la Dignidad: Historia de la Unión de Pueblos y Organizaciones del Estado de Guerrero, Movimiento por el Desarrollo y la Paz Social.* Mexico City: UNAM.

CHAPTER 4

The Case of Sepur Zarco and the Challenge to the Colonial State

IRMA A. VELÁSQUEZ NIMATUJ

This work has its beginnings in the lives of fifteen Q'eqchi' women who were originally from communities surrounding Sepur Zarco, one of the 138 small villages in the municipality of El Estor, which is in the department of Izabal, northeastern Guatemala, more than three hundred kilometers (185 miles) from the country's capital. For six years, from 1982 to 1988, these fifteen women experienced sexual and domestic slavery imposed by the Guatemalan military, which had occupied that area amid the internal armed conflict that occurred in the country from 1960 to 1996.

In 2011, the organizations Mujeres Transformando el Mundo (MTM, Women Transforming the World), the Unión Nacional de Mujeres Guatemaltecas (UNAMG, National Union of Guatemalan Women), and Estudios Comunitarios y Acción Psicosocial (ECAP, Community Studies and Psychosocial Action), working together on the project "Mujeres rompiendo el silencio: Fortalecimiento de conciencia para mujeres sobrevivientes de violencia sexual durante el conflicto armado" (Women breaking the silence: Strengthening awareness for women survivors of sexual violence during the armed conflict), asked me to produce an expert report on the cultural ruptures experienced by women of different ages when the military intervened in their region. With the support of these three collectives, I began the process of writing the report, which was a painful but also beautiful privilege that allowed me to approach the facts, the region, the surviving women, the direct witnesses, and the documents, such as copies of reports and references. This chapter is based on the information that I collected for this work.

In 2012, after more than thirty years of silence, the women of Sepur Zarco decided to seek help in the national courts. In February 2016, Court A for High-Risk Crimes sentenced Lieutenant Colonel Esteelmer Francisco Reyes Girón to 120 years in prison, and the former military commissioner Heriberto Valdez Asij to 240 years in prison, for crimes against humanity, forced disappearances, and the deaths of Dominga Coc and her young daughters, Anita and Hermelinda.

Part of the information contained in this chapter is based on the expert cultural report that I wrote for the trial initiated by the female survivors of Sepur Zarco in the Guatemalan courts, referred to above (Velásquez Nimatuj 2013). I conducted research from December 2011 to April 2013. During that period, I identified constant acts of sexual violence against women in their communities in the years 1982–86. These were part of a scheme of cruel and inhuman treatment planned by the state and executed by members of the military occupying the region. First, soldiers arrived in the communities and murdered all the women's husbands and eldest sons. They captured the widows, many of them pregnant, and made them their sexual slaves. Second, they raped the women collectively or individually in the military outpost, in their homes, by the rivers, and in many other locations. Third, they forced the women to perform domestic work for the military outpost, including cleaning the facilities, cooking for a unit of approximately four hundred soldiers, and doing laundry, among other jobs. And fourth, they tortured and murdered several women. Those women who survived were subjected to systematic cultural, emotional, and physical violence and were held against their will for years. All these crimes marked, and altered forever, the cultural frames of reference in the lives of these women.

During the investigation, I identified sociocultural elements that were destroyed in the women's individual and communal lives. I documented cultural ruptures that modified or destroyed their extended families, their systems of authority, their properties, their medicinal knowledge, and their spirituality and solidarity. The sexual abuse inflicted on the survivors' bodies and minds marked a turning point in the women's lives and has prevented them from reinitiating a normal life. At a personal level, and as a Maya K'iche' woman, I felt a kind of joy in knowing that my work as a social anthropologist had contributed to supporting the claims filed by the women in the

Guatemalan courts, in their search for justice and some kind of reparation for themselves, their families, and their communities.

My work consisted of the elaboration of fifteen life histories. As such, I was able to confirm that their stories all agree in that the military's inhuman attacks ended their husbands' lives, that the women were subjected to unprecedented sexual violence, and that their cultural practices were also annulled. All the violence of the 1980s was carried out in order to guarantee the security of property owned by large landowners around Sepur Zarco. The military installed detachments in outposts to prevent the community from making legal claims to the lands and to prevent guerrilla groups from emerging. In 1980, insurgents were operating in the central and western parts of the country, on the opposite side of Guatemala from Sepur Zarco. In 1982, a group of Indigenous men from the Sepur Zarco area began petitioning to gain legal title to the landowners' estates. They were captured and disappeared by the military. Soldiers then came and destroyed their homes and raped women related to the men who had petitioned for land. The large landowners sought to control the lands of the Q'eqchi' people, as well as exploit their labor force, so they could continue to generate income. The survivors' testimonies make evident that the sexual assaults they suffered were, in reality, just an extension of the colonial relationships of dependence and exploitation that have historically prevailed in Guatemala. Demecia Yat summarized it like this:

> There are people responsible for ordering the murder of all the men in our communities. We were poor and living in a small village. That's why we thought they wouldn't bother us, but our "crime" was simply that we lived too close to the large landowners. For this reason, the soldiers burned and stole our animals, and even the corn we had harvested. They left us without homes, without clothes, without food, without animals, and without husbands. Then, they began to rape us. So, we began living off what people would give us, off what they would give us out of kindness; in the middle of the war we had to ask for food, because we had ended up on the street, without anybody [to help us], with nothing. (Velásquez Nimatuj 2013, 34)

Culture and Its Interconnections

Given that my work is focused on identifying and understanding cultural ruptures, I have revisited the concept of *culture* to argue that it must be understood as a symbolic system that is translated into shared meanings by the women and men of a community. I argue that the systems and processes of their collectivity are linked to their own history but are also affected by the national history of the place where they live, as well as by the prevailing political, economic, and social processes operating there. For this reason, women's culture is connected to their history, territory, social class, identity, gender, and race. Cultural and social spaces cannot be analyzed independently of those interconnections because culture does not exist (and is not reproduced) in a vacuum (Velásquez Nimatuj 2011, 98). In the case of the Q'eqchi' women, their life histories, as well as their identities as women and as Q'eqchi', revolve around and are connected to—among other things—the land, their political struggles, and their family stability. It is for this reason that they tried to defend their lands, as Manuela Ba remembers:

They kidnapped our husbands [because] they were struggling for the legalization of our lands. The sacred earth gave us food, gave us life. We had our home there, our animals. We all lived there. That's why the commissioners, together with the large landowners, made a list with the names of the men in the community who were working for this legalization. That's why [our husbands] were taken away. (Velásquez Nimatuj 2013, 41)

The culture and identity of the women revolved around reproduction and agricultural survival and were linked to the cultivation of crops, which guaranteed food sovereignty for the community's families. The women were working to preserve the right to life and the right to own their lands, their territory. However, as María Ba Caal narrates, that world was soon destroyed:

One early morning in 1982, around 5:00 am, I was preparing the corn dough, when dogs began barking desperately. I got scared and told my husband, but we had no time to react, as twenty soldiers surrounded our home. Juan Sam, the community's commissioner, was with them. With the hammocks we had in our house, they tied up my husband and my two eldest sons: eighteen-year-old Santiago Cac, who was part of the school committee, and fifteen-year-old Pedro. I followed them to the school, where they kept them for one day and one night, and then I saw the soldiers take them away. That was the last time in my life that I saw my husband and sons. (Velásquez Nimatuj 2013, 37)

For lack of space, I am not going to go in detail about the cultural ruptures I investigated. Instead, I will present a general view of the atrocities suffered by the women of Sepur Zarco, so that I can connect their experiences to the national and international historical contexts in order to bring to light the relationship between the crimes committed in the historical past and the impunity that the Guatemalan state enjoys with respect to the crimes against the poor, rural, monolingual, and widowed Indigenous women who survived the attacks.

Historical Context

In 1982, still within the framework of the Cold War (1945–89), the Maya population throughout Guatemala was labeled as an "internal enemy" and subjected to institutional violence at the hands of the military. The institutions enabling this violence included the Patrullas de Autodefensa Civil (PACs, Civil Self-Defense Patrols), the judiciary, and the military commissioners. This structure of interconnected state institutions of violence was recognized by the minister of national defense, General Héctor Alejandro Gramajo (1986–2004), in his memoir (Gramajo Morales 1995).

In those years, the Maya collectivities had little access to food and basic services such as drinking water, sewers, health care, and education. In the 1980s, Maya men working as day laborers on the large farms that produced export crops such as coffee, sugar, and other products were supposed to earn Q0.25 daily (the equivalent in quetzals to about US$0.25). However, workers usually did not get more than Q0.05 daily. Families laboring on farms that produced coffee, bananas, cotton, and cattle were aware of the exploitative conditions under which they labored. They worked to get organized and fight for the legal possession of their territories, petitioning for land in order to guarantee their access to food and to facilitate subsistence food production. The price paid by the Maya for their demands of legal certainty with respect to their territories, access to arable land, fair wages, the end of racism, and access to social services, among other basic rights, was a disproportionate and irrational state violence carried out by the military that ended in genocide.[1]

---

1. In its May 10, 2013, sentencing of General José Efraín Ríos Montt, Court A for High-Risk Crimes recognized that in Guatemala, under his presidential administration, genocide was executed against the Maya-Ixil people. See Centeno Martín (2018).

Several studies have documented the genocide of the Maya people from the end of the 1970s to the mid-1980s. This devastation was the work of civic action military projects, which used psychological control, as well as PACs, which patrolled and suppressed communities through violence and enforced taxes.[2] Under the government of the Protestant general Efraín Ríos Montt, a campaign of "guns and beans" was initiated, and PACs' functions were increased, which was key for executing the massacres. The government's scorched-earth counterinsurgency policy transformed more than 440 Maya small towns into ashes and clandestine cemeteries; more than six hundred communities were massacred, and more than 1.5 million people were forcefully displaced, fleeing to the mountains and seeking refuge in southern Mexico. Thousands of Maya girls and adult women of all ages suffered sexual violence perpetrated by the military. Even today, the exact number of women who were sexually assaulted during the war is unknown. In fact, sexual violence was publicly discussed in Guatemala in March 2010, during the Primera Tribunal de Conciencia Contra la Violencia Sexual hacia las Mujeres (First Tribunal of Consciousness Against Sexual Violence Toward Women), where the sexual violence inflicted on women from different Maya ethnic groups was denounced, debated, and documented.[3] When the Permanent Peoples' Tribunal held a session on Guatemala in 1983 in Madrid, Spain, gendered and sexual violence was invisible, normalized as part of war (see chapter 7 in this volume). The intervening period—from this 1983 session, to the 2010 tribunal, to the 2016 Sepur Zarco trial—marks significant change for the recognition of sexual violence in Guatemala. In 2008, Guatemala passed Latin America's most comprehensive piece of antiviolence legislation, which called for establishing a specialized court system to process cases related to various forms of violence against women starting in 2010 (see the introduction to this volume). These courts are known as *tribunales de sentencia penal de delitos de femicidio y otras formas de violencia contra la mujer y violencia sexual* (sentencing courts for the crime of femicide and other forms of violence against women). Instances of femicide, sexual assault, and gendered violence—whether physical, psychological, or economic forms—are

---

2. The PACs were created in 1981. Indigenous men from across the country were forcibly recruited by the military and integrated into them.

3. Hundreds of children were also assassinated, beheaded, stolen from their parents, or kidnapped after the massacres and given in adoption to families inside and outside of Guatemala.

supposed to be tried in these courts. This recent history is far removed from the situation that Indigenous women encountered during the civil war.

In the early 1980s, family life in Sepur Zarco unfolded amid a national environment of violence. Unequal power relations between ladino landowners (mestizo descendants of Spanish and Indigenous peoples) and Q'eqchi' leaders were exacerbated by the extreme state violence and repression by the military (Grandin 2007; Sanford 2003). These unequal power relations marginalized the Maya people racially, economically, and culturally, and were thus a form of structural violence. This violence greatly intensified beginning in 1954, when a coup d'état supported by the United States overthrew the government of President Jacobo Árbenz Guzmán.

Indigenous Women and Violence

When we compare the life histories of the women from Sepur Zarco with Guatemala's long history and the collective history of the Maya people, we become aware that the first breaking point for Indigenous people was the Spanish invasion of 1524, when Indigenous peoples of what is now Guatemala were subjected to previously unseen levels of physical and sexual violence, exploitation, and subjugation in all areas of their lives. Attempts to annihilate their world views have not stopped since that time. The violence against Indigenous women has been constant, and it cannot be understood separate from the long history of their communities.

The extremely violent actions by the military against Sepur Zarco's women and families in 1982–86 constitute unjustifiable levels of violence on the bodies, minds, and sexualities of Q'eqchi' women. Antonia Choc remembers:

> The day after my husband's detention, the soldiers returned and got the women out of our homes and burned them down; we ended up without our husbands, with nothing. Then, they took us to the Poombaak camp. I was pregnant, and on the way there, I was stopped by approximately ten soldiers, who raped me. Trembling and hurt, I stood up however I could, and frightened, I arrived at the camp where they had corralled us; there, we were accused of feeding the guerrillas. As a consequence of these rapes, I lost my baby and started to get sick; even though I was ill, I was then forced to give services to the military in the outpost at Sepur Zarco. (Velásquez Nimatuj 2013, 44)

Before 2010, little was mentioned about the sexual violence inflicted during the twentieth-century genocide, which had hardly been investigated. However, if we look at the historical record, we find that sexual violence has always been present in the lives of Indigenous women. This is why *mestizaje* (miscegenation) is a complex and painful topic for Indigenous women in Guatemala. The colonial era was three centuries of economic ignominy and physical and sexual violence against Indigenous women, continual sexual violation, and, in some cases, disdain for the children that were the product of the rapes. In that period, women also became domestic and sexual slaves. The number of Indigenous women separated from their places of origin, cultures, and families is currently unknown. The number who were forced to build new homes and found new towns to the benefit of the dominant elites is also unknown. These processes of displacement are not only historical but also ongoing, amid a settler colonialism that continues today. Thousands of women in the colonial era spent their whole lives in the tribute-labor system known as *repartimiento de hilados* (distribution of fabrics), in which they were obligated to provide unpaid labor weaving cotton and wool textiles. Thousands of others never enjoyed the right to breastfeed their children, because even this was denied to them by the colonial elite. Instead of being able to raise their own children, they had to breastfeed the children of the elite.

Guatemalan independence in 1821 did not bring freedom to Indigenous women. On the contrary, a system of forced labor meant that they had to leave their families. Likewise, the liberal period (beginning in 1871) and the introduction of coffee did not translate into economic development for Indigenous peoples, particularly women. The commercialization of coffee brought the integration of Guatemala into the world economic system starting in 1840, but it also converted Indigenous women into arms for work and wombs for birthing the peasant sons and daughters who were needed for the harvests. On the large coffee farms, Indigenous women also encountered sexual violence. For a small number of elites, coffee brought immense wealth, but for women, forced to work on the large farms all their lives, it meant a violent system of control over their bodies, their strength, and their sexuality. For generations, it was very difficult to break away from this system of control.

The beginning of the twentieth century did not mitigate the situation for Indigenous women. Quite the opposite. It brought another period in which the magnitude of the sexual violence suffered is still not fully known, in need of critical documentation by historians. The various ways in which women resisted throughout the twentieth century are also yet to be interpreted. We have to consider the lives of Sepur Zarco's women—the daughters, mothers, and grandmothers—within this historical framework. The physical, emotional, and sexual violence that the state of Guatemala inflicted on them during the armed conflict cannot be understood as distinct from this longer history of violence.

The testimonies of the Q'eqchi women that I heard and documented between 2010 and 2016 (from the First Tribunal of Consciousness Against Sexual Violence Toward Women until the Sepur Zarco trial) give evidence of rapes perpetrated by the military, of women kept in captivity, and of the domestic labor they were forced to perform for the troops and military high commanders. After murdering the women's husbands and, in some cases, their older sons, the military left the women vulnerable, in charge of the youngest children. These conditions facilitated their subjugation by the soldiers. Those who refused to comply with what was being demanded of them were tortured and murdered.

The Guatemalan Civil War legally ended with the signing of peace accords in December 1996. However, this event did not mean that Q'eqchi' women were able to heal from the violence that had been inflicted on them. For example, Vicenta Col emphasized that "the military destroyed us because [what they did] was a massive disappearance; the soldiers finished off the communities."[4] Magdalena Pop also stated:

> in that time I was sexually raped; the military transformed me into a slave at their disposal. It was a true and deep bitterness, to be used and be dropped off all bloodied as if we were a thing, worse than an animal. They would get us at the outpost, in the rivers, in our homes, in the mountains, wherever they wanted, and in front of our kids who screamed whenever they witnessed those attacks. I was inconsolable. I wanted to die, I did not want to live, I asked God to bring me death; I wanted to flee from my own body. The soldiers filled us with illnesses, and we never received any medical attention during those years; we could not even say what we had, what was affecting

---

4. Throughout the text, some quotes appear with no citation; this practice is to protect the physical integrity and personal safety of the witnesses.

us, what we felt in our [intimate] parts; this is why I feel anger, pain, and hatred toward the men who did this. (Velásquez Nimatuj 2013, 27)

Despite what Sepur Zarco's women lived through, they were able to face their external and internal pain and go to the courts to obtain justice for the atrocities that the military had inflicted on their bodies and dignity. This process was not easy, as Carmen Xol states: "during all our history, justice was never on our side. It never supported us." This is why Antonia Choc argued that denouncing the crimes they suffered was a complex process:

I felt that I was not ready, that I could not speak. I was afraid: I felt alone. There weren't any organizations willing to support us. And to be honest, I feel everything arrived a little bit too late, because many of our sisters died from all that raping, from fear, from pain when they could not find their relatives. And now they are not able to see this. (Velásquez Nimatuj 2013, 45)

The women did not give up despite suffering from their wounds for more than two decades, despite facing illnesses and pain in their reproductive organs, and despite feeling a spiritual, physical, psychological, emotional, cultural, ethnic, and social breakdown, without ever receiving any attention from the state. For this reason, the minimal restitution that the courts mandated for them after they won the trial in 2016 has to be used to seek a reparation that promotes healing according to their reality and present condition. Without comprehensive, integrated support and accompaniment, the survivors will never be able to have a healthy life.

Location of Sepur Zarco

Two routes go to the community of Sepur Zarco: both are complicated and require transit on dirt roads that are in a state of disrepair. The first access is through the municipality of Telemán, Alta Verapaz. After going through the Polochic Valley, one has to head toward the Pueblo Viejo River, which ends in Sepur Zarco. The other route is through the municipality of Mariscos, Puerto Barrios. One has to take the highway toward the Atlantic, cross Playa Dorada and Pataxte, and reach an African palm plantation and several other large farms with small population centers, including San Miguel,

Río Zarquito, and Chavilán. The final stretch of road is through another large African palm plantation, fifty kilometers across, but one has to get a permit at the entrance gate to be able to traverse this property.[5] This road concludes in Sepur Zarco. In addition, this is the only highway that leads to the community of Las Tinajas. To get there, one has to pass three rivers (Zarco, Las Tinajas, and Pueblo Viejo). Las Tinajas is the large farm and population center where the majority of the survivors claim their husbands were taken after being detained, the site of one of the six military detachments in the region. Another military detachment settled in Sepur Zarco, where the women were forced to give "service to the military": cooking, cleaning, washing clothes in the river, and enduring sexual servitude. Regarding this "service," Manuela Ba stated:

> Each one of the women who survived was forced to make tortillas three times per day, for all the soldiers, from Sunday to Sunday for six years whether we were living inside or outside the outpost. To prevent them from torturing us, we would buy corn with our own money. Many women were forced to exchange the few animals they owned for corn in order to feed the soldiers. Back then, each pound [of corn] would cost Q0.50, and they would force us to give them two pounds for breakfast, two for lunch, and two for dinner. Also, we had to make logs for cooking and wash their uniforms; we also had to buy the soap, since they would not give it to us. (Velásquez Nimatuj 2013, 43)

The military, then, imposed a system of rape and sexual and physical abuse on all women.

---

5. African palms began to be planted in this region between 1995 and 1997. The plantation described here is registered as part of an anonymous society that hires temporary workers for two months; we cannot know the exact number of workers on the plantation. During the armed conflict, this land was mainly the site of rice or corn farms, or cattle ranches. Back then, the farms had permanent residents who lived on-site with their families and received, as a result of their labor, a land parcel to plant their own food staples. The surviving women explained that residents who did not rise up or question anything were left alone for a time, but the farm and ranch owners began to kick them out after the peace accords were signed. These residents were left without any benefits or land, becoming part of the poverty belt that continues to grow in Guatemala.

Land as a Factor of Repression

When we analyze the survivors' testimonies, we find a common thread in their stories: the struggle to obtain legal certainty (titles) over the land they owned. They started organizing in the late 1970s because Sepur Zarco was, and continues to be, a large estate with community lands on which some ladino families—owners of large farms in the surrounding areas—wanted to claim ownership. The large landowners would hire men from the communities as day laborers and pay them Q0.05 or Q0.10 per day. The situation of exploitation and legal uncertainty of land titles led the Sepur Zarco community members to organize a cooperative in order to obtain legal titles to the land where they lived and to demand fair wages as workers on the large farms.

In the interviews I carried out with women survivors, the women explained that by 2010 the families living in Sepur Zarco had been settled on that land for approximately forty-seven years, after migrating into the area. Due to the local residents' attempts to regularize land claims during the armed conflict, the large farm owners—the "alleged owners of the land," as expressed by one woman—accused them of being insurgents. Another woman recalled Walter Overdick García, who was mayor of the municipality of Panzós during the massacre of May 29, 1978.[6] Together with another large landowner, he began harassing the Indigenous population so that they would not legalize their land claims. However, the Q'eqchi' continued their quest for legal certainty, and so the large landowners negotiated with the military to settle in detachments in the region and prevent any Q'eqchi' insurgency— that is, to provide security for the landowners.

As of 2020, the agrarian conflict has still not been resolved. The community of Sepur Zarco continues to be at a legal impasse, contending with an ongoing boundary dispute with José Ángel Chan, who, according to his Indigenous neighbors, "has trespassed their boundaries and does not want to respect the *extensión* [land] kept by the Q'eqchi' elders and families." This conflict is ongoing, despite the fact that after the 1996 peace accords the Fondo de Tierras (Department of Land) measured the parcel in question and

6. Regarding the Panzós massacre and its historical context, see CEH (1999), Grandin (2007), IEPALA (1980), Pitarch, Speed, and Leyva Solano (2008), Proyecto Interdiocensano (1998), Sanford (2003, 2009), Soriano Hernández (2006), and Vilas (1994).

found that Sepur Zarco possesses an extension of twenty-nine *caballerías* and forty-six *manzanas*,[7] a land measurement that coincides with a 1976 survey, before the beginning of the repression. This survey confirms Sepur Zarco's claim against Chan.

Representatives of the Sepur Zarco survivors have tried negotiating with Chan, but he has not accepted, and this uncertainty about the ownership and possession of the land has led the women to say that they and their children, "have possession of the land, but do not have the paperwork." The survivors have stated that "during the conflict, the large landowners originally respected the community boundaries because they were afraid of insurgency, but when the peace [accords] were signed, they began trespassing even more, and now they do not respect the communities at all."

Gender and Ethnic Equality

In order to understand why the Q'eqchi' women in Sepur Zarco faced such inhuman sexual violence by the state and the military, we must adopt a perspective that simultaneously includes both gender and class oppression, given that in Guatemala these kinds of oppression are structural and historical, forming part of the foundation of the country. Gender and class oppression have been key pillars in Guatemalan nation-building, used by the economic and cultural elites to control and subjugate the Indigenous people. This connection is expressed by the survivors as part of their life experience. Magdalena Pop, for example, told us as we were reconstructing her life story, "Look, *compañera*, I am asking myself, why did all this happen to us?" And she answered:

> Because the wealthy see that we are poor; the large landowners believe that they own all the land; they look at us as women with no education, who only speak Q'eqchi'. This is why the large landowners wanted to take the land from us; they were the ones who invited the soldiers to come in for us, they opened the doors to them. (Velásquez Nimatuj 2013, 28)

---

7. These are units of area. A *caballería* in Guatemala is equivalent to 64 *manzanas* or just over 45 hectares (112 acres). The land extension mentioned here is approximately 1,351 hectares (3,338 acres).

We also have to consider racism, which operates as social construct, just as gender and class oppression do. This kind of oppression has been difficult to understand for the middle-class ladinos or mestizos, who both ignore and reproduce the discriminatory characteristics of the conservative elites. This attitude is shared by leftist sectors that prioritize the economic struggle and minimize the weight of racial oppression.[8] However, for the women of Sepur Zarco, the connection between forms of oppression is clear. Vicenta Col stated: "The military was looking at us as poor Indigenous women; this is why they did whatever they wanted to do with us; they would rape us, they would laugh at us, saying: 'look at the poor *indias* (female Indians), they are all alone'; this is why we were not able to defend ourselves from the rapes, as they would also let us see their weapons" (Velásquez Nimatuj 2013, 31).

In Guatemala, like in other regions of the world, ethnic claims have been subsumed in the struggle for economic rights (Omi and Winant 1986). Even today, despite the advances made by Indigenous movements in international spaces such as the United Nations or tribunals like those discussed by Morna Macleod (chapter 7), and despite international frameworks that guarantee inalienable rights to Indigenous peoples, it is argued that ethnic claims signify the creation of extremist groups wanting to fragment states, or that Indigenous groups are simply demanding "hardly deserved" privileges.

Even though professionals, activists, lawyers, and members of civil society, among others, might support, for example, Indigenous claims to fair wages, Indigenous people are to this day denied many rights, including self-determination, territorial autonomy, or a voice on economic, political, or

---

8. Class oppression as a political doctrine and theoretical framework took shape with Marxism at the end of the nineteenth century. It has three key pillars: philosophical materialism, economic doctrine, and scientific socialism (Bottomore 1983). I consider it necessary, and healthy, to analyze with critical eyes how the revolutions emerging from the Americas (revolutions that had socialist doctrine as their ideological framework and political project) made theoretical and practical contributions to the struggles against deep social inequality and yet, simultaneously, rejected a focus on the concrete demands of Indigenous peoples, particularly women. Take, for example, the 1944 October Revolution in Guatemala; the government of President Salvador Allende in Chile (who arrived to power with a socialist proposal through a democratic process in 1970); or the 1959 fall of Fulgencio Bautista's dictatorship in Cuba, which led to the construction of a socialist country. In none of these three historical processes—all of them key moments in the history of the world—were the Indigenous or Afro-descended populations seen as subjects who could have their own projects and demands.

other projects that affect their lives. Indigenous people are also restricted from decisions on how to use the natural resources of their territories; for this reason, laws have been created for the appropriation of community resources. Indigenous peoples therefore must make simultaneous demands about Indigenous/ethnic rights and economic rights—often referred to as *doble militancia*, or double rights claiming. Often such *doble militancia* is not accepted because if all these claims were to become a reality, they would undermine the bases upon which states have been built, which allow for the subjugation of the original peoples. This situation has perpetuated the small bourgeoisies as well (Casaús Arzú 1992). Today, even though the economic, political, cultural, and social rights of Indigenous peoples are accepted at the level of discourse, these rights have not become materialized in public policies or in the reestablishment of the Guatemalan state.[9]

The interaction of class, ethnic, and gender oppressions has been studied; however, it is not easy to analyze this interaction in practice, as to do so one must look at different institutions concurrently (Davis 1981; hooks 1992). Feminist theory encourages discussion about the complexity that exists when putting theory into practice. I found that the feminist approach referred as intersectionality was most useful for me as a theoretical framework for the expert report. Popularized by Kimberlé Williams Crenshaw (1995) and emphasizing the intersection of race, gender, and class in individuals and groups and their links to structural causes of multiple oppressions and inequalities, intersectionality theory allowed me to present to the court, in a logical and coherent way, the multiple oppressions and crimes against Q'eqchi' women that were facilitated, allowed, promoted, and financed by the state, together with the region's agrarian elite, between 1982 and 1988.

Racism and the Q'eqchi' Grandmothers

Given the size of the Indigenous population in Guatemala, representing more than 50 percent of the total population of the nation and more than 90 percent of the local population in some regions, the category of racial oppression is key to an understanding of Sepur Zarco. The rapes suffered by

---

9. The exception on the South American continent is the Plurinational State of Bolivia, which in 2009 recognized these rights and transformed them into law, a move that was signified in the country's new official name.

the women of Sepur Zarco during the armed conflict cannot be understood outside of a context of the racism that, as a mechanism of oppression, has existed in the country since 1524. Racism was institutionalized in the era of Creole independence after 1821. It was strengthened during the liberal period and the age of coffee (dating to 1871), and it continues to be reproduced to this day, placing Indigenous women (and men) at the bottom of the social pyramid of the country.

Racism as oppression has been constantly documented and denounced by Indigenous women and men, individually and collectively.[10] However, the laws in the country have not typified this oppression as a crime, in part because the very same justice system has been utilized to legitimize or deny racism. That is, the state and its institutions are the main generators of racism, though obviously not the only ones.

Neither national nor international legal frameworks have been able to change the fact that in a country such as Guatemala, racism continues to determine the life of Indigenous people.[11] In theory, Indigenous persons can appeal to the rights guaranteed to them in Articles 4, 58, 66, 71, 76, and 143 of the Guatemalan Political Constitution of 1985, as well as to the rights recognized in various international resolutions: the Convention 169 of the International Labour Organization, ratified by Guatemala in 1996; the International Convention on the Elimination of All Forms of Racial Discrimination, ratified in 1983; the Convention on the Elimination of All Forms of Discrimination Against Women, ratified in 1982 (and applying directly to Indigenous women); the International Covenant on Economic, Social and Cultural Rights, ratified in 1988; the Convention on the Rights of the Child, ratified in 1990 (and with articles dedicated to Indigenous

---

10. Several archives contain reports of acts of racial exclusion: Defensoría de Pueblos Indígenas de la Procuraduría de los Derechos Humanos (Office of Indigenous Peoples of the Ombudsman for Human Rights), Defensoría Maya (Office of the Ombudsman for Maya Peoples), Ministerio Público (Office of the Public Prosecutor), Defensoría de la Mujer Indígena (National Office for the Defense of Indigenous Women), and the UN Verification Mission in Guatemala (MINUGUA).

11. In 2003 the Procuraduría de los Derechos Humanos (PDH, Ombudsman for Human Rights) received around 136 reports of discrimination and racism. The majority of claimants were women discriminated against for wearing their traditional regional dress, but the PDH archive for that year also includes reports from men and women who faced persecution for practicing their religiosity in Maya altars located in public spaces, or political exclusion for belonging to an ethnic group or for speaking a Maya language.

boys and girls); the International Covenant on Civil and Political Rights, ratified in 1992; the Agreement on Identity and Rights of Indigenous Peoples, signed by Guatemala and the Unidad Revolucionaria Nacional Guatemalteca (Guatemalan National Revolutionary Unity) in 1995 in Mexico; and the UN Declaration on the Rights of Indigenous Peoples, approved by the United Nations in 2007.

National and international legal instruments guarantee the rights of all Indigenous women and men—urban, rural, children, seniors, illiterate, disabled—to equal access to resources and a life with dignity. This guarantee includes, among others, the right to wear one's regional traditional clothes in any space; to communicate and get an education in one's native language; to move around in and access public spaces, from educational to political to leisure; to access public services; to organize according to one's own customs; to practice one's spirituality without persecution; and to be free from physical assault, dishonor, or insult in private or public spaces. However, in daily life, these rights are not fully respected—as is evident in the atrocious crimes suffered by the Q'eqchi' women together with their families and communities in Sepur Zarco, and the more than thirty years that passed before the perpetrators of these crimes were tried in special courts created for that purpose. More than three decades transpired before the Q'eqchi' women could become empowered as women who have value and have the right to truth, justice, and reparation.

The women of Sepur Zarco were subjected to rape, sexual atrocities, servitude, and retention against their will. They witnessed the torture, death, and disappearance of their husbands, sons, and daughters, the burning of their properties, and the destruction of their crops and animals. All these violations were perpetrated with the complicity of the state (which did not try to stop the perpetrators), since they were being done to Indigenous women, who are seen as beings with no value. The prevalent racial hierarchy of Guatemala includes social relationships, structures, and institutions that historically and currently subordinate Indigenous women and men. Racism is not only an ideology of prejudices that emerge and are reproduced within the basic framework of ideas.[12] It is also not simply an isolated or individual

---

12. For an analysis of the racism faced by a middle-class Indigenous sector, see Velásquez Nimatuj (2011, chapter 2).

behavior, as in specific acts of discrimination. To the contrary, racism is a collective and social oppression that keeps entire populations subjugated.

Fundamentally, racism is a complex system of oppression that confers privileges on the group in control of economic and cultural power at the national level. These privileges are passed on to the members of this group, even if they do not ask for them, on the basis of their racial identity. For example, it is not a coincidence that the greatest part of the national budget in Guatemala is invested in the country's capital city rather than in the regions where the majority of the poor Indigenous population lives. According to data from international organizations, 73 percent of the country's Maya population lives in conditions of poverty, with 26 percent living in conditions of extreme poverty (MSPAS, OPS, and OMS 2016, 9). This poverty exists despite the fact that Maya people, who constitute just over half of Guatemala's population, pay taxes, of which their communities see only the most minimal services in return. According to the annual report on human development from the UN Development Programme (2019) for Guatemala, the poorest municipalities in the country continually have the highest numbers of Indigenous people.

In other words, the racism of the state and its institutions is systematic, permanent, and framed in a system of power relations that are not always evident. We cannot forget that racism frequently operates in a hidden manner, as has been documented by Michael Omi and Howard Winant (1986). These authors argue that institutional racism is not always explicit. In Guatemala, exclusion, segregation, and racial discrimination against Indigenous women are not written in laws because it is not necessary to do so; racism permeates daily life as a socially accepted fact, operating and oppressing as if it were a legal structure.

Indigenous women in Guatemala, throughout history, have been excluded due to their racial identity. Indigeneity and the assumption of this perceived identity, including stereotypes associated with indigeneity, are used by the state and the elites—those people who built and have always controlled the state and its institutions in order to exclude others and perpetrate violence. The state and the elites have systematically prevented Indigenous peoples from accessing education, health care, infrastructure, fair employment, and, above anything else, justice. In short, Indigenous people's right to life has been denied to them and their families. The lives of the women of Sepur Zarco show how racism always operates and is interconnected with other systems of oppression and exploitation—in this case, patriarchy and capitalism.

As it is a complex system of power, racism cannot be simply reduced to specific cases of discrimination, to instances of prejudice, or to concrete acts of segregation. Racism includes these three types of violations, but it goes beyond them. This is why, in Guatemala, structural racism—the racism of public and private institutions and that of the state and daily life—can be partly contested by building justice through recognizing, judging, and punishing the intellectual and material authors of racist acts, be those persons or institutions. In fact, in the Sepur Zarco case, only two of the men who executed the heinous violations against the Q'eqchi' women were tried and convicted; the rest continue to live under the blanket of impunity. Likewise, justice has yet to be achieved in the case of women from other Indigenous communities who experienced rapes by members of the military during the years of the internal armed conflict, who still feel ashamed or afraid to speak out, and who are not yet ready to use the national courts.

The Sepur Zarco case demonstrates how much harm structural racism can do, harm that can be seen when we compare the survivors' life histories to the statements they presented in court. Rosaro Xó explains what many suffered:

> After they killed my husband, they raped me. Because I did not want to be taken to the outpost, I fled to the mountains together with my four children, but we had no food, not even water, and the military kept chasing us. We lived like that, running from one place to another, in the mountains. Then, my children got sick, and they began dying one by one. At the end, I came down from the mountain alone, sick and in rags. (Velásquez Nimatuj 2013, 22)

If the women from Sepur Zarco had been white women, ladinas, and daughters of the elite, they would not have had to face those atrocious crimes. Catarina Caal also took refuge in the mountains:

> I had been living for about four years in the mountain of San Balscuando. One day, my daughter was underneath a tree, when, all of a sudden, the military bombed us. My daughter was pregnant and could not escape. I was able to hide behind a rock. There, I witnessed how the soldiers and patrolmen

clutched my daughter and, using only a machete, opened her stomach and took her baby out. I was able to see that the one who slit her more with the machete was the patrolman Tzuc Xol. My daughter and her baby were murdered, and their bodies burned. Days after, I went back with other neighbors to find the remains and ashes of my daughter and grandson in order to bury them, but we couldn't find them. They have both remained in the mountain, without a grave. (Velásquez Nimatuj 2013, 24)

The racial hierarchy, built and maintained by the elite controlling Guatemala, has allowed, promoted, covered up, financed, and prevented the end of these war crimes—crimes against humanity, which now some of the survivors, even at the end of their lives or while ill, are explaining and denouncing before the national justice system. Even if belatedly, the survivors are demanding accountability for these crimes.

The women's search for justice has been an uphill struggle. This is why it was important that on February 26, 2016, Court A for High-Risk Crimes convicted Esteelmer Francisco Reyes Girón to 120 years in prison and Heriberto Valdez Asij to 240 years in prison. The sentence was a step forward for the women of Sepur Zarco, as it demonstrated they had not lied about their experiences. However, justice for the survivors, for their children, and for the memory of those who died, has yet to be achieved within a state that is criminal, racist, and patriarchal, and that refuses to heal the historical wound that has not stopped bleeding.

Sobering as a Researcher, Frustrating as an Activist

To carry out the work with the women from Sepur Zarco, I was fortunate to have access to a wealth of written sources about the region, recordings, and meetings with specialists who produced other expert reports. I was able to participate in discussions with organizations of women activists and professionals who supported the process, but above all, I had the privilege of knowing, sharing with, and interviewing each of the Sepur Zarco women who courageously presented their complaint to the justice system in September 2013. Meeting them was an enlightening, if sobering, experience for me. Hearing the details of their lives, the lives of their parents, understanding how the settler-colonial system of the plantations of Alta Verapaz in which they were born marked them, and learning how, in various ways, they broke that slavery was inspiring. I also learned from their frustration and helpless-ness at the slowness of the justice system in dealing with their demands on account of their being Indigenous, poor, monolingual, illiterate, and rural women. My work as an expert on the case showed me the racist blindness of the judges who began to demand, thirty years after the fact, "scientific evidence" from the bodies of the raped women or their children who were born as part of the rapes. I was a witness to the fact that for the Guatemalan system, members of the army were not guilty if the women did not physically prove the violence or sexual slavery they lived through for six years.

In this process, I came to reaffirm that for Indigenous women, psychologi-cal marks are not enough evidence, nor are the diseases affecting their minds or bodies. The destruction of their communities, or the disappearance or murder of their husbands and children, is not enough. For women who sur-vived the genocide in Guatemala, the settler-colonial justice system requires "scientific" evidence to determine the veracity of their stories. Thus, the more I worked on my expert report, the more I understood that this was a strategy to delay the administration of justice to Indigenous women who lived at sub-sistence levels. The process of recording these actions over several years was sobering as a researcher, but as an activist it was frustrating and infuriating, because it involved seeing a system that legitimizes crimes against humanity.

Within this framework of contributing as a committed researcher, devel-oping a quality expertise, I found that a series of questions began to arise for me. These questions came slowly but intensely, beginning with the geno-cide trial against the Guatemalan general and former president Ríos Montt, who was declared guilty by the Court A for High-Risk Crimes on May 10, 2013, but whose sentence was withdrawn ten days later by the Constitutional Court. This trial and its outcome exposed the arbitrariness of the system and revealed the alliances between the small economic elite and the justice sys-tem. Both sectors came together as allies because they need a country with fragile institutions to maintain impunity, on the one hand, and subordination of Indigenous peoples, on the other. This impunity, which we Indigenous people have faced since May 2013, led me to ask myself whether my work could be an instrument that supports justice in Guatemala, that contests the historical impunity that devastates and disarticulates the poor, racializing them as people without rights and without future.

So my first set of questions is related to the methodology that I used for the expert opinion: What tools should I use to carry out useful research work for groups, communities, or towns that trying to recover from a genocide? Is the interview valid? How do I work in areas of armed conflict where those who managed to survive do not know whether this survival is a privilege or a disgrace, for all that the war took from them, and where what they least want is to swim in the sea of pain that my questions force them to return to? What is an appropriate methodology that does not perpetually victimize survivors of crimes against humanity, individuals who cannot live as perpetual victims?

At the end of 2005, I returned to Guatemala and began to work in political advocacy processes in order to transform, from the standpoint of Indigenous peoples, some state institutions. There, I noticed that most meetings ended with discussion of the human injuries and losses that the war left across its nearly four decades. Sometimes the Indigenous men and women did not want to learn how to develop a logical framework or a budget and asked me, instead, whether the funds they could access, rather than trying to transform state institutions, could be used to find their disappeared loved ones.

My second set of questions is about my position as a researcher in the processes in which I have participated, building or translating the memory of my surviving brothers and sisters. In this work, the language demanded by the justice system has led me to question my relative privileges of obtaining academic training, of surviving the genocide and of having not faced sexual violence. How do I confront the emotions, the sense of conscience, and the courage that overlap when I document crimes against humanity, crimes perpetrated against people with whom I share a racial identity? With each woman I interviewed, I ended up emotionally beaten; each trip I made dragged me into internal silence and permanent irritation, provoking anger and even hatred for the state and its elites. I felt that I was interviewing women from my family, and it was difficult for me to maintain the fragile line that the investigation requires. For me they were not informants or survivors, but women in whom I saw reflected the long history of oppression that precedes me as a K'iche' woman and that faced the women of my town, from the Spanish invasion to the present. For this reason, given the reality of the Sepur Zarco women, it has not been easy for me to be a researcher or to position myself as an apolitical professional; that has been impossible.

My last set of questions regards the usefulness of my work. The genocide, the human and cultural destruction, the deranged sexual violence that I documented in Sepur Zarco—in which members of the army raped women immediately after killing their husbands, in front of their children or members of the community—is beyond reason. Learning from the slavery and labor exploitation that the women experienced in the 1980s, and their fight to seek justice, I felt that my work should have utility not only for women in that community, but also for women who fight in other settings. We have to continue learning how to bring cases and lawsuits before the courts so that the state applies justice and ensures nonrepetition for the sake of the bodies and lives of Indigenous women in Guatemala and across the world. How can research contribute to ensuring that the sexual violence faced by Indigenous, rural, monolingual, and poor women does not remain silenced, is not buried under the cloak of impunity, but is instead aired in a way that sets normative precedents for the country and for humanity? Faced with this challenge, can our work dismantle the aberrations that the institutions themselves carry out and that threaten the basic principles of life, collective rights, and access to reparative justice?

My experience preparing expert opinions has shown that the demands of survivors of state violence not only include legal processes but also collective moral processes; a society cannot be built by sweeping away the crimes faced by Indigenous women and hiding them under the national carpet. For me, the process of investigation and activism demands the due judgment of those who violated the fundamental rights of Indigenous women.

In this scenario, where the fight is not on the battlefields but in the spaces of justice and memory, I ask myself: To what extent are the social sciences committed to the towns where we come from? And to what extent do Indigenous researchers keep our work from being reduced to the "safe areas and themes" that universities dictate and that imply disconnection with communities that are being attacked? Can we extend the academic work beyond the thesis or the doctoral dissertation? How do we create strategies to accompany communities after we publish a book or article about them?

Perhaps my broadest question is this: Amid a world economic system that supports the oppressive apparatus that permanently vomits up crimes against humanity, that seeks to erase memory in order to make those who are in power strong and keep the majority of peoples down, how can the academy support universal justice and not contribute to turning survivors into expressions of sympathy or representations that facilitate our professional careers?

Conclusion

The lives of the women of Sepur Zarco point to and are an example of the sexual violence, together with the obligatory work, to which Indigenous women have been subjected throughout history by the sectors controlling the state and the economy. This subjugation was central for building and consolidating the wealth that has been concentrated and kept within small group of elites, whose descendants, in this twenty-first century, are still enjoying the privileges inherited from the sixteenth. And this wealth has been buttressed on the bodies and minds of Indigenous women, who, historically, have never been assumed to have dignity.

In Sepur Zarco, the permanent periods of servitude to which Maya women have been subjected are crystallized. This servitude was always imposed through violence, and, although with different faces, it has remained and has been reinforced throughout different historical periods. The armed conflict in Guatemala, as has been demonstrated in many studies and expert reports, is a time period in which the modern state built precisely the conditions for the exacerbation of the physical, sexual, emotional, racial, and economic violence that has always been inflicted on Maya women. Because of this, even today, in the eyes of the state and the perpetrators, the sexual violence against Indigenous girls, adult women, pregnant women, and elderly women does not constitute a crime, nor does the detention of Indigenous women in military outposts. For the state and the perpetrators, such crimes were simply an extension of older atrocities from the armed conflict that concluded in 1996. Certainly, these crimes continue to be reproduced in the postwar era.

References

Bottomore, Tom. 1983. *A Dictionary of Marxist Thought*. Oxford: Blackwell.

Casaús Arzú, Marta Elena. 1992. *Guatemala: Linaje y racismo*. San José, Costa Rica: FLACSO.

Centeno Martín, Héctor. 2018. *Comisión del Esclarecimiento Histórico: Guatemala, entre la memoria del silencio y el silencio de la memoria*. Informe de CMI, no. 13. Salamanca: Universidad de Salamanca.

Comisión para el Esclarecimiento Histórico (CEH). 1999. *Conclusiones y recomendaciones: Guatemala memoria del silencio*. Guatemala City: CEH.

Crenshaw, Kimberlé Williams. 1995. "Mapping the Margins: Intersectionality, Identity Politics, and Violence Against Women of Color." In *Critical Race Theory*, edited by Kimberlé Williams Crenshaw, Neil Gotanda, Gary Peller, and Kendall Thomas, 357–83. New York: New Press.

Davis, Angela. 1981. *Women, Race, and Class*. New York: Random House.

Gramajo Morales, Hector Alejandro. 1995. *De la guerra . . . a la guerra: La difícil transición política en Guatemala*. Guatemala City: Fondo de la Cultura Editorial.

Grandin, Greg. 2007. *La última masacre colonial: Latinoamérica en la Guerra Fría*. Guatemala City: Avancso.

hooks, bell. 1992. *Black Looks: Race and Representation*. New York: Routledge.

Instituto de Estudios Políticos para América Latina y África (IEPALA). 1980. *Guatemala: Un futuro próximo*. Madrid: IEPALA.

Ministerio de Salud Pública y Asistencia Social (MSPAS), Organización Panamericana de la Salud (OPS), and Organización Mundial de la Salud (OMS). 2016. *Perfil de salud de los pueblos indígenas de Guatemala*. Guatemala City: MSPAS, OPS, and OMS.

Omi, Michael, and Howard Winant. 1986. *Racial Formations in the United States: From the 1960s to the 1980s*. New York: Routledge.

Pitarch, Pedro, Shannon Speed, and Xochitl Leyva Solano, eds. 2008. *Human Rights in the Maya Region: Global Politics, Cultural Contentions, and Moral Engagements*. Durham, N.C.: Duke University Press.

Proyecto Interdiocesano de Recuperación de la Memoria Histórica (REMHI). 1998. *Guatemala: Nunca Más*. 4 vols. Guatemala City: Oficina de Derechos Humanos del Arzobispado de Guatemala (ODHAG).

Sanford, Victoria. 2003. *Violencia y genocidio en Guatemala*. Guatemala City: F&G.

Sanford, Victoria. 2009. *La masacre de Panzós: etnicidad, tierra y violencia en Guatemala*. Guatemala City: F&G.

Soriano Hernández, Silvia. 2006. *Mujeres y guerra en Guatemala y Chiapas*. Mexico City: UNAM.

UN Development Programme. 2019. *Human Development Report 2019: Inequalities in Human Development in the 21st Century: Guatemala*. Accessed October 21, 2020. http://hdr.undp.org/sites/all/themes/hdr_theme/country-notes/GTM.pdf.

Velásquez Nimatuj, Irma Alicia. 2011. *La pequeña burguesía indígena comercial de Guatemala*. Guatemala City: Soros, Serjus, Avancso.

Velásquez Nimatuj, Irma Alicia. 2013. "Peritaje Cultural. Caso: Violaciones sexuales a mujeres q'eqchi' en el marco del conflicto armado interno (1960–1996) de Guatemala caso Sepur Zarco, municipio de El Estor, departamento de Izabal." Ministerio Público MP001-2011-118096. Unpublished manuscript.

Vilas, Carlos Maria. 1994. *Mercado, Estados y revoluciones: Centroamérica, 1950–1990*. Mexico City: UNAM.

CHAPTER 5

Confronting Gendered Embodied Structures of Violence

Mam Indigenous Women Seeking Justice in Guatemala and the United States

LYNN STEPHEN

G endered violence in transborder communities is linked to gender inequality, multiple masculinities, racism, ongoing settler colonialism, and uneven institutional terrain. Within these complex structures, Indigenous women bravely navigate their lives. Their strategies to flee violence and improve their lives, as well as their faith and hope that they can find safety and security, need to be seen as acts of heroic proportions. Those who work in institutions dedicated to fighting gendered violence and achieving gendered justice are also heroes and heroines often swimming against the tide.

My work as an expert witness for Mam female refugees has embedded me in ongoing emotional, intellectual, and strategic relationships with people and structures stretching from Oregon to Mexico to Guatemala.[1] The pro-

---

1. Mam is one of twenty-two Mayan languages spoken in Guatemala. Mam is spoken in the departments of Huehuetenango, Quetzaltenango, and San Marcos in Guatemala, and in the state of Chiapas, Mexico. It has approximately five hundred thousand speakers (Dirección General, n.d.). Mam also refers to an Indigenous ethnic group. Most of the Mam women whose asylum cases I have worked on or interviewed in Guatemala and in the United States are from Huehuetenango. This department has a population of 1,024,324, representing about 7.8 percent of Guatemala's total population. The department's population is majority Indigenous (57.5 percent), from nine different ethnic groups (Mam, Tectiteco, Acateco, Jacalteco or Popti', Chuj, Kanjobal, Aguacateco, K'iche', and Chalchiteco), and it has a 23 percent illiteracy

cess of taking in the stories of Indigenous women asylum seekers and listening to the experiences of gendered violence—as described by survivors and their family members in court and in interviews in Guatemala and the United States—has deepened my own understanding of structural and embodied violences borne by Mam Indigenous refugees. This in turn has permitted me to offer support and allyship, albeit limited, to such women through pro bono work on their asylum cases as an expert witness. This chapter begins by discussing my positioning, as well as two crises that directly engaged with my volunteer work as an expert witness and my research on gendered violence in Guatemala. I use the concept of *gendered embodied structures of violence* in this chapter to bring together militarized, paramilitarized, kinship, and masculinized governance and justice and the bodies that these forces act on—including my own (see Speed 2019)—and I link this concept to settler colonialism. Through an examination of how gendered embodied structures of violence have functioned currently and historically in Mam communities in Huehuetenango, and using one detailed example, I demonstrate that we cannot separate public and private violence, or state and nonstate actors. The sections that follow also discuss how I came to be involved in collaborative research on gendered violence in Guatemala and the United States, the transborder intersectional feminism that informs my work, insights from Indigenous feminists, and gendered structures of violence across time, borders, and bodies.

Positionings

First, I want to situate myself in relation to the women whose asylum cases I have worked on in the United States, and whose cases I have observed in specialized gendered violence courts in Guatemala. I am a white, Queer, highly educated professional woman who grew up in a lower-to-middle-class household in the Chicago area. Politicized by the time I was a teenager and fortunate to have learned Spanish while growing up, I became aware as a preadolescent of the ties between the consumption of food in the United States and those who produce it. This knowledge came through my family's participation locally in the United Farm Workers–organized boycotts

---

rate, a 71 percent poverty rate, and a 21.2 percent extreme poverty rate (Instituto Nacional de Estadística 2014, 14, 23, 25).

of grapes and lettuce. This personal history and placemaking has followed me through much of my research and into this project. My understanding of gendered embodied structures of violence emerged over several decades of conducting research with Indigenous populations in Mexico and Central America, as well as with Indigenous and non-Indigenous immigrants and refugees in the United States, primarily in California and Oregon.

My past work has explored how Indigenous peoples who migrate experience multiple border crossings as they move over boundaries of ethnicity, race, class, gender, sexuality, region, and nation-state and reconstitute their identities and communities along multiple dimensions in multiple sites (Stephen 2007, 2012). These border crossings and spaces of movement are constituted by historical and ongoing processes of settler colonialism that have resulted in the racialization, inequality, dispossession, and structures of violence that continue to affect Indigenous communities and women today. As pointed out by Shannon Speed (2019, 240), the framing of such sites as spaces of "coloniality"—a term suggesting vestiges of colonial processes that are the underside of and part and parcel of modern states—distracts us from the historical continuity that undergirds "the settler-colonial imperative of dispossession, extraction, and elimination." I find Speed's application of the concept of settler colonialism to shifting forms of capitalism in Latin America and the United States to be a useful path for connecting to the gendered violence I discuss in this chapter.

Interlinked Crises

In spring 2017, news reports about increasing numbers of immigration raids with no arrest priorities became common in the United States. Many people who were simply "encountered" by Immigrations and Customs Enforcement (ICE) officers while these latter were in search of a specific person were picked up as collateral: arrested, detained, and put in deportation proceedings. In many cases, these individuals were men and women going to work, waiting for transportation, buying gas, waiting for children to finish school or a sports game, or going on a family outing. After hearing about one such case in the Northwest on the six o'clock news, I had an emotional break. I began crying and shaking, and I accidentally dropped a white salad plate that I was loading into the dishwasher. I watched it break into a shower of white shards spreading across the living room floor like a map of cascading pain across my body and the continent. After a pause, I reached into the dishwasher and grabbed a full-size dinner plate and tossed it up into the air. After it arched up, it too crashed to the floor, spreading its fragments far and wide. I repeated the action two more times. Then I stood crying, staring at the pieces on the floor. A few minutes passed, and I slowly walked to the closet and took out a broom and dustpan. I methodically swept up the white, sharp fragments. After several passes, the broken pieces were in my trash can. The wooden floor was clean, but my emotional state remained shattered. This event marked a watershed for me in my work as an expert witness for Indigenous women fleeing gendered violence and asking for asylum in a hostile political climate in the United States.

A second watershed event came in June 2018, when U.S. attorney general Jeff Sessions reversed a 2016 ruling by the Justice Department's Board of Immigration Appeals that had granted asylum to A.B., a Salvadoran woman who fled to the United States after suffering long-term violence and after going to the Salvadoran police, who did nothing about it. Sessions's ruling had broad implications for the future of asylum in the United States, further inhibiting the ability of women to escape violence, both domestic and otherwise. Sessions's reasoning was based on an argument that domestic violence victims are not persecuted as members of "a particular social group" (*Matter of A-B-*, 27 I&N Dec. 316 [A.G. 2018]). A few years earlier, in the precedent-setting case of Ms. Cifuentes from Guatemala, the Board of Immigration Appeals had found that "married women in Guatemala who are unable to leave their relationship" counted as a social group for the purposes of asylum (*Matter of A-R-C-G-*, 26 I&N Dec. 388 [BIA 2014]). The Board of Immigration Appeals found that in Guatemala spousal rape is common and police fail to enforce domestic violence laws. Sessions disagreed and undid this precedent. In part Sessions's ruling stated:

> I do not believe A-R-C-G correctly applied the Board's precedents, and I now overrule it. The opinion has caused confusion because it recognized an expansive new category of particular social groups based on *private violence* . . .
>
> . . . . when the applicant is the *victim of private criminal activity*, the analysis must also consider whether government protection is available, internal relocation is possible, and persecution exists countrywide. . . .

. . . . Generally, *claims by aliens pertaining to domestic violence or gang violence perpetrated by non-governmental actors* will not qualify for asylum.

. . . The mere *fact that a country may have problems effectively policing certain crimes—such as domestic violence or gang violence—or that certain populations are more likely to be victims of crime, cannot itself establish an asylum claim.* (27 I&N Dec. 316, 318 [A.G. 2018], italics added)

In this one 2018 ruling, Sessions attempted to slam the door of the U.S. asylum system on women whose cases for asylum are based on gendered and domestic violence. At the same time, Sessions threw up a major obstacle for the transborder research and advocacy work that I had been doing with Mam refugee women.

Fortunately, the American Civil Liberties Union and the Center for Gender and Refugee Studies challenged Trump administration policies that seek to gut asylum protections for immigrants fleeing domestic violence, gang brutality, and more, an increasingly harsh set of policies aimed at limiting access to asylum and other forms of immigration. In December 2018, Judge Emmet Sullivan of the U.S. District Court in Washington, D.C., found that the asylum policies pushed by Sessions, "which instructed asylum officers to 'generally' deny such domestic violence and gang violence–related claims, violate immigration laws" (CGRS 2018; see also CGRS 2019). The ruling suggested that it was still possible for people who have suffered domestic violence and gang violence to seek asylum within existing U.S. immigration law. However, the reality is that the Sessions ruling has made it more difficult for those of us working on gendered asylum cases to maneuver the system. In general, it has resulted in lawyers' and advocates' needing to work with new definitions of "social group" and "political opinion" in order to help women quality for asylum.

The Sessions ruling was also accompanied by increasing numbers of women seeking asylum and severely overcrowded immigration courts. As of October 2020, more than 1,246,000 backlogged cases were in the immigration court system (TRAC Immigration 2020). At that same time, 275,845 (22 percent of the backlog) were from Guatemalans. The year 2019 was marked by a significant number of asylum requests from women, children, and families, many of whom presented themselves to Border Patrol or at ports of entry. From October 2018 to May of the following year, 593,507 people were detained, and 332,981 (58.5 percent) were a part of a family unit, defined as "individuals (either a child under eighteen years old, parent, or legal guardian) apprehended with a family member by the U.S. Border Patrol" (U.S. CBP 2019a). Of the nearly six hundred thousand detained, 56,278 (9.8 percent) were unaccompanied minors. Just in the month of May 2019, 144,278 people were detained at the U.S.-Mexico border—a majority of whom arrived from Guatemala and Honduras as families with children (see U.S. CBP 2019a). A significant number of them were Indigenous, particularly from Guatemala. These numbers decreased in 2020, partially as a result of a series of restrictive policies including the Migrant Protection Protocols (MPP). The MPP, colloquially known as "Remain in Mexico," forced about sixty thousand people to wait on the Mexican side of the border until their asylum cases were to be heard in the United States. The U.S. Supreme Court ruled in March 2020 that the program should remain in place after a federal appeals court found that it violated national and international law (Liptak and Kanno-Youngs 2020). MPP was drastically scaled back in the wake of the COVID-19 pandemic to virtual closure by the Trump administration.

Sessions's pernicious 2018 ruling had one unintended benefit: it made clear the basic contradiction in the way that states (and thus laws related to domestic violence) attempt to differentiate different types of violence as either (1) private violence perpetrated by nongovernmental actors, or (2) nonprivate or public violence perpetrated by state actors. My research suggests that Mam women refugees are survivors of multiple, overlapping forms of gendered violence that are not separable along this dichotomy. What is often termed "private," domestic violence cannot be parsed from interlocking forms of public violence. State, nonstate, and private actors are all linked in networks of violence and authority. The rest of this chapter further develops this argument.

The historical case study here of gendered violences in Huehuetenango (and elsewhere) demonstrates that women and their bodies have been viewed as part of territories and sites of control—from the household to the municipality to the department and beyond—by competing groups of men who have exercised multiples forms of masculine authority through time. The response of women, girls, and their supporters (often including men) to masculine authority exercised through violence is initially to attempt to persevere but eventually, after accumulated episodes of violence, to flee for their lives. That is what brings many through the perilous escape route of

Mexico to the U.S. border, seeking relief from suffering, and hoping to find safety and asylum.

Gendered Embodied Structures of Violence

Sessions's ruling vexed my heart, soul, and analytic creativity. My challenge here is to communicate the "in the skin" sense of accumulated terror, trauma, and heroic recovery demonstrated by Mam women refugees who flee to seek asylum; to explicate how their experiences of violence are tied to historical, structural systems of control and authority; and to convey my own embodied emotional, physical, and intellectual experience in working as a researcher and expert witness with these women and their families. *Gendered embodied structures of violence* is a concept whose purpose is to connect historical and structural violence with embodied experience. As suggested by Cecilia Menjívar (2011, 39–74), everyday violence and interpersonal violence are interwoven with structural violence, symbolic violence, political violence, and state terror. These interrelated forms of violence are naturalized in what Menjívar calls "multisided violences" (see also Speed 2014). As Menjívar further notes, gender ideologies create spheres of social action that "normalize expressions of violence" and that "justify punishments" for deviation from expected gender roles and gendered physical and social spaces (59). The women with whom I have worked have suffered multiple injustices and have engaged in creative use of multiple legal systems to try to leverage justice (see Hernández Castillo 2016; chapter 2 in this volume).

As discussed by Rachel Sieder (2017, 9), I also believe that it is "vital to historicize understandings of gender violence . . . locating different forms of gender oppression within specific national and local histories of racialization and colonization." Also useful here is Speed's (2019, 26) analysis of how the neoliberal form of capitalism, as mediated through the ongoing logics of settler colonialism, has resulted in an "unregulated neoliberalism . . . killing off its multiculturalist counterpart." In Latin America, as the state divested from public goods and services and privatized formerly public institutions and resources, dispossessed Indigenous peoples were recognized in some state constitutions and accorded limited, primarily cultural (not land or materially based) rights. This process was aptly called multicultural neoliberalism.

The price for these limited rights was an accelerated accommodation for global capitalist investment, which in Mexico and Guatemala blossomed together with the integrated drug, weapon, and human trafficking businesses controlled by organized crime. This process consolidated from the mid-1980s through the 2010s. Accompanied by ongoing and extremely violent struggles for territory and profit, the business models of many projects of global capitalism include "neoextractivist impulses that look remarkably similar to those at work in the initial stages of world colonization, bringing with them the intertwined mandates of dispossession and labor extraction" (Speed 2019, 26–27). In Mexico and Guatemala, as Speed notes, states are central to these dynamics.

Guatemalan Indigenous communities are embedded—as am I—within the structures of the settler-colonial capitalist state, currently in its global neoliberal, "multicriminal" phase (Speed 2016). More specifically, the Mam refugees and I coexist in a shared settler-colonial political economy that includes ever-harsher U.S. immigration and security policies; increased defense and securitization of the U.S.-Mexico border and the Guatemala-Mexico border; and community and regional borders patrolled by security committees, police, and other local and regional actors. This shared political economy also involves the consolidation of organized crime businesses, which extend throughout Central America, Mexico, and parts of the United States. As settler-colonial neoliberal states and their organized crime affiliates have deepened their presence at the local level, these disputes over territorial control along with increased drought and lack of employment have driven many to leave. For women, this decision is often made in the context of multiple violences that have become normalized as a part of community life. Their lives are embedded in settler-colonial structures of violence.

The concept of *gendered embodied structures of violence* deliberately disrupts an assumed public/private binary and makes visible plural forms of violence and suffering through their everyday, processual, and structural forms of operation (see Fluri and Piedalue 2017, 538–39; Menjívar 2011, 29). By speaking of gendered embodied structures, we challenge the idea that gendered and other violences can be directly imputed to distinct state or nonstate actors. States implicitly or explicitly delegate their power to nonstate actors, as seen through ongoing processes of colonialism (settler and otherwise) that continue to unfold in Guatemala through extractivism, the ceding of Indigenous territories to organized crime and affiliated groups, and the counterreaction of citizen security groups that have the indirect approval of many local and regional parts of the Guatemalan state apparatus (see chapter 4). Historically, for example, the boundaries between state and nonstate actors in the perpetration of violence have been blurred by the relations between Guatemala's army and its supervision of state-mandated Patrullas de Autodefensa Civil (PACs, Civil Self-Defense Patrols). The Mam women refugees and their families have carried gendered embodied structures of violence with them through multiple generations. Morna Macleod analyzes the process of how this violence went from invisible to visible in human rights tribunals in Guatemala, and Irma A. Velásquez Nimatuj offers evidence of its long-term historical continuity (see chapters 7 and 4, respectively). I have become personally connected to these structures of violence through my work as a researcher and expert witness for asylum cases based on gendered violence.

Transborder Research and Expert Witnessing: From Oregon to Huehuetenango

In July 2015, I began an ongoing collaborative project with several community-based organizations (CBOs) and immigration attorneys in Oregon to interview Mam refugee women and adolescents who were fleeing multiple violences and seeking asylum. Two local CBO workers came to my office at the University of Oregon to meet with me and request my help in supporting the asylum cases of Mam women, who had begun to arrive in Oregon in increasing numbers over the previous two years. They knew of my work with Indigenous immigrants in California and Oregon as a researcher (Stephen 2007), pro bono expert witness for asylum cases from Mexico and Guatemala (see Stephen 2016, 2017, 2018), and teacher of Latinx immigration history and Latinx filmmaking (see "Latino Roots," n.d.). For the last two decades, I have framed my work as *collaborative activist ethnographic research* (see Stephen 2007, 321–25; 2013, 17–27; Hale and Stephen 2013). Collaboration implies cooperation, having a share or part in a process. In this case it involves actively working with immigrant rights CBOs and immigration lawyers who are seeking to obtain asylum for Guatemalan Indigenous refugees. It also requires knowledge of the politics of location (Grewal and Kaplan 1994): we must understand the differences and similarities between ourselves as researchers and those with whom we collaborate. Activism means an alignment with and commitment to a particular sociopolitical process. In this project, the commitment is to achieving the protection and security of asylum within the U.S. immigration system for refugees who have suffered multiple forms of violence. Ethnography invokes the self and rich description and interpretation as a means to knowing, while research suggests a process of uncovering information and interpretations. This project involves interrogation of my own position as an ethnographer and the relationship between ethnography and expert testimony (see Stephen 2018). My research also encompasses fieldwork in Guatemala in the summers of 2015–19, interviews with Mam refugees and families in the United States and Guatemala, observations of court cases and analysis of case files of femicide and gendered violence carried out against Indigenous women in Guatemala, and an analysis of all this information together in conversation with Mam interlocutors and those who advocate for them.

The collaborative plan I worked out with the CBO staff and attorneys involved devoting some of my research funds and time, as well as hiring two graduate students. Our collaborative activities included setting up and conducting interviews, transcribing the interviews, preparing summaries of the interviews in Spanish for the clients to review and correct or change, and then translating these summaries into English as the basis for declarations. We also offered the audio interview and entire transcription to the women's lawyers and legal team so as to facilitate their preparation of the asylum cases. These materials also proved helpful to me, complementing my research in Todos Santos and other areas in Huehuetenango and Quetzaltenango, and facilitating my writing of expert opinions about the national, regional, and local conditions within which a person's particular experiences took place.

Interviews were conducted in Spanish with a Mam translator. Most were done in the offices of the CBOs or immigration legal services, which the asylum seekers had already visited. These interviews—as well as my own later process of testifying as an expert witness—were among the most difficult parts of the work, emotionally.

The purpose of providing expert testimony and reporting is to put an individual case of gendered violence into a larger context for the judge. The expert must show that what happened to one woman is part of a larger pattern of ongoing violence, that this violence affects women in particular as members of a social group, and that the violence involves a pattern of impunity for those who commit it and/or are responsible for prosecuting those who do. Working as an expert witness requires trying to disrupt what are often racial, ethnic, national, and gendered stereotypes and providing nuanced and accurate contextual information. An initial and important part of doing this work is first deciding whether the petitioner's declaration and other supporting documents appear to be consistent with what the anthropologist expert witness understands the on-the-ground situation to be. The evaluation of information for an expert asylum report functions in much the same way as the decision of whether to include a source of information in an ethnography. While expert reports do not contain an explicit theoretical framework, they are interpretive, as is ethnography.[2]

In order to build my credibility as an expert witness while also broadening my knowledge of the context surrounding the Mam women's lives in Guatemala, I made four trips to Todos Santos Cuchumatán and other parts of Huehuetenango between 2016 and 2019. The collaborative work I began in 2015 to support asylum cases blossomed into a comparative project on Indigenous women's access to justice (or not) in Guatemala's specialized gendered violence courts and in U.S. asylum courts. To understand the obstacles that women and others encounter in accessing the formal justice system in Guatemala, I engaged in a study of Guatemala's specialized courts for violence against women. Prior to 2008, the only legal spaces where women could bring complaints against perpetrators of violence were local courts known as Juzgados or Tribunales de la Paz (local courts called Justices of the Peace). But in that year, and owing to the efforts of Guatemalan women's movements, the country passed comprehensive antiviolence legislation and established a specialized court system to process cases related to violence against women (see Beck, forthcoming). Instances of femicide, sexual assault, and gendered violence in physical, psychological, and economic forms are supposed to be tried in these specialized courts, which began operating in 2010. Together with my colleague Erin Beck (a professor of political science at the University of Oregon), I have conducted four rounds of fieldwork across three different locations in Guatemala, where three of Guatemala's thirteen specialized courts are located: Guatemala City (the capital and largest population center), Quetzaltenango (the second-largest city and home to a significant Indigenous population), and Huehuetenango (a regional city close to the Mexican border with a majority Indigenous population).

Beck and I have conducted over eighty-five interviews with activists, congressional representatives, service providers, psychologists, judges, lawyers, survivors, and survivors' family members. We have also undertaken ethnographic observations in three city centers and several rural communities and

---

2. The ideas and prose in this paragraph draw from Stephen (2018).

logged roughly ninety hours of ethnographic observations of oral trials and deliberation in courtrooms, often involving Indigenous survivors of gendered violence and Indigenous defendants. We have collected statistics on criminal reports, court cases, and sentencing outcomes, as well as case files and final sentences for key cases. We have also researched what happens to women who bring their cases to local judges. Analyzing this data, we uncovered advances but also ongoing barriers to accessing courts, particularly for Indigenous women living in remote communities, and critical weaknesses that negatively affect those who engage with and work in the courts such as lawyers, judges, clerks, translators, and public prosecutors. This research has made me acutely aware of the kinds of obstacles Mam women refugees encounter in trying to find support and an escape from gendered violence in Huehuetenango. It has also revealed to me the ongoing dangers faced by women and their families even if they successfully file a court case and receive a sentence of prison time for those accused of gendered violence. After serving prison time—and without undergoing rehabilitation— perpetrators of violence can return to the communities where the survivors live and continue to threaten them and their families. And in prison, they can become connected to others who can help them threaten and retaliate against the women and their families who filed the court cases.

Part of the collaboration has involved working with a range of actors and institutions in Guatemala who support Indigenous women seeking protection from gendered violence. These include the Defensoría de la Mujer Indígena (National Office for the Defense of Indigenous Women) in Huehuetenango, and Fundación Sobrevivientes (Survivors' Foundation) in Guatemala City, which handles gendered violence and femicide cases in Huehuetenango, the capital, and elsewhere in Guatemala. We are also building relationships with local Mam women's groups such as Asociación de Comadronas del Area Mam (Mam Area Association of Midwives) in Concepción Chiquirichapa, Quetzaltenango; Asociación de Mujeres Río Isquizal (Río Isquizal Women's Association) in San Sebastián, Huehuetenango; and the Oficina Municipal de la Mujer (Municipal Women' Office) in Todos Santos, Cuchamatán. We have discussed the 2008 femicide law, knowledge about the law, specialized courts, and the challenges that these groups have faced in supporting women in the courts. Through triangulating our court observations (where detailed stories are told from a variety of viewpoints by witnesses), interviews with Indigenous women's organizations, and interviews with individual survivors and their families, Beck and I have developed an understanding of the complex context of gendered violence in Huehuetenango and Quetzaltenango.

Transborder Intersectional Feminism: A Perspective

The collaborative research we have developed is framed by intersectional feminism. The structures of violence that young, poor, and often Indigenous women and girls experience in Guatemala and on their journeys from Guatemala through Mexico to the United States occur in a transborder context that requires an intersectional analysis. The concept of intersectionality, first widely used by legal and critical race studies scholar Kimberlé Williams Crenshaw (1995, 358), illuminates "the various ways in which race and gender shape multiple dimensions" of the life experiences of women of color. In her analysis, Crenshaw discusses the dynamics of structural and political intersectionality that she observed while working in a shelter for battered women in Los Angeles. At the shelter, she encountered significant numbers of immigrant women fleeing domestic violence. She notes that shelters must not only address domestic violence inflicted by batterers, but also "confront the other multilayered and routinized forms of domination that often converge in these women's lives, hindering their ability to create alternatives to the abusive relationships that brought them to the shelters in the first place" (358). She further notes that many of the women are also "burdened by poverty, child care responsibilities, and the lack of job skills. These burdens, largely the consequence of gender and class oppression, are then compounded by racially discriminatory employment and housing practices" (358). In discussing U.S. immigration law—particularly an amendment to the 1990 Immigration Act to "provide immigrant spouses in a bona fide marriage, an escape from the beatings, the insults and the fear" (Lee 1993, 780) (meant to protect immigrant women who are battered or exposed to extreme cruelty by U.S. citizen and residents)—she notes that the law leaves undocumented immigrant women and their undocumented batterers completely unprotected. Many such women are reluctant to report abuse for fear of partners or other family members being deported.

The intersectional violence that Crenshaw documents in the United States around immigrant women and other women of color—poverty, lack of employment options and skills, racial discrimination in housing and employment—is deeply connected to the transborder structural violence that links

U.S. citizens and consumers to Central American refugee women and girls. Transborder violence can refer to transnational networks of violence that spread across the boundaries of nation-states, such as the smuggling networks of humans, drugs, guns, and cash that stretch from Central America, through Mexico, and into the United States. It can also refer, however, to structures of violence that cross regional, class, ethnic, language, and racial boundaries, as well as to U.S.-supported historical violence such as the genocide and deliberate gendered violence that accompanied the Guatemalan Civil War (1960–96). This gendered violence continues today. Guatemala has the fifth-highest femicide rate in the world. In the nine years prior to October 2017, at least 7,273 women were murdered. A woman is killed approximately every twelve hours, with an average of fifteen femicides per week. The year 2016 saw 51,131 complaints about gendered violence of all kinds across Guatemala (Pocón and Sánchez 2017; Instituto Nacional de Estadistica 2017).

Gendered violence continues for Indigenous girls and women who migrate from Guatemala and cross Mexico in their quest to get to the United States. In the forty Mam asylum cases for which I have provided expert testimony and reports, a majority cite ongoing threats from local *maras* (gangs), who threaten the women with rape or worse for spurning their advances either in their home communities or in towns in Mexico. Local gangs may be working with the larger organized crime groups that control drug production and transport routes through departments such as San Marcos and Huehuetenango, which border Mexico, and then into the United States for the large drug market there.

Many girls and young women who flee have parents who migrated to the United States in the 2000s in search of a way to financially support their children, who were often left in the care of grandparents, other relatives, or godparents. These young women, many of them left unprotected in the absence of fathers or husbands, are seen as "available" for exploitation by men and boys. Indigenous women often face further discrimination in local communities or along the journey to the United States. Many find themselves without any source of support or advocacy.

Women Refugees: From Guatemala to Oregon

From 2004 to 2019, a dramatic increase took place in both undocumented and legal immigration from Guatemala to the United States. Until 2011, the average annual figure for all migrants was 56,737 (Jonas and Rodríguez 2014, 60). After 2011, the numbers grew bigger, with many refugees fleeing drug, gang, and paramilitary violence. The 2010 U.S. Census registered 1,044,209 people of Guatemalan origin. By 2019 this number was up to 1,683,093, with 16,727 in Oregon (U.S. Census Bureau 2011, 2019). Indigenous people are strongly represented among post-2010 Guatemalan immigrants in Oregon and elsewhere. Their presence can be seen through the legal and social service institutions of the state. Language interpretation requests from the Oregon Judicial Department for 2017, for example, included fifteen different Indigenous languages, among them six Mayan languages from Guatemala. The highest number of requests were from Mam speakers (Rahe 2018). In 2019, an Oregon immigration judge commented that a significant number of cases from Guatemala involve Indigenous language translation. As of August 2020, of the 7,817 pending immigration cases in Oregon, 3,188 (about 41 percent) are from Guatemala (TRAC Immigration 2020).

While making the journey from Guatemala to Oregon has always been a high-risk proposition, the danger increased significantly beginning in the 2000s. For Central Americans passing into Mexico over its southern border, the journey is perilous. While no official statistics exist, unofficial estimates claim that between 70,000 and 150,000 Central Americans have disappeared in recent years while trying to cross Mexico—numbers similar to those who died in the Salvadoran and Guatemalan Civil Wars (Telesur 2014). The migrants are subject to violence, extortion, kidnapping, and murder by organized crime groups and corrupt Mexican police and other security officials. Cartels and cartel-affiliated gangs and businesses control integrated routes that reach deep into Central America, through Mexico on trains and other forms of transportation, and into the United States. In June 2019, the Mexican government sent fifteen thousand members of the newly created Guardia Nacional (National Guard) to its northern and southern borders (Graham 2019).

According to U.S. Customs and Border Protection (CBP), in fiscal year 2014 (FY2014, i.e., October 2013–September 2014), 68,445 family units (primarily women and children) were apprehended at the U.S. border. These numbers decreased in FY2015 but then rose again in FY2016, to 77,674, with 23,067 of these family units being from Guatemala. This number decreased by only 3 percent in FY2017, to 75,722, with 14,827 of these family units coming from Guatemala (Johnson 2019). However, FY2018 saw a significant increase, with 84,405 family units "apprehended," 42,757 of those from

Guatemala (U.S. CBP 2018). Between October 2018 and May 2019—only nine months—149,081 family units and 24,638 unaccompanied minors from Guatemala were "apprehended" by CBP (U.S. Customs and Border Protection 2019b). The numbers rose significantly from 2014 to 2019.

In Oregon, the period from 2013 to 2019 was marked by an increase in undocumented Mam women and others from transborder Guatemalan communities. Many women also came with some of their children. Almost all were seeking to escape multiple forms of violence and reunite with family members in rooted transborder communities, according to more than forty interviews I have conducted with Mam women, children, and adolescent refugees in the Northwest who fled violence after 2014.

Most of the women have children, are living without male protection—spouses are most often absent or deceased—and have suffered from ongoing harassment, including sexual assault or attempted sexual assault, kidnapping, and extortion. Most report that local forces of the Policía Nacional Civil (PNC, National Civil Police) do not protect them, take their complaints seriously, or work to prosecute criminals. Most also mention the presence of local gangs who they believe are connected to their experiences of physical assault, robbery, attempted or actual sexual assault, extortion, and intimidation. Some attribute possible involvement to local police. Several are fleeing violent husbands who subjected them to severe domestic abuse, in addition to the other violence they experienced. All the cases I have worked on involve women who have suffered from multiple forms of interlocking violence that include domestic violence, militarization, paramilitarization, state security interventions, and local gang activity. Below, I share a specific story to demonstrate how gendered embodied structures of violence work through time in one family. The names are pseudonyms, and the dates and details are changed to protect identities and ensure security.

Gendered Embodied Structures of Violence Through Time: Pedro and Petrona's Story

Pedro was born in the mid-1980s in a small hamlet in a Mam-speaking municipality of Huehuetenango. Mam is his first language. He was a small child at the time that Guatemala was recovering from its bloody civil conflict, which left many communities devastated. The population of his community was ravaged by the war, with many killed, displaced, or disappeared. The presence of the Ejército Guerrillero de los Pobres (EGP, Guerilla Army of the Poor) made the community a target for repression from the military and, after the war, from PACs. Between 1982 and 1996, men between the ages of eighteen and sixty were organized into these civil patrols and were required to patrol in twenty-four-hour shifts. PACs were used to suppress the EGP and other guerillas, but also to control communities through a mandatory labor tax. In addition, civil patrols empowered the locals who led these units, linking them to local military bases and commanders. After the civil patrols were disbanded in Pedro's community in the mid-1990s, new local security committees were formed and all men were obligated to participate.

Pedro left his community in the mid-2000s to go to the United States, but he returned after a short period of time. When he returned at the age of seventeen, he was forced to join a local security committee. Not wanting to engage in meting out severe punishment and torture to community members, he fled to another village several hours away. He was brought back by the local patrol leader to be publicly punished, humiliated, and tortured. He was whipped, thrown into very cold water, forced to break up large rocks as hard labor, and, when unsuccessful, thrown into a cold jail cell. Once liberated, he fled to the regional capital.

There, he was able to establish a life by working in a cafeteria. The owner was a former soldier named Ramón. After some time, Pedro met Petrona, who periodically came in to order food. They began to live together in common-law marriage and had a child. As Pedro happily recalls, when his child was a couple of years old, two other Mam-speaking people began working with Pedro, and he was able to speak his first language at work. That happiness didn't last long. One day his boss, who had previously fought against the EGP, accused Pedro of being a guerilla or son of a guerilla fighter because of his place of birth and the fact that he was speaking Mam. Pedro's once-nice boss became abusive and threatening. When Pedro told someone at work that he was thinking of reporting the abuse to local authorities, his boss threatened to kill him and harm his family. He then fired Pedro and told him to never come back. A few days later, Pedro was severely assaulted by four men and a woman, who told him that he deserved the attack for being the son of a guerilla fighter. Severely injured, Pedro fled to Mexico without informing his wife of what had happened. He later migrated to the United States, settling in the Pacific Northwest. The story continues with specifically gendered violence aimed at Pedro's wife, Petrona.

Petrona was born in 1990 in a small Mam-speaking hamlet in Huehu-etenango. She did not attend school and knows very little Spanish. She remembers that her father was forced to participate in civil patrols during the war. He resisted and was severely beaten for noncompliance. Due to this treatment, he died when Petrona was just six years old. In order to survive and feed her children, Petrona's mother began a new relationship. Petrona's stepfather systematically beat her, her siblings, and her mother for years. He also raped her mother. Petrona's mother refrained from reporting this abuse to local police, out of a fear that her husband would kill her if she did so, as well as a certainty that local police seldom responded. Petrona left the house at age fifteen to try to make a living. Her mother fled to Mexico to escape the abuse and sexual violence. Petrona worked as a maid for another family in a small town and then got a job at a laundry mat in the regional capital, where she met Pedro, who had fled the security committee of his hometown. After two years of dating, they began to live together as common-law wife and husband. She worked at the laundromat and on the weekends sold food at the local park. She and Pedro had a son.

Things were going fine, until one day when Pedro came home from work looking really beat up. Then, when he began a new job, he suddenly disappeared, and she didn't know what happened to him. About eight months later, while waiting for transport home from work, she was kidnapped, blindfolded, taken two hours out of town, raped at knifepoint, and severely beaten. The people who kidnapped her called her racial slurs in Spanish, referring to her identity as a Mam Indigenous person. They demanded to know where her husband was, showing her his picture. "You are going to have to learn to respect Ramón," they screamed at her. After spending a week in a local medical clinic, she borrowed money, hired a local smuggler, and fled to the United States. She left her son in Guatemala with her sister.

Petrona turned herself in at a legal port of entry on the U.S.-Mexico border and attempted to share her story in Mam. There was no interpreter available. Finally, after at least a month of detention in Arizona, she was able to reach a relative who paid for her $10,000 bail and a bus ticket. The relative lived in a city where there were many other people from her home community. There she received information about how to file for asylum. After two years, she ran into her husband by chance, and they began to live together again and filed for asylum together. They subsequently moved to Oregon, where their case was transferred. I served as an expert for their case. They were both granted asylum in 2018.

Pedro and Petrona's stories illustrate the historical and contemporary connections between past forms of gendered and racial violence and its continuation into the present. They also demonstrate how the structures and processes of masculine violence and authority that were entrenched during the decades-long Civil War continue to act on Indigenous women's and men's bodies today, drawing a connecting line between the Guatemalan army, PACs, present-day security committees, and organized crime. Petrona's husband was targeted by an ex-solider on the basis of his indigeneity and place of origin. Ex-soldiers and officers of the Guatemalan military run many small businesses in regional towns and cities. Because many towns in Huehuetenango have been thoroughly penetrated by organized crime groups, it is easy to hire assassins and thugs. Pedro was targeted by his former employer. Petrona was brutally raped and kidnapped as a proxy for her spouse. As a woman left with a small child, she was seen as unprotected and vulnerable. She was kidnapped and raped in an effort to get her to reveal the whereabouts of her husband, which she did not know. Most women do not report such violence to the police; there are major incentives for remaining silent.

Petrona is a bearer of accumulated gendered violences, which have manifested literally on her body and that of her husband. The sequence of gendered violences she experienced includes physical abuse from a stepfather as a child and rape and assault as an adult. The first incidence of violence occurred within the structure of her family. The physical abuse she suffered was part of a continuum of violence that included the sexual assault of her mother, and the physical abuse of Petrona, her siblings, and her mother. This violence was not reported to local police; Petrona's mother feared retaliation and police inaction. These police were members of the PNC. Although the PNC had been restructured and reformed by the early 2000s and was deployed close to where Petrona lived, the police did not provide her with protection. Nonintervention by state actors permits impunity by nonstate actors such as Petrona's stepfather.

As an adult, Petrona survived a violent rape and severe physical beating at the hands of several men who appear to have been hired by her husband's former boss Ramón, an ex-soldier who accused her husband—and her, indirectly—of being related to former guerillas in the EGP, viewed as the enemy of the Guatemalan army during the Civil War. Former soldiers such as Ramón continue to hold authority and power directly through their positions in regional economies but also through their connections to police, current soldiers, and, in some cases, organized crime networks. Ramón, a former state actor, was able to foment gendered violence against Petrona with impunity, even hiring people to carry out that violence. If we put together the trajectory of gendered embodied structures of violence that were perpetuated and permitted by the Guatemalan military, PNC, local organized crime, and a male-controlled family structure in the community where Petrona grew up, we can see how they converge literally in her body through time.

Accumulated Gendered Violences

In what follows, I discuss the accumulated gendered violences that have formed continuous, interconnected structures in Todos Santos Cuchumatán, Huehuetenango, in which I have conducted some recent short-term research. This section is based on my own research as well as that of Jennifer Burrell (2013) and Ellen Jane Sharp (2014). I offer it to complement the detailed case study of gendered violence as told through the stories of Pedro and Petrona. I also offer it to concretely document the historical interconnections between state and nonstate actors and to suggest the impossibility of separating their actions, networks, or structures through time.

Following the militarization of the municipality of Todos Santos in the early 1980s, first by the EGP, and then by the Guatemalan military, a culture of fear, insecurity, and suspicion set in. Over a two-year period, the municipality suffered the burning of 150 homes, the rape of women, and the detention, torture, and dismemberment of more than two hundred male community members (Burrell 2013, 29, 179n9; Ikeda 1999). This action was followed by disappearances, murders, and kidnappings. Many locals fled to the mountains and to Mexico. Some remained in Mexico until late into the 1990s.

The Guatemalan state under the dictatorship of General Efraín Rios Montt (1982–83) appointed rural mayors and brought the power of the state to local communities through the so-called Thesis of National Stability, in programs that included PACs and local militias that often acted on behalf of the army to control access to communities and suppress guerilla groups. These civil patrols carried out torture, killings, and other crimes as well as informing on community members.

Researchers who have worked in Todos Santos have reported that the civil patrols there did not engage in armed combat during their first seven years (1982–89) (Perera 1993; Carrescia 1989) and were nonaggressive even after that (Burrell 2013, 35). The PACs did, however, contribute to a consolidation of power and to a general culture of distrust. After the PACs had been in operation for a little more than a decade, the Guatemalan state established local-level state institutions of justice. While justice and local policy were administered before the war through *fiscales, ixcueles, regidores*, and mayors (elders who held the highest positions in the civil-religious hierarchy) (Burrell 2013, 157–58), authority shifted to PAC leaders linked to local army commanders during the conflict. As noted by Rachel Sieder (2011, 175), "the civil patrols effectively became a part of community authority structures and norms" and were a "form of communal collective defense." The patrols were both part of a state system—one that operated through the everyday actions and normalization of patrolling—and also a state effect, demonstrating what Sieder describes as the "power of the counterinsurgency state" (175).

Following the 1996 signing of peace accords in Guatemala, the Guatemalan National Police, which was notorious for working with the Guatemalan military to carry out counterinsurgency operations during the conflict, was demobilized. Under the rubric of the peace accords, a new police force, the National Civil Police (Policía Nacional Civil or PNC), was to be established that would be autonomous from the military, subject to a new security law, trained in a new six-month course at the National Police Academy (Academia de la Policía Nacional Civil), and subject to community involvement in recruitment in order to reflect the multiethnic character of Guatemala. Community involvement was to encourage recruitment from local communities. Unfortunately, most of the old national police officers were rehired. By 1999, the PNC had 17,399 members deployed, and only 36.5 percent were new officers (Byrne, Stanley, and Garst 2000, 1).

In the early 2000s, several years after the PACs were ended, Todos Santos formed local security committees. Anthropologist Ellen Jane Sharp (2014) refers to these committees as vigilantes, contrasting with Jennifer Burrell (2013, 139), who uses the local term *comité de seguridad* or simply *seguridad*. Both authors agree that *seguridad* (referring to local security committees) filled what was perceived as a security vacuum, drawing on past practices of the PACs: "constant surveillance within communities, rapid and collective response to detain interlopers, and the occasional summary and spectacular use of physical violence" (Sieder 2011, 176). Sharp and Burrell both suggest that local security committees were able to achieve a great deal of power and continue the culture of surveillance, use of physical violence, and empowerment of male leaders that emerged under the PAC system. As the security committees geared up, local youth gangs clashed with them, becoming higher profile and more violent by 2010.

Testimonies that I have received during interviews from recent female refugees who fled Todos Santos suggest that the two local gangs have escalated into more serious crimes such as extortion, kidnapping, and rape, building on a preexisting culture of hypermasculinity and control that is "adaptable across a range of anxieties, worries, and contexts" (Burrell 2013, 37). This culture of hypermasculinity builds on local experiences of participation in the PACs, some local security committees, gangs, and the violence perpetuated by some members on the PNC.

Burrell and Sharp both condemn the culture of *seguridad* that took hold in Todos Santos, dominating daily life. Burrell (2013, 156) writes that *seguridad* "exercised control over the local judiciary, publicly humiliated community members by dunking them in the fountain, and in short, brought back the kinds of 'forcivoluntary' paramilitarized forms that characterized the war years" (see also McAllister and Nelson 2013). Sharp (2014) documents fathers having to flog their sons and engage in other forms of physical punishment to exercise authority over unruly youth. If they did not, the security committee would.

Both Sharp and Burrell note that the security committees built a culture of masculine power. Burrell (2013, 158) writes: "generational conflict is expressed through the criminalization of youth rebellion and the subsequent remilitarization that quells it." This youth rebellion and remilitarization are built on a complex, historical culture of masculine control and impunity. While the culture of masculinity promoted by *seguridad* is very different from that of the local youth gangs, both cultures are rooted in the patrol and control of territory. Women figure as subordinate or even disposable parts of both cultures of masculinity.

Women and Their Bodies as Part of Territories

During the Guatemalan Civil War, the army, guerillas, and civil patrols vied for control of Indigenous territories in the western highlands of Guatemala.

The establishment of *seguridad* in Todos Santos was also about control of Indigenous territory. Strongly linked to ideas of Indigenous sovereignty, control of territory is a baseline of autonomy. This sovereignty and control of territory continues to be contested, both through the occupying presence of security forces or the youth gangs or the PNC, and through the space of the local legal apparatus, the local Juzgados de la Paz, where judges preside. Such judges are often from outside of the region and usually do not speak local Indigenous languages. The gendered occupation of territory not only identifies geographic space and the sacred local landscape, but also operates on the gendered bodies found within Indigenous territories. In the power struggle that has emerged between *seguridad* and gangs in Todos Santos, women's bodies—and men's—are understood as part of the territory each group strives to control. While I have amply discussed the type of control *seguridad* attempted to exercise and its consequences, here I explore in more detail how the occupation of specific places in Todos Santos and these sites' identification with one of the local gangs—either Los Azules (The Blues) or Los Rojos (The Reds)—reads onto bodies.

Conversations with two men who recently fled Todos Santos Cuchumatán revealed details about local gang activity. One man reported that Los Azules and Los Rojos had divided up the *territorio* (territory) of Todos Santos. He fled after gang members threatened him because of his involvement with a particular woman. The gang members claimed this woman's body as part of their territory and thus as their possession. Another man stated that the local gangs could call in their larger affiliates when needed. He suggested that the Los Azules might be affiliated loosely with the organized crime groups who controlled routes through the municipality, into Huehuetenango.

Interviews carried out between 2016 and 2019 suggested that local women have observed violence against women that they believe is carried out by gangs. Cristina (a pseudonym), age twenty, related to me a 2015 incident of rape and femicide when I asked about violence against women and girls.

CRISTINA: There is violence here for women. They killed a girl. She was walking to school, but she never arrived. They found her raped and dead in the hamlet of Chicoy. They also found a handicapped person who had been killed there in Chicoy as well as a boy who was killed there.

LYNN: Why there in Chicoy?

CRISTINA: There is no PNC in Chicoy. A lot of families are afraid there. . . . You have to really watch what you wear because of the gangs. For example, if you are walking around with red shoes or a red sweater, they [Los Azules] will tell you that you can't wear that. This happens in the center of town too.

Cristina went on to describe how Los Azules can also police women and their clothing choices. She warned me that one has to be careful about what color they are wearing if they cross into Los Azules' territory: "If you have on something red and they see you, they will take it off of you and beat you." She suggested that corruption in the PNC works to the advantage of local gangs, who are able to easily get out of the local jail, even if they are arrested.

CRISTINA: Now there are soldiers from the army that are also patrolling here. They have more force. The gangs used to beat up the PNC. And there also was a problem with corruption of the PNC. They would let the gang members out of jail for a bribe. And they hardly ever go to the more distant hamlets. If they do detain a gang member, then they just pay a bribe of Q2,000 or Q10,000, and they are let out. . . . But there is a problem because some soldiers also rape women.

LYNN: And what about the local security committees? Do they protect women?

CRISTINA: Well, the people from *seguridad* threw those from the *maras* into the drainage ditches, they broke rocks on their feet, and they beat them up. But the community here rose up recently against the security committee because they started to punish everyone. If you disagreed or fought with them, they would throw you in jail and throw you in cold water. Women too. There was a girl from here who was out taking pictures, and they captured her and threw her in the water.

My conversation with Cristina reaffirms the vulnerable position of women within the logic of male territorial control, whether it is in relation to the two gangs, *seguridad*, the PNC, or, in some cases, the Guatemalan army.

Gendered Violence Structures Across Time, Borders, and Bodies

Serving as an expert witness for Mam women refugees seeking asylum became harder when Donald Trump assumed the U.S. presidency in January 2017. With every passing week of the Trump administration, I began to feel an increasing desperation to take on as many pro bono asylum cases as I could. It seemed that we needed to get as many asylum cases into the system as possible in order to prevent people from being deported back to certain danger and death. Many of the Mam women refugees faced continued high levels of violence or death if they were returned to Guatemala, where they could be confronted by those who seek to harm them.

By March 2017, I was working about twenty extra hours per week above my teaching and research job, writing expert reports and preparing to testify. I was working on the reports in the evenings and on the weekends. I had lengthy conversations with lawyers and pored over newspaper stories and reports to further buttress the information I could include. As the underlying logic of the Trump administration's immigration policy became clear, I become more and more worried and obsessed with completing cases. At the beginning of this chapter, I described an emotional break I experienced under the stress of serving as an expert witness in an increasingly hostile political atmosphere.

After that event and a night's retreat in a local hotel, I felt the emotional and physical weight of my accumulated anger, frustration, dashed hopes, and feelings of uselessness and immobility take up residence in my body. Headaches, shoulder pain, fitful sleep, and a desire to drink wine every evening alerted me to the need to regroup. I spoke with several friends who experienced similar reactions from doing the same kind of work. "Take a break," "try meditation," "have some fun," I was advised. I began to read about secondary trauma and reached out to a few lawyers with whom I was working. Yes, they too had such feelings and had to work very hard to not be overwhelmed by the stories of their clients and the challenging political climate. Later that year, when I interviewed judges, lawyers, and advocates who support survivors of gendered violence in Guatemala, they all commented on the importance of *autociudado* (self-care) and the effort that takes.

My body, of course, was also bound up in the gendered structures I thought and wrote about in relation to the Mam women refugees, as were the bodies of the lawyers who defended them and everyone who is an antiviolence advocate in Guatemala, whether in the specialized justice system for femicide and gendered violence or in NGOs or women's organizations.

One of my solutions was to take a mindfulness-based stress reduction class and to mediate daily. An awareness of the here and now did provide relief and space for a pause and appreciation of the small joys in my life. It also made me aware of what a luxury it is to be able to consciously take time to do that. Such tools have also helped some of the Mam refugee women, most of whom suffer PTSD and other forms of trauma. The act of centering the physical and emotional experiences of accumulated trauma in myself pushed me to pay renewed attention to the historical weight of generations of gendered violence in the bodies of the Indigenous women with whom I was working. I want to highlight how historical structures of gendered violence are embodied and carried through subsequent generations by repeated cycles of male authority and control directed at Indigenous peoples, and particularly at Indigenous women.

Ongoing Settler Colonialism, Heteropatriarchy, and Paternalism

Mam women fleeing multiple violences must be seen in the larger historical frame of settler-colonial violence that began with the usurpation of Maya kingdoms and territories by the Spanish and some Indigenous allies. This violence has continued under the modern Guatemalan nation-state, which has alienated the territory, forms of government, justice, and social organization of its Indigenous peoples. Shannon Speed (2017, 786) convincingly argues that ongoing processes of dispossession of Indigenous labor, land, and resources indicate "a state of ongoing occupation, in Latin America as elsewhere in the hemisphere." She further suggests that while the processes through which racialization occurred and racial hierarchies were established in the Americas varied over distinct histories and landscapes, "they nevertheless were directed to similar aims of Native elimination through direct physical or assimilationist violences, and to the ongoing control of . . . populations" (787). Following Saldaña-Portillo (2017), Speed (2018, 787) notes that while racial mixing as an assimilationist strategy was employed in the United States and Latin America at the same time, it led to different outcomes. In Latin America, Indigeneity remained a distinct part of national identities, accompanied by the erasure of Afro-descendants. In the United States, indigeneity was "discursively eliminated (by mixing with whites, Indians literally disappeared)."

Settler-colonial histories of violence, bloodshed, genocide, rape, and other forms of gendered violence are part of Guatemalan Indigenous physical territories and bodies. Racial justifications for violence—whether during the colonial period or in the era of independence—have always been gendered. The brutal treatment of, genocide against, and displacement of Maya peoples from their territories historically and currently are significant factors in the ongoing intersectional violence experienced by Indigenous Mam women in their search for safety, asylum, and relief from violence. The historical structures of gendered violence—including the Guatemalan military, paramilitary civil patrols, community security committees, and organized crime groups—converge in women's bodies, which, as their targets, incorporate the accumulated history of structural violence. Being conscious of repeated patterns of gendered trauma allows us to connect the physical symptoms of trauma manifested in women's bodies with the structures and processes that facilitate ongoing violence.

Settler colonialism suggests an ongoing process and adaptable structure—not an event—whereby colonial agents occupy Indigenous territories and assert state sovereignty over land, governance, and judicial processes. Settlers seek to permanently occupy and end the colonial difference and mainstream settler logics of belonging (see Wolfe 2006; Veracini 2011). Scholars Maile Arvin, Eve Tuck, and Angie Morrill (2013, 13) have outlined the important ways in which settler colonialism is linked to heteropatriarchy and heteropaternalism (i.e., to social systems in which heterosexuality and patriarchy are seen as "normal"). As they explain, these social systems are based on an assumption that "heteropatriarchal nuclear-domestic arrangements in which the father is both center and leader/boss should serve as the model for the social arrangements of the state and its institutions."

We also have to examine the ways that states engage with heteropatriarchal and paternalist constructions of the family through masculine authority and through policies that govern inequalities and displacement. This phenomenon often results in the naturalization of women's obedience and their subordinate position in relation to many forms of masculine authority. State immigration policies, such as those currently promoted by the Unites States, need to be seen as a kind of state violence that directly affects access to justice for women like the Mam women I have discussed here, by leaving them in a legal limbo (Ashar et al. 2016; Menjívar 2006). The treatment some people receive in immigration detention is another kind of state violence.

Conclusions

When states incorporate and normalize social systems of heterosexuality and patriarchy and elevate men to be "in charge" of state institutions, the family, and kinship systems, we cannot argue that violence is wholly "private" or "public." When Petrona was violently assaulted by members of local organized crime circles, who acted with impunity, hired by an ex-soldier in order to punish her Indigenous husband for the perceived crimes of his forebears, there is no separation of state and nonstate actors. When local police did not intervene after Petrona was brutally beaten as a child, and after her mother was raped and assaulted by Petrona's stepfather, there is no line between family violence and state violence. Native women theorists like Arvin, Tuck, and Morrill (2013), Speed (2017, 2019), and others shine a bright light on the ways that gendered embodied structures have affected Indigenous women for hundreds of years. My own research and corporeal experience pushed me to recenter the knowledge gained through embodied experience and allow it to guide me to a theoretical conclusion.

In early July 2019, I testified in an immigration court to support the case of Julia (a pseudonym) and her two daughters, who had been stigmatized as "daughters and grand-daughters" of a guerilla fighter, receiving ongoing threats and physical punishment from local community members. Julia has suffered lifelong trauma since being left at the age of eight in the jungle after an attack by the Guatemalan army on a community of Mam families on the border between the municipalities of Ixcán and Barillas. The 1982 attack killed hundreds of people, including over fifty children. She bears physical scars on her head, feet, and legs from her childhood, but she bears many more nonvisible scars of the multiple traumas and accumulated violence she has carried in her body for decades. Her experiences of violence in the war have been joined with persecution, physical beatings, and most recently rape perpetrated by those who wanted to punish her for having a father and perhaps other family members in the EGP. Her daughters have also suffered persecution, carrying the war on and in their bodies. My own emotional state returned to "fragile" during the hearing, and I could not leave behind the images of what was described in the testimonies given. I hugged Julia and her daughters as we left the court, and they wanted to take pictures with me and their lawyer. The images captured our tenuous hope, but also emotional exhaustion and pain. I returned from the hearing bone-tired and slept fitfully. The Sessions ruling was invoked at the hearing. Because she was suffering from a severe health problem, Julia was unable to testify, and the hearing was continued. As of March 2020, immigration courts in Oregon are closed due to the Covid-19 pandemic, and it is unclear when Julia's case will resume. As of this writing she does not know yet whether she and her daughters will receive asylum.

My hope is that my reflections here can help combat the ideas that undergird Sessions's 2018 ruling and perhaps future rulings that falsely attempt to separate gendered violence into domestic and public spheres. Sessions's ruling suggested that survivors of domestic abuse and gang violence generally would not qualify for asylum in the United States under federal law because such violence is "private." It is not. The historical, gendered embodied structures of violence discussed here document how the Guatemalan state is bound to a wide range of actors. The perseverance, tenacity, and sheer willpower of women who survive multiple gendered violences generated through these structures and who bear these violences in their bodies means that they have the right to asylum and the protections it offers.

References

Arvin, Maile, Eve Tuck, and Angie Morrill. 2013. "Decolonizing Feminism: Challenging Connections Between Settler Colonialism and Heteropatriarchy." *Feminist Formations* 25 (1): 8–34.

Ashar, Sameer, Edelina M. Burciaga, Jennifer M. Chacón, Susan Bibler Coutin, Alma Nidia Garza, and Stephen Lee. 2015. *Navigating Liminal Legalities Along Pathways to Citizenship: Immigrant Vulnerability and the Role of Mediating Institutions.* Report. University of California, Irvine. https://socialecology.uci.edu/sites /socialecology.uci.edu/files/users/pdevoe/rsfreport_final_2-16-2016.pdf.

Beck, Erin. Forthcoming. "The Uneven Impacts of Violence against Women Reforms in Guatemalan Intersecting Inequalities and the Patchwork State." *Latin American Research Review* 56 (1).

Burrell, Jennifer. 2013. *Maya After War: Conflict, Power, and Politics in Guatemala.* Austin: University of Texas Press.

Byrne, Hugh, William Stanley, and Rachel Garst. 2000. *Rescuing Police Reform: A Challenge for the New Guatemala Government.* Washington, D.C.: Washington Office on Latin America.

Carrescia, Olivia, dir. 1989. *Todos Santos: The Survivors.* New York: Icarus Films. Film, 58 min.

Center for Gender and Refugee Studies (CGRS). 2018. "Court Rules Trump Policies Denying Asylum Protections to People Fleeing Domestic and Gang Violence Are Illegal." University of California Hastings College of the Law. December 19, 2018. https://cgrs.uchastings.edu/news/court-rules-trump-policies-denying-asylum -protections-people-fleeing-domestic-and-gang-violence.

Center for Gender and Refugee Studies (CGRS). 2019. "New Guidance Requires Fair Process for Domestic Violence, Gang Asylum Claims at the Border." University of

California Hastings College of the Law. January 14, 2019. https://cgrs.uchastings .edu/news/new-guidance-requires-fair-process-domestic-violence-gang-asylum -claims-border.

Crenshaw, Kimberlé Williams. 1995. "Mapping the Margins: Intersectionality, Identity Politics, and Violence Against Women of Color." In *Critical Race Theory*, edited by Kimberlé Williams Crenshaw, Neil Gotanda, Gary Peller, and Kendall Thomas, 357–83. New York: New Press.

Dirección General de Educación Bilingüe Intercultural. n.d. "Guatemala, un País con Diversidad Étnica, Cultural y Lingüística." Guatemala Ministerio de Educación. Accessed September 10, 2020. http://www.mineduc.gob.gt/DIGEBI/mapa Linguistico.html.

Fluri, Jennifer L., and Amy Piedalue. 2017. "Embodying Violence: Critical Geographies of Gender, Race, and Culture." *Gender, Place & Culture* 24 (4): 534–44. https://doi.org/10.1080/0966369X.2017.1329185.

Graham, Dave. 2019. "Mexico Says It Has Deployed 15,000 Forces in the North to Halt U.S.-Bound Migration." Reuters, June 24, 2019. https://www.reuters.com /article/us-usa-trade-mexico-immigration/mexico-says-it-has-deployed-15000 -forces-in-the-north-to-halt-u-s-bound-migration-idUSKCN1TP2YN.

Grewal, Inderpal, and Caren Kaplan. 1994. *Scattered Hegemonies: Postmodernity and Transnational Feminist Practices*. Minneapolis: University of Minnesota Press.

Hale, Charles R., and Lynn Stephen. 2013. Introduction to *Otros Saberes: Collaborative Research on Indigenous and Afro-Descendant Politics*, edited by Charles R. Hale and Lynn Stephen, 1–29. Santa Fe, N.Mex.: School for Advanced Research Press.

Hernández Castillo, Rosalva Aída. 2016. *Multiple InJustices: Indigenous Women, Law, and Political Struggle in Latin America*. Tucson: University of Arizona Press.

Ikeda, Mitsuho. 1999. "The Cultural Involution of Violence: A Guatemalan Highland Community and Global Economy." Center for Studies of Communication Design, Osaka University. Accessed September 10, 2020. http://www.cscd.osaka-u.ac.jp /user/rosaldo/991008CIVgua.htm.

Instituto Nacional de Estadística. 2014. *Caracterización departamental Huehuetenango 2013*. Report. Gobierno de Guatemala. https://www.ine.gob.gt/sistema /uploads/2015/07/20/yYXFscGDOuzXzAzSVWOzGnaa1WSaqajj.pdf.

Instituto Nacional de Estadística. 2017. *Estadísticas de Violencia en contra de la Mujer 2014–2016*. Report. Gobierno de Guatemala. https://www.ine.gob.gt /sistema/uploads/2017/12/28/20171228115248NvGE8QaDqrUN7CbitcK2fqc8 Rt5wIvMj.pdf.

Johnson, Jeh Charles. 2019. "United States Border Patrol Southwest Family Unit Subject and Unaccompanied Alien Children Apprehensions Fiscal Year 2016." U.S. Customs and Border Protection. Last modified June 17, 2019. https://www.cbp .gov/newsroom/stats/southwest-border-unaccompanied-children/fy-2016.

Jonas, Susan, and Nestor Rodríguez. 2014. *Guatemala–U.S. Migration: Transforming Regions* Austin: University of Texas Press.

"Latino Roots in Oregon." n.d. University of Oregon. Accessed September 10, 2020. http://latinoroots.uoregon.edu/archives/.

Lee, Maxine Yi Hwa. 1993. "A Life Preserver for Battered Immigrant Women: The 1990 Amendments to the Immigration Marriage Fraud Amendments." *Buffalo Law Review* 41:779–805.

Liptak, Adam, and Zolan Kanno-Youngs. 2020. "Supreme Court Revives 'Remain in Mexico' Policy for Asylum Seekers." *New York Times*, March 11, 2020. https://www.nytimes.com/2020/03/11/us/supreme-court-mexico-asylum-seekers.html.

McAllister, Carlota, and Diane M. Nelson, eds. 2013. *Aftermath: War by Other Means in Post-Genocide Guatemala*. Durham, N.C.: Duke University Press.

Menjívar, Cecilia. 2006. "Liminal Legality: Salvadoran and Guatemalan Immigrants' Lives in the United States." *American Journal of Sociology* 11 (4): 999–1037.

Menjívar, Cecilia. 2011. *Enduring Violence: Ladina Women's Lives in Guatemala*. Berkeley: University of California Press.

Perera, Victor. 1993. *Unfinished Conquest: The Guatemala Tragedy*. Berkeley: University of California Press.

Pocón, Roni, and Glenda Sánchez. 2017. "Mensualmente mueren 62 mujeres de forma violenta en Guatemala." *Prensa Libre*, October 31, 2017. https://www.prensalibre.com/guatemala/justicia/mensualmente-mueren-62-mujeres-de-forma-violenta-en-guatemala.

Rahe, Mallory. 2018. *Estimates of Migrant and Seasonal Farmworkers in Agriculture, 2018 Update*. Report. Oregon Health Authority, Public Health Division. https://digital.osl.state.or.us/islandora/object/osl:421298.

Saldaña-Portillo, Maria Josefina. *Indian Given: Racial Geographies Across Mexico and the United States*. Durham, N.C.: Duke University Press.

Sharp, Ellen Jane. 2014. "Vigilante: Violence and Security in Postwar Guatemala." PhD diss., University of California, Los Angeles.

Sieder, Rachel. 2011. "Contested Sovereignties: Indigenous Law, Violence and State Effects in Postwar Guatemala." *Critique of Anthropology* 31 (3): 161–84.

Sieder, Rachel. 2017. Introduction to *Demanding Justice and Security: Indigenous Women and Legal Pluralities in Latin America*, edited by Rachel Sieder, 1–28. New Brunswick, N.J.: Rutgers University Press.

Speed, Shannon. 2014. "A Dreadful Mosaic: Rethinking Gender Violence Through the Lives of Indigenous Women Migrants." In "Anthropological Approaches to Gender-Based Violence and Human Rights," *Gendered Perspectives on International Development* WP304, 78–94. https://gencen.isp.msu.edu/files/8914/5201/1092/WP304.pdf.

Speed, Shannon. 2016. "States of Violence: Indigenous Women Migrants in the Era of Neoliberal Multicriminalism." *Critique of Anthropology* 36 (3): 280–301.

Speed, Shannon. 2017. "Structure of Settler Capitalism in Abya Yala." *American Quarterly* 69 (4): 783–90.

Speed, Shannon. 2019. *Incarcerated Stories: Indigenous Women Migrants and Violence in the Settler-Capitalist State*. Chapel Hill: University of North Carolina Press.

Stephen, Lynn. 2007. *Transborder Lives: Indigenous Oaxacans in Mexico, California, and Oregon*. Durham, N.C.: Duke University Press.

Stephen, Lynn. 2012. "Conceptualizing Transborder Communities." In *The Handbook of International Migration*, edited by Marc Rosenblum and Daniel Tichernor, 456–77. New York: Oxford University Press.

Stephen, Lynn. 2013. *We Are the Face of Oaxaca: Testimony and Social Movements*. Durham, N.C.: Duke University Press.

Stephen, Lynn. 2016. "Gendered Transborder Violence in the Expanded United States–Mexico Borderlands." *Human Organization* 75 (2): 159–67.

Stephen, Lynn. 2017. "Guatemalan Immigration to Oregon: Indigenous Transborder Communities." *Oregon Historical Quarterly* 118 (4): 64–93.

Stephen, Lynn. 2018. "Gendered Violence and Indigenous Mexican Asylum Seekers: Expert Witnessing as Ethnographic Engagement." *Anthropological Quarterly* 91 (1): 321–58.

Telesur. 2014. "Central American Mothers Begin Search for Missing Children in Mexico." November 21, 2014. https://www.telesurenglish.net/news/Central-American-Mothers-Begin-Search-for-Missing-Children-in-Mexico-20141121-0043.html.

TRAC Immigration. 2020. Immigration Court Backlog Tool. Syracuse University. Accessed October 10, 2020. https://trac.syr.edu/phptools/immigration/court_backlog/.

U.S. Census Bureau. 2011. *The Hispanic Population: 2010*. Report C2010BR-04. https://www.census.gov/prod/cen2010/briefs/c2010br-04.pdf.

U.S. Census Bureau. 2019. Hispanic or Latino Origin by Specific Origin. 2019 American Community Survey 1-Year Estimates Detailed Tables. Table B03001. https://data.census.gov/cedsci/table?q=Hispanic%20or%20Latino%20by%20types%20&tid=ACSDT1Y2019.B03001.

U.S. Customs and Border Protection (CBP). 2018. "U.S. Border Patrol Southwest Border Apprehensions by Sector FY2018." Last modified October 23, 2018. https://www.cbp.gov/newsroom/stats/usbp-sw-border-apprehensions.

U.S. Customs and Border Protection (CBP). 2019a. "Southwest Border Migration FY 2019." Last modified November 14, 2019. https://www.cbp.gov/newsroom/stats/sw-border-migration/fy-2019.

U.S. Customs and Border Protection (CBP). 2019b. "U.S. Border Patrol Southwest Border Apprehensions by Sector Fiscal Year 2019." Last modified November 14, 2019. https://www.cbp.gov/newsroom/stats/sw-border-migration/usbp-sw-border-apprehensions.

Veracini, Lorenzo. 2011. "Introducing Settler Colonial Studies." *Settler Colonial Studies* 1 (1): 1–12.

Wolfe, Patrick. 2006. "Settler Colonialism and the Elimination of the Native." *Journal of Genocide Research* 8 (4): 387–409.

CHAPTER 6

Gender-Territorial Justice and the "War Against Life"

Anticolonial Road Maps in Mexico

MARIANA MORA

nternational Women's Day, March 8, 2018, marked a political inflection point for the residents of Morelia, a *caracol* (regional cultural and administrative center) of the Ejército Zapatista de Liberación Nacional (EZLN, Zapatista National Liberation Army). The festivities that day followed a quarter-century of social mobilizations by the rebel army in the state of Chiapas, Mexico. A new generation of Indigenous Tseltal, Tsotsil, Tojolabal, and Ch'ol Zapatista women, born after the 1994 EZLN uprising against the Mexican state, organized an international *encuentro* (meeting) that highlighted particular ways of naming femininized political actions and thus the conditions of violence and oppression against which they struggle. Their words set the tone for a collective political agenda that positioned gendered violence within a dense web of structural racialized violences, whose current manifestations are intimately linked to narco-state interests, specifically in the ways that organized crime, in complex association with government officials, fuels acts of extreme violence in the country.

I begin this chapter with a detailed description of the 2018 *encuentro* and the speeches of Zapatista women such as Maribel, from the Indigenous Ch'ol *caracol* Roberto Barrios. The women denounced gendered violence—that which inflicts physical acts of pain, humiliation, and degradation onto a gendered body—as closely linked to acts of dehumanization, territorial dispossession, and the destruction of ways of being/acting in the world. Current states of violence, Zapatista women suggest, are enmeshed within this colonial matrix; decolonizing struggles thus necessarily seek to transform the conditions that make gendered violence permissible.

The testimonies of women such as Maribel inspired me to ask the following questions: In what ways do their analysis of gendered violence align with the political formation of a new generation of Zapatista women, and to what extent do their words echo with other Indigenous women struggling in different regions, including those living outside the confines of the Mexican nation-state? How does this understanding of colonial gendered violence collapse dominant narratives in Mexico and push forth certain conversations within feminist debates? And what political alliances—both among groups of women and with men in their communities—are enabled by such understandings? These questions guide the context of this chapter, and they have a starting point in the political analysis elaborated by Maribel during the gathering.

The event, known as the Primer Encuentro Internacional, político, artístico, deportivo y cultural de mujeres que luchan (First International Political, Artistic, Sport, and Cultural Meeting of Women Who Struggle), grouped together more than seven thousand Indigenous, Afro-descendant, and mestiza women from Latin America and the United States as well as women from other regions of the globe. For four days we met on a grassy hillside dotted with more than a dozen wood-planked buildings overlooking one of the valleys that stretches into the Lacandon Jungle. From March 7 to March 10, participants organized workshops on diverse themes such as struggles over body/territory, personal defense trainings, the affirmation and dignification of women's bodies, collective reflections on struggles against forced disappearances and against social environmental destruction, and child-rearing based on alternative constructions of gender, all of which took place alongside poetry readings, documentary film screenings, and performances of music, dance, and theater. The diversity of events registered and communicated knowledges through the body, on affective sensory planes, and across social memories.

This was hardly the first Women's Day event to be held in Zapatista territory; regional celebrations have been held annually since soon after the uprising, usually with the discrete participation of male counterparts. The *encuentro* of 2018 was distinct, however, because all men over the age of twelve remained on the outside boundaries of the barbed wire, their roles displaced to the margins and focused on that silent yet fundamental logistical work required to carry forth any endeavor of this magnitude (those behind-the-scenes tasks such as cooking and cleaning that are typically relegated to women). Throughout the days of the *encuentro*, men, many of whom hold important *cargos* (political responsibilities) within the autonomous governing bodies of the *caracol*, took on the mundane tasks of sifting through kilos of dried beans in search of small pebbles before washing this basic staple and cooking it in large aluminum containers over fire pits; carefully cutting strips of stickers in the form of name tags for the suitcases or backpacks of those present; and running hundreds of errands between the *caracol* and Altamirano, the nearest town with required supplies, alongside all other logistical support requested by the women. Similarly, in the weeks prior to the event, men prepared much of the necessary infrastructure, including painting signs, installing a water system for showers, digging holes for latrines, and transporting women from the different regions to the *caracol*.

The men's largely invisible labor sustained the more public work and coordination of the event carried out by Zapatista women from the five *caracoles*. Women held public roles: managing the electricity, fixing the sound system, announcing where and when specific events were to be held, and taking the stage during theater productions, musical performances, and speeches, including the rendering of testimonies. The affirmation of women's capacity to handle all the public and visible aspects of the *encuentro* sent a powerful, multipronged message to multiple audiences. To their male counterparts, who were essentially invited to experience this inversion of gender roles, the event announced that *andar parejo* (walking equally) sometimes means walking behind so as to transform unequal footings. To those women in attendance who occupy racialized positions of privilege and are thus accustomed to being agents of change, the gathering announced that Zapatista Indigenous women generated the conditions to visibly make and move history. And to those who have historically been subordinated, as is the case of other Indigenous women from the region, their actions conveyed an example and vision of collective dignity.

In order to set the stage for the dialogues that would follow, the first day of the *encuentro* was dedicated exclusively to speeches from dozens of Zapatista women representatives from the five different Zapatista *caracoles*. It was there that Maribel, from the *caracol* Roberto Barrios, located in the northern region of Chiapas, on the border with the state of Tabasco, began her intervention, recognizing the escalation of cases of femicide and other extreme forms of sexual violence throughout the country. She recalled that only a decade before, the murder of women appeared to be concentrated in the northern border town of Juárez. Now, though, this national emergency of ever-increasing femicides threatens women in other cities and states, especially in the State of Mexico, Guerrero, and Veracruz. Maribel explained that femicide is yet another form of violent death, an extreme expression of violence occurring alongside those slower, less visible deaths brought on by "hunger and misery." To stress this point and draw connections to the lived experiences of women from the valleys of the Lacandon Jungle, Maribel associated the current moment of violence with those social memories marked by indentured servitude on the *fincas* (agricultural estates), whose property owners were almost always ladinos, or non-Indigenous people of European descent. These landed estates and the status of Indigenous peoples as peons extended well into the 1970s in Chiapas. On these *fincas*, Maribel recalled not only the hunger and rampant illness, but also the multiple forms of sexual violence inflicted on Indigenous women, including "abuses suffered at the hands of the *capataz* [overseer]." The "prettier" young girls, she noted, were raped by the *patrón* (estate owner), "regardless of whether they were married or single." She continued:

> Now, these times are repeating themselves, we are enduring conditions such as what our grandparents endured on the *fincas*, only now these take on other forms, such as kidnappings, disappearances, femicides, a never-ending list of injustices. . . . And what are we going to do with all of these problems, are we only going to go complain to the *capataz* government, so they come back to us only to respond [with statistics] of how many women have been murdered? Who is going to solve this problem? If before we weren't afraid of the seventy thousand soldiers in our [Zapatista Indigenous] territory [during the counterinsurgency operations of the 1990s], we aren't going to be afraid now.

As someone who has participated in activities in Zapatista autonomous municipalities since 1996, I was struck by how Maribel and her counterparts were inviting all present to situate the violence fueled by current narco-state territorial disputes within broader (neo)colonial conditions. Her intervention, though a fundamental aspect of more extended dialogues between Indigenous and Afro-descendant women, had been virtually absent from dominant public spheres and debates in Mexico. For a majority of feminist

organizations—with the marked exception of collectives such as the Coordinadora Nacional de Mujeres Indígenas (CONAMI, National Coordination of
Indigenous Women) and certain Casas de la Mujer Indígena (CAMI, Indigenous Women's Centers)—cases of femicide are seen as part of life in a patriarchal state.[1] Little consideration is given to how sexism intermeshes with
other forms of racialized domination and exploitation. For many male-led
Indigenous organizations, colonial forces are expressed primarily through
territorial dispossession, environmental destruction, and state-sponsored
repression of community leadership (Durán Matute and Moreno 2018).
And finally, human rights organizations defending victims have tended to
demarcate cases into spheres, dividing matters of grave human rights violations such as murders and femicides from efforts to undermine Indigenous
collective rights and claims to autonomy and self-determination. In contrast, Maribel establishes a continuum between colonial forms of gendered
violence—rape of Indigenous indentured women by the estate owner or
capataz—and contemporary acts such as femicide that have been partially
spurred by the proliferation of physical violence across the country since the
federal government began its so-called war on organized crime in 2006.[2]

As I listened to Maribel and watched the reactions of those around me, I
could not help but situate the *encuentro* within the global era of #MeToo, in
which high-profile Hollywood cases have appeared alongside massive social
media denouncements of quotidian acts of sexual harassment and violence
suffered by regular people. This movement has brought attention to the
physical and physiological violence experienced by the thousands of individual women who have had the courage to stand up and speak out. While
the extensive public debate generated by #MeToo has undoubtedly left an

---

1. CONAMI was founded in 1997 to articulate political actions by Indigenous women in
Mexico. In 2013 it began a project titled "Community Gender Emergency," which involved
analyzing cases of violence against Indigenous women from their own cultural perspective. As
part of its analysis, CONAMI insists that "to understand the current context of violence that
we are living [in], it is necessary to recognize the history of discrimination and colonization
that we have been subjected to as women and Indigenous peoples, that is why it is essential
to construct from within our collective memory." See Jurado Mendoza, Don Juan Pérez, and
CONAMI (2019).

2. The Mexican state's use of military actions to curtail narco-economies became a priority
under the Calderón administration (2006–12) and continued as such under the Peña Nieto
administration (2012–18). This conflict between the state and organized crime has resulted in
more than three hundred thousand murders and forty-five thousand forced disappearances.

important mark, including struggles against the backlash that women survivors face for speaking out, its emphasis has largely been on sexual violence in the workplace, the academy, and urban centers. This focus risks obscuring other realms and dimensions of sexual violence.

Maribel's speech, in contrast, connected gendered violence to those acts that impede the survival of a collective body, its relationship to territory, its distinct ways of being, and its understanding of the world. Her presentation invited *encuentro* participants to simultaneously listen (very carefully) to the actions of Indigenous women—including Tseltal, Tojolabal, Tsotsil, and Ch'ol women, as well as others who had gathered for the *encuentro*—and question epistemological assumptions that may (unwittingly) prioritize certain definitions of gendered violence, hence silencing other understandings and alternative constructions of justice.

Engagements, Positioning, and Un- and Relearning

This task of questioning dominant epistemologies has consumed much of my political energy over the course of two decades. I often state that my theoretical political education took place not so much during my formal academic training as during the years that I participated in solidarity work within Zapatista communities, primarily in the *caracol* where the *encuentro* was held, with the women whose daughters would organize that 2018 meeting. During the latter half of the 1990s and into the 2000s, as I engaged in workshops and popular education training to promote women's participation in Zapatista communities, I was forced to unravel and question many of the epistemological premises through which I had been taught to understand the world (including my place in it).

What initially pulled me toward the Lacandon Jungle was the poetics of Zapatismo, which grounds the political in the body and the earth, and which invites a diverse, disjointed "we" to (re)imagine a collective political horizon (rather than a prescribed path to social transformation). Even though I was too young to have participated in Marxist social movements, I grew up in their aftermath and, despite recognizing the relevance of their legacy, I felt repelled by the weight of masculinized vanguard leadership. In contrast, I was intuitively drawn to a calling that emerged from a knowledge base that marginalized both a male and a Eurocentric perspective, and that I came (very slowly) to understand, along with its profound contradictions.

The daily, often apparently insignificant, practices of women's agricultural collectives in communities forming part of Zapatista Indigenous municipalities played a critical role in this processual (un)learning.[3] When I arrived in Chiapas in 1996, I began participating in K'inal Antzetik, a women's NGO whose feminist activities centered on supporting the Tsotsil and Tseltal artisan cooperative Jolom Mayaetik, yet whose work expanded to include accompanying roles with community collectives and educational initiatives in Zapatista regions. During the 1980s, the liberation theology–inspired Catholic Church (under Bishop Samuel Ruiz), the first NGOs in the state, and the Instituto Nacional Indigenista (INI, National Indigenous Institute) all promoted women's production collectives, where groups of Indigenous women engaged in activities such as cultivating vegetable gardens, raising chickens or rabbits, or making bread, in familial community spaces. Such tasks necessarily required certain levels of collective decision-making, the administration of funds, and some basic skills in areas such as mathematics and accounting. Within fairly liberal progressive spheres, these activities were labeled as Indigenous and peasant women's "empowerment," yet, as is most often the case, those who participated in such projects redirect the activities toward what was most meaningful to them, regardless of the project's "official" objectives. Though K'inal Antzetik was initially hesitant to support our work with the collectives, arguing precisely that these had been initiatives long promoted by reformist institutions, the NGO ultimately agreed that the endeavor was worth the effort because of the way that community women grafted their own meanings and goals onto the projects.

Between 1996 and 2000, I organized popular education workshops with friend and social activist Hilary Klein in Tseltal and Tojolabal communities. The women with whom we worked stated time and again that their political formation—what they described as "learning to open our eyes," to "raise our heads when we are asked to speak," and to "not feel shame to participate"— was anchored in activities involving harvesting vegetables, kneading bread,

---

3. Zapatista territory is divided into municipalities that group together anywhere from fifteen to thirty-five communities with Zapatista civilian support bases. These municipalities are then grouped together into five *caracoles* (regions) that are in turn governed by the Zapatista Juntas de Buen Gobierno (Good Government Councils) and political-administrative commissions, responsible for implementing autonomous education, health, agricultural, and justice systems, among others. These autonomous municipalities geographically overlap with official municipalities, thus creating a highly disputed terrain. See Mora (2017).

or planting corn in the collective cornfield. Their mundane tasks were often accompanied by exchanges and collective reflections on their own life experiences and those of generations past who had lived in the valleys of the Lacandon Jungle.

Women's leadership in Zapatista autonomous municipalities oftentimes begins with the acceptance of a *cargo* within one of these collectives, a leadership role that requires organizing the rest of the women, facilitating collective decision-making (such as how to use the collective funds raised through the sale of their products), and negotiating certain needs with the men in their community. From these experiences, a woman might choose to move into other community responsibilities by learning midwifery or working as a health promoter in the community clinic, by training to be a primary school teacher, or by accepting a *cargo* within her autonomous municipality's political-administrative commissions (education, agriculture, health, and justice) or a place on the municipality's autonomous governing body.

In my book *Kuxlejal Politics: Indigenous Autonomy, Race, and Decolonizing Research in Zapatista Communities* (2017), I describe how my years of solidarity work with these women's collectives profoundly influenced how I came to understand the political as part of the daily construction of autonomy within Zapatista territory. Rather than resting my gaze on those cultural political practices typically considered to be the backbone of Zapatismo, such as decision-making in the assemblies through *mandar obedeciendo* (governing by obeying), I focus on women's production collectives. From them emerges a fundamental theorization of the political that then filters into, and grants meaning to, other practices within autonomous communities. In the women's collectives, the political is inseparable from tasks of social reproduction: from physically toiling in the soil and harvesting that which will nourish others, to supporting one another through collective self-reflection on their lives as Tseltal and Tojolabal women in relation to the rest of their communities, to *kaxlanes* (non-Indigenous people or those external to the communities), and to the state. In the book, I refer to *kuxlejal* politics—*kuxlejal* meaning collective-life existence in Tseltal—as those practices emerging on the margins of the state that sustain a social life as part of being/making territory. The political is inseparable from the act of living for a people who for centuries have survived both direct and indirect state-sponsored genocide.

Just as my previous accompaniment role in women's production collectives has shaped my gaze, and hence determined what I could and could not see as part of the daily practices of autonomy, so too has the active, oftentimes critical, participation of community members in the research process itself. As I describe elsewhere (Mora 2011, 2017), both men and women community members collaborated in my fieldwork by transforming the methods I had originally proposed, discussing the transcribed interviews, and even directly interpolating my interpretations, questioning my analysis, or providing alternative understandings. In *Kuxlejal Politics*, I describe at length the ways that Zapatista community members subjected my research to the same practices of autonomy that they undertook in their lives, hence forcing me to situate research itself as an object of analysis. The book locates the subtle yet profound ways that community members questioned the colonial logics of anthropological knowledge production and redirected the research process so as to incorporate that which made political sense to them. The responses to my questions on the history of the region and on the daily practices of autonomy not only directly informed my research topic—the interaction of Zapatista autonomy with the Mexican neoliberal state—but also critically reflected much broader political ideas that came from decades of collective praxis. Without the active participation of community members in the research process, I would have probably not seen how both men and women point to the Mexican state's continued reproduction of racialized colonial conditions, or how femininized notions of the political point to antiracist decolonial horizons.

For that reason, the task of writing *Kuxlejal Politics* was a profoundly humbling experience, one that moved me countercurrent to the inertia of academic arrogance that piles in layers alongside those pages of publications, whose material unfolding seems to uncritically suggest that one has something to say, and that a doctoral degree and publication record legitimate one's ability to speak as an "expert." Certainly, the years I had participated in political work in Chiapas and my activist training as an anthropologist could be read through such a "legitimating" register. Yet I have learned that affirming that I have something to say as a light-skinned Mexican mestiza women researcher involved in social struggle results in a double bind: it pushes me up against the silencing force of male-centered, Eurocentric academic authority, where I will never be a "legitimate" voice; but it also leads me to question whom I silence, or what epistemological forms of naming/ acting I am occluding by speaking. This work requires a delicate maneuvering: a commitment to listen and sit still, only to then listen again by shifting positions and leaning forward in a different sort of way. It presents an ongoing challenge in the forging of political alliances across racialized gendered differences. In terms of the concrete task of writing, such constant shifting of what could be considered a fairly stable knowledge base—I had after all spent two decades listening to particular stories and conversations—meant that at the end of the writing process I finally came to understand elements I had not perceived before. Let me elaborate.

Hearing Embodied Histories

The time of the *fincas*, the time of the estates, the period between the end of the nineteenth century and, roughly, the 1970s, a period that in Ch'ol is referred to as the time of the *mosojantel*, and in Tojolabal as the *baldío*, the historical period labeled by elders as a time of "pure suffering," of enslaved conditions, was a time when male life energy was extracted through the deliberate exploitation of that which their muscles, tendons, and bones could endure, and women were subjected not only to similar bio-extraction but also to the sexual violence of the *patrón*, who controlled living conditions and could access women's bodies. During the years I spent in Morelia, the testimonies of the times of the *fincas*—oftentimes conveyed in the collective sense, *we lived* rather than *I lived*—consistently acted as a counterpoint to autonomy. The *fincas* were the negative reference point through which to explain current forms of struggle.

Narratives of the times of the estates were and continue to be consistently conveyed. Recognizing their relevance, I would diligently and respectfully listen to those memories during fieldwork, as I (mistakenly) understood them to be part of a narration of the past.

Yet the memories of the estates are profoundly registered on the body. During collective intergenerational interviews with Tseltal and Tojolabal women, those lived experiences of pain and humiliation, of being treated as if they were "nothing and nobody," were often conveyed through (not interrupted by) tears as the body remembered and decided to speak for itself. Tseltal intelectual Juan López Intzin (2014) refers to this profound intergenerational pain as *p'ajel-uts'inel*, a historical continuum of grievances that attack in multiple ways the "grandeur and dignity" of humanity along-side nature, what in Tseltal would be comparable to the concept of racism. Such collective pain was invariably followed by anger, especially for younger generations, who expressed a commitment to heal deep social wounds through the struggle in autonomy. The pattern of listening and relistening to the testimonies of life on the *fincas*, of recognizing the weight of *p'ajel-uts'inel* at an emotional, intersubjective, intergenerational level, resulted in my understanding those narratives not as references to the past, but as a way of speaking of the present, of naming racialized and gendered forms of exploitation and oppression within the current Mexican state formation. Such social memories register on the body as that which continues to be painful, to bleed through and across bodies and generations. Justice, in this sense, is granted meaning through the ways that actions of social transformation respond to colonial wounds.

During the women's *encuentro* in 2018, Capitana Erika, a member of the political-military structure of the EZLN, referred in her opening address to the gendered racialized configuration displayed through the *finca*, as a colonial enterprise. She first spoke of her own personal trajectory: prior to joining the ranks of the EZLN, she had as the only economic option to work as a domestic servant, from which she learned that "mistreatment comes not only from men, but from other women as well." She then went on to refer to the figure of the *patrón-marido*, the estate owner/boss/husband.

In Zapatista Tseltal communities, such as Morelia, where the *encuentro* was held, the *patrón* is also referred to as the *patrón-gobierno*, the estate owner-government, a term that in Tseltal is described as the *ajvalil*, a figure of power that can be both the estate owner and a government official, or a fused combination. In the region of the Lacandon Jungle, estate owners often vied for political office and became the face of local government (many of those same families continue to hold political office today at the municipal, district, and state level). At the same time, Indigenous communities experience the state as a *patrón* who governs through the constant infantilization of the local population and makes decisions for those deemed too ignorant to make demands or participate in decision-making for themselves.

In her speech, Capitana Erika added a further dimension to the figure by fusing the *ajvalil* to that of the husband. In doing so, she evoked colonial gender constructions that hinge on the continual inferiorization not only of Indigenous women but also of Indigenous men, whose devalued sense of masculinity in relation to mestizo or ladino men further downplays (oftentimes violently so) their female counterparts. Hence, the reconfiguration of colonial violence is also internalized within communities as part of its reproduction. Capitana Erika's continual use of the *patrón-marido* throughout her speech was a powerful reminder in a women's *encuentro* that directing all energies against male counterparts fails to unhinge underlying colonial violences; addressing gendered violences necessarily requires undermining current manifestations of such racialized logics centered on territorial dispossession.

A "War Against Life": Embodied Colonial Histories in National Pan-Indigenous Autonomous Spaces

The *encuentro* took place a few months prior to the July 1, 2018, presidential elections in Mexico. It was designed to leave a social imprint that collectively names and thus mobilizes against manifestations of gendered oppression and exploitation at a specific historical juncture. Similarly, the event was situated within broader political mobilizations by Indigenous organizations and communities grouped under the Congreso Nacional Indígena (CNI, National Indigenous Congress) and its Concejo Indígena de Gobierno (CIG, Indigenous Government Council).[4] After listening to Maribel and Capitana Erika, specifically their insistence on locating the continuation of colonial forms of violence in their current struggles for justice as Indigenous women, I was interested to see whether a similar emphasis was visible in the public interventions of women CIG members.

As we shall see, within the historical particularities of the struggles of their pueblos, these public figures reiterated in diverse ways that colonial conditions are not a thing of the past, bracketed historically in the colonial era and distanced from a postcolonial present. Rather, colonial conditions continue to actively shape their lives and struggle today, specifically through the continual occupation of their territories and related attempts at dispossession, alongside those actions that mine their ways of being/existing in the world. Surprisingly, such a specific act of naming has found insufficient echoes among non-Indigenous allies, including within broader feminist cir-

---

4. The CNI was founded during the peace dialogues between the EZLN and the Mexican government in 1996 as a network of Indigenous communities and organizations sympathetic to the rebel army's demands, particularly for Indigenous collective rights of autonomy and self-determination so that they might "reconstitute their peoples in an integral manner in light of the permanent process of conquest that has destroyed, mutilated, fragmented, and exterminated them" (CNI n.d.). After an extended period of silence nationally, the CNI resurfaced in 2017 when its members met to decide how to shift the terms of discussion during the 2018 presidential elections and disrupt the virtual omnipresence of political parties as that which sets the terms of the political terrain.

cles, and for that reason we must pause on their words if we are to forge the diverse forms of collective action proposed by the women's *encuentro*.

The CIG, created in 2017, is an alternative governing body made up of one male and one female council member from each of the ninety Indigenous regions whose communities or organizations participate in the CNI. Each pair, elected according to the political cultural practices of their community or organizational assemblies, commits to actively participating in national and regional discussions as well as bringing those discussions back to their collective to be debated. They similarly agree to engage politically according to the ethical-political principles established by the CNI: serve and do not be served; construct and do not destroy; obey and do not order; propose and do not impose; convince and do not defeat; go below and not above; represent and do not replace.

During an assembly held on May 29, 2017, the CNI named María Patricia de Jésus (commonly known as Marichuy), to be spokesperson for the CIG and a potential independent presidential candidate. At the time, the EZLN/CNI attempted to shift national and regional electoral debates by mobilizing signatures for Marichuy. During a period of eight months, members of the CIG traveled to hundreds of cities, towns, and villages throughout the country, to the locations where Marichuy was invited by collectives and organizations. In these grassroots events, they would both present the CIG as an alternative governing body for Indigenous and mestizo people (and I will add Afro-Mexican) and listen to what was specifically affecting the lives of those present. At the end of each meeting, CIG members would then invite participants to support Marichuy as an independent presidential candidate by adding their signature to a petition. The official guidelines set by the Instituto Nacional Electoral (INE, National Electoral Institute) require signatures from 1 percent of registered voters in each of seventeen states, amounting to almost nine hundred thousand signatures for an independent presidential candidate to be officially included on the ballot. This collective effort resulted in almost three hundred thousand signatures being presented to the INE, an insufficient number for Marichuy to be included on the July 1 ballot, yet an impressive demonstration of support for alternative forms of political participation and government.[5]

5. The CIG and CNI successfully mobilized legal defense efforts so that Indigenous forms of political participation, based on consensus decision-making, would be recognized. This allowed the sum of individuals in an assembly decision to be included alongside individual signatures.

The question of whether this mass mobilization was truly intended to shape the electoral field or, conversely, merely intended to place certain topics front and center in community discussions was highly debated during those months. This latter position is what women members of the CIG generally argue, as is evidenced in video interviews gathered for *Flores en el desierto* (Flowers in the desert), a beautiful and carefully designed testimonial project headed by journalist Gloria Muñoz Ramírez (2018). CIG member Guadalupe Vázquez Luna (2018), Tsotsil from the highland town of Acteal in Chiapas, insisted that the objective was not to win the presidency, which only represents "death and destruction," but rather to redirect public attention toward all the injustices that have piled up, "all the conflicts, the deaths, the disappearances . . . that is why we have to defend our lands, our lives, our rights." According to Lupe, as she is commonly called, the CIG wanted to fracture the implicit consensus that frames public issues during national moments such as presidential campaigns so as to vehemently insist on tackling the underlying causes of violence in the country.

In a parallel video interview, CIG representative Rocío Moreno (2018), from the Coca Indigenous community of the island of Mezcala, on the lake Chapala, which borders the states of Jalisco and Michoacán, explicitly named these current conditions a "war against life." This war, Rocío explained, has historical origins in the numerous attempts to erase the presence of Indigenous (and Afro-Mexican) peoples: "the only way to struggle is to organize, so they don't disappear us." This attempted erasure—what Patrick Wolfe (2006, 387) refers to as the "settler-colonial logic of elimination"—has diffused and spread from Indigenous bodies to non-Indigenous bodies through the forced disappearances of the narco-state.[6] Rocío associates attempts to "disappear us" both with historical mechanisms that gravitate between silencing and physically removing Indigenous communities and with a current widespread mechanism of producing the physical absence of Indigenous,

---

Similarly, despite the fact that the INE required signatures to be registered on a digital platform, the CNI legal defense team successfully argued that such measures discriminated against populations with little to no internet connection. According to the CNI, more than 10,500 signatures were captured on paper rather than on the digital platform (CNI 2018).

6. Wolfe (2016, 387) describes this "settler-colonial logic of elimination" as taking place both through physical violence and through apparently more benign (i.e., "positive") forms such as assimilation policies. The combined effects of such elimination principles push Indigenous peoples toward genocide, though settler colonialism is not reducible to genocide.

Afro-Mexican, and Mestizo individuals through narco-state terror. CIG members consciously link current expressions of extreme violence to the extended bleeding of colonial violence across multiple sectors of the social body. These connections are central to the collective mobilizing efforts, and they represent a profound analysis of current expressions of violence. Before turning to this analysis, however, I would like to briefly describe who the women CIG members are and how they draw on specific life experiences to frame the contemporary moment as a "war against life."

When I listened to the life testimonies of these women, I noticed that many participate in their communities and organizations through roles centered on social reproduction and pedagogy activities—that is, they help sustain the material and spiritual conditions for their people's continued existence in relation to their territories, and they facilitate the production of collective knowledge. Some CIG women members are traditional doctors or midwives or come from matrilineal lineages of traditional healers; others participate in their communities by growing food staples and medicinal plants; and still other women members are educators. Marichuy herself is a traditional *curandera* (herbalist doctor), a profession that allows her to identify misbalances that express themselves through pain and then suggest possible remedies to nourish the body and help it heal.

CIG member Gabriela Molina Moreno (2018), Comca'ac from the state of Sonora, studied in a culinary school in the state capital of Hermosillo, where she researched the traditional ingredients found in the dishes of her people, those that strengthen the body rather than cause harm. She recognizes such knowledges as central to combating diabetes and other illnesses that have become epidemic in the territory of her peoples. Osbelia, Nahua from the town of Tepoztlán, Morelos—who, at eighty years old, is one of the oldest CIG members—studied at a normal school (teacher's college) during the 1950s and 1960s, at a time when schooling for Indigenous women was a rarity. She earned her degree in the city of Cuernavaca, with a thesis focusing on health issues in her community. Myrna Dolores Valencia Banda, Yoreme (Mayo) from the state of Sonora, is a secondary school teacher in her village; and Lucero Alicia, Kumiai from the state of Baja California Sur, followed in the footsteps of her mother and other women clan members, who are not only teachers but also healers and spiritual guides.

During her interview for *Flores en el desierto*, Myrna Dolores Valencia Banda (2018) suggested that such chosen professions inform the ways that women CIG members engage in leadership roles, given that they view their responsibilities as part of daily life. She described being an authority figure as "being a guardian of life, [whose role is] to preserve life and defend people as a collective." Through such statements, women like Myrna suggest that decolonial gendered justice centers on creating the conditions that advance the well-being of a collective. Struggles must be directed at (re)establishing socio-environmental balances, beginning with political actions that Melissa Forbis (2006) once described as politics through "a handful of herbs." Similarly, the pedagogical process of collective learning is critical to social transformation and intergenerational development of leadership (Romero-Hernández et al. 2014).

Women CIG Members' Views on the "War Against Life"

If such horizons of justice inform the political actions of women CIG members, how do these women name the makeup of this "war against life" that seeks to erase them? In the video interviews for *Flores en el desierto*, women members of the CIG speak of their own lives as part of their communities and organizations. They refer to the continual occupation of their territories through diverse means, pointing to the private business interests, oftentimes in alliance with non-Indigenous local elites, as well as state-sponsored extractivist economies, infrastructure development projects, tourism, and narco-economies that continue to settle on their lands. They condemn the numerous effects of such multidimensional occupations: labor exploitation, forced displacement, assassinations, political repression, and the constant and systematic acts against their peoples, treated like foreigners on their own land. The combined effects severely debilitate a collective tenacity to survive as a people, facilitating an existence of slow deaths punctuated by extreme acts of violence.

Rocío Moreno (2018) refers to the encroachments on the lands of the Coca peoples as historical cycles of invasions that include both direct actions by non-Indigenous private interests and juridical underpinning, including legal frameworks that negate Mezcala as an Indigenous community. Lake Chapala is a popular tourist center and weekend leisure site a few hours from the city of Guadalajara, with Mezcala being the last community to remain in the area. In recent years, businessmen, developers and local elites have attempted to occupy their lands, not only through the illegal invasion of communal spaces, but also through private infrastructure projects that further deplete community resources, including building a small dam to collect water for private use. Rocío states that the community assembly determined the dam to constitute an additional "invasion," yet the state response has been to criminalize those who defend their territory. The state's actions have included "issuing arrest warrants against eleven members of their community" and supporting repressive measures, such as that of a "businessman who formed an all-women's paramilitary group, Las Águilas de El Pandillo. He armed women that wanted to [violently] confront us."

At the same time, these forms of land encroachment occur on a terrain shaped by everyday encounters that consistently point to Coca peoples as inferior to their non-Indigenous neighbors, and thus as out of place on their own lands. Rocío explained that when she taught classes at a nearby university, students complained that an "Indian" was their professor. Similarly, she describes the first time she recognized herself as Indigenous in the sense that such an identity marks a constructed and internalized sense of inferiorization. She was only seven years old when she traveled to the municipal center of Poncitlán, Jalisco, where—as is common among members of the popular class—she grabbed a seat at a food stall to order a taco, only to receive a sharp scolding by her uncle, who didn't want her to be mistreated for being an "Indian." She recalls that "there was no law, nothing, but it was already instilled inside our heads, we had appropriated in ourselves the idea that this was not our place, we didn't belong." Such everyday actions, Rocío highlights, brand her body as not belonging in her own home.

For her part, Bettina Lucila Cruz Velazquéz (2018), Zapotec from the Isthmus of Tehuantepec, and leader of the Asamblea de Pueblos Indígenas del Istmo de Tehuantepec en Defensa de la Tierra y el Territorio (Assembly of Indigenous Peoples of the Tehuantepec Isthmus in Defense of Land and Territory), refers to the "new presence of colonizers" that occurred in the first decade of the 2000s when Spanish transnational investments established wind-powered generators on Zapotec territory in conjunction with Mexican state incentives (Planeta Latino Radio 2018). Bettina explains that the Mexican state imposed this energy project for the public good and "national" interest; not only did this understanding of the "nation" exclude Indigenous peoples, but those affected communities were denied their right to be consulted. The turbines not only alter the landscape, thus affecting agricultural activities, but also destroy local flora and fauna and contaminate the water and soil. She argues that they form part of a long list of extractivist development projects in her territory, including gold, iron, silver, and salt mines.

Myrna Dolores Valencia Banda (2018), Yoreme from the state of Sonora, refers to the destruction of the Mayo River in her people's territory due to agro-industrial exploitation that has turned the "water that is life, into what is now death," contaminating both the river and the underground water sources. Myrna links this project of "death" by private interests to a spiraling narco-economy that destroys her community's young people by turning them into consumers. The image she paints is tragic: young men and women meander through the streets, while others sit on benches in heavily intoxicated states. The combined effects of both extractivist and narco-economies are also described by Gabriela Molina Moreno (2018), who explains that in recent years her peoples have been threatened by mining companies and organized crime. At the same time, the presence of narco-traffickers has justified the quasi-permanent presence of marines on the island of Tiburon. "Instead of taking care of our territory," she says, "[these marines] defend organized crime."

It is with these embodied knowledges that women CIG members listened to what collectives, organizations, and communities throughout the country conveyed during their visits as they traveled alongside Marichuy. The collective analysis emerging from hundreds of exchanges led to them naming conditions in Mexico and beyond as a "war against life." In the town of Totonacapan, Veracruz, Marichuy provided such a description by linking territorial destruction and dispossession to narco-economies, a resulting terrain that renders permissible acts of extreme violence such as femicides, assassinations, and forced disappearances. Though she speaks specifically of communities in Veracruz, she refers to a concern of Indigenous peoples across the country: social geographies where the state and transnational companies destroy the land and the peoples.

> They don't care if they contaminate the water that runs under the earth and that is the life source for our communities. They sow death with their "intelligence," with the liberation of gas, and with their toxic spills. They strip and destroy the earth by sowing death, destruction, exploitation, contempt. and repression against us. . . . What they do here, in Totonac territory, they want to do in Nahua territory, in Tepehua, Popoluca, and Tikmay territory [etc.]. They sow fear, they disappear our peoples, and the narco-violence appears

less and less different from what the mining companies do, what companies that extract hydrocarbons through fracking do, those that commercialize and traffic our immigrant brothers and sisters on these lands, those that kill women only for being women. . . . [They] discriminate [against] our peoples to justify to themselves the dispossession and the violence. . . . And now they are doing that in the entire country, regardless of whether we live in the cities or in the countryside; or whether we are peasants or journalists; or students or housewives; or whether we are white or brown. (CNI 2017c)

Though Marichuy refers above all to capitalist exploitation, thus creating the assumption among many of her supporters that class struggle is what continues to prevail, the testimonies described above render inextricable the logics of capital from colonialism and gendered racisms. Marichuy suggests that the forced occupation of Indigenous territories, those historical cycles of invasion that Rocío Moreno identifies, alongside the systematic devaluation of both human and nonhuman forms of life, are physical expressions of elimination that engender forms of territorial control and push those inhabitants to the brink of collective death. Such expressions of occupation are then repeated and further entrenched through acts of femicide, assassinations, and forced disappearances within a narco-state economy. In this sense, colonial violences continue into the current day; they establish the historical terrain on which an extractivist narco-state finds anchor. As other CIG members have suggested, through overt strategies of elimination founded on the bio-social erasure of Indigenous and Afro-descendant peoples, the state's project of turning life energy into waste has now expanded to other sectors of society, while at the same time continuing to concentrate its effects on Indigenous and Afro-Mexican regions of the country.

Extraction, Narco-Economies, and Gendered Violence

In several speeches during her tour, Marichuy explicitly associated struggles against land dispossession and environmental destruction (primarily propelled by extractivist and narco-economies) with struggles against gendered violence. She stated that by inflicting violence onto women's bodies, state-sanctioned forces attack the life projects and the potentiality of the biological life of entire peoples. In that sense, gendered violence is inextricably linked to environmental destruction and territorial occupation, what *comunitaria* (community) feminists refer to as the association between body and territory (Cabnal 2010; Paredes 2013). Surprisingly, Marichuy made this connection between *body as territory* and *territory as a socio-natural body* most explicitly not when speaking in an Indigenous rural town, but rather when speaking in an urban periphery of Mexico City, in the district of Netzahualcóyotl

Neza, as the municipality is commonly called, was most recently populated through the waves of primarily Indigenous and peasant migrants that came to the city starting in the late 1940s, on lands that form part of the ancient Lake Texcoco, home to the fifteenth-century Mexica-Chichimeca monarch, poet, and architect Netzahualcóyotl (hence the name). Those that arrived in search of employment opportunities settled on what were then the largely barren lands of Neza, and they built precariously constructed homes, only to later negotiate property titles or install water, electricity, and drainage systems. It is now site to some of the highest rates of violent crime, particularly cases of femicide, in Mexico. In recent years, those cases have skyrocketed; in 2018, the state of Mexico had the highest concentration of cases of femicide in the country—108 cases officially reported—with Netzahualcóyotl along with two other municipalities, at the top of the list (Salinas Cesáreo 2019).

While most events of Marichuy's tour focused almost exclusively on speeches from her and other CIG members, her November 27, 2017, visit to Neza was preceded by a series of group discussions among the participating organizations and collectives on those issues that most affect local residents: water and territory, dignified housing, education and culture, and women and femicides (Orepeza 2017). Marichuy's event began with a brief summary of what had been debated thus far. Women and men spoke of structural racism and everyday forms of discrimination suffered by their mainly Indigenous grandparents who first populated these lands; of the subsequent generations that were stigmatized for being from *nezahualodo* (Neza-mud, in reference to the lack of effective water and drainage systems, along with the absence of sufficient paved roads); and of the city's use of nearby lands for garbage dumps, whose noxious odors reflect broader processes of social decomposition, including the exacerbated levels of violence and insecurity, as well as the lack of dignified housing and public spaces.

Marichuy spoke of femicide as a violence that cuts across all other issues. She began her speech by establishing a direct relationship between the lives of women, the earth, and Indigenous communities, "As women we want ourselves alive, in the same way we want our mother earth alive, and our communities alive. We want to be free in the way we want our territories to be free, and our people in solidarity and with consciousness" (CNI 2017b). She went on to name forms of capitalist exploitation that extract collective life energy, hence depleting socio-environmental life. These process of bio-extraction are based not only on labor exploitation and the violent dispossession of natural resources, but also on the fragmentation of communities, with their ways of organizing and political decision-making. While she recognized that colonial capitalist forces concentrate violence in Indigenous (and, I would add, Afro-descendant) communities, such acts progressively expand to those who live in the cities, not only because historical migration patterns of Indigenous peoples tend toward urban centers, as is the history of regions like Neza, but also because violent acts tend to multiply and expand outward. She continued:

> To defend and organize ourselves as women . . . [is the] only way we will be able to break out of the trap that those in power have placed over us, that not only puts our lives as women at risk, but also the life of our mother earth, and thus the sum of all life. When they rape, disappear, jail, or murder a woman, it is as if all the community, the neighborhood, the pueblo, or the family has been raped. . . . They seek through such fears and grieving to colonize and pervert our collective heart, to own us and turn us into merchandise. (CNI 2017b)

While recognizing the pain caused by acts of violence directed at individual women, Marichuy draws from social memories of struggle against colonialism to highlight how acts that dominate women's bodies attack a collective (Smith 2005). Acts that seek to control the social and biological reproductive roles of women occur in conjunction with actions that attempt to dominate the earth as a life mother, along with her resources. Though such statements risk reinscribing essentializing narratives of women as equal to nature, and of Indigenous women as inextricably linked to the earth, Marichuy takes this association to a different plane by pointing to parallel processes of destruction: the rampantly accelerating destruction of the earth's forests, oceans, rivers, and valleys in recent decades is paralleled by the spiraling mutilation and torture of women's bodies, not only in Mexico, but in many regions of the globe. Marichuy continues:

Thus, to act against the lives of women, against their integrity, dignity, and rights, is to act against life itself, and for our pueblos this is profoundly destructive, given that the sacred collectivity that we imagine, that we exercise and for which we struggle, is that which we fundamentally defend as Indigenous women. When the blood is women's blood, we are all wounded, it is the wound of our mother and our daughters, our grandmothers, our mother earth. (CNI 2017b)

While Marichuy seems to refer to women in a universal sense, here she focuses on what is lived and felt specifically by Indigenous women. She considers Indigenous women's struggles to be anchored on defending the existence of a collectivity because life is sacred and sustained through connections to the spirits and other beings. For that reason, both Indigenous male leaders (who often prioritize territorial struggles above all else), and mestiza feminist leaders (who tend to focus exclusively on patriarchal violence as inflicted on individual women's bodies) fail to locate the inextricable link between women's bodies, the earth, and territory. When groups adopt colonial capital interests, they turn against themselves in a self-destructive modality that threatens humanity in its entirety, along with the natural environment of which we are part. Marichuy ends her speech by calling for the construction of alliances across and between collectives: between men and women, among Indigenous peoples, and between Indigenous and non-Indigenous people: "That is why our struggle is not only of women, or the victims and their families; it is a struggle that also calls to men, it is a struggle that corresponds to us as collectives, and as collectives of collectives, to dismantle power that is essentially *machista* [chauvinist] and patriarchal" (CNI 2017b).

The urgent challenge for feminist struggles thus becomes how to collectively counter the "war against life"—a continued expression of colonial conditions that differentially affect a plurality—all while decentering racialized, gendered hierarchies and contesting continued territorial dispossessions.

Final Reflections: Anticolonial Road Maps and Alliances Between Women

The day after the public event in Neza, women CIG members, including Marichuy, participated in a public presentation at the Universidad Nacional Autónoma de México (UNAM, National Autonomous University of Mexico). Two separate yet interrelated events marked the women's presence on campus. The first consisted of a physical walk through Ciudad Universitaria (CU, University City, the main UNAM campus) alongside Araceli Osorio Martinez, the mother of femicide victim Lesvy Berlin Rivera Osorio. In May 2017, Lesvy, an UNAM student, was found murdered on campus, the morning after she had been seen with her boyfriend and another man. Though the exact circumstances of her death were still under investigation in November 2017, when Marichuy visited, autopsy reports had determined that her death was caused by strangulation. On October 18, 2019, Jorge Luis González Hernández, Lesvy's boyfriend, was sentenced to forty-five years in prison for her femicide.

Marichuy and the other women CIG members walked through a section of CU, beginning in the location where Lesvy's body was found, close to the School of Engineering. They exchanged words in a small, makeshift wooden platform under the shadow of pine trees, the soil carpeted with petals, surrounded by pink crosses and handwritten signs, "Ni UNAMas" (Not one more in UNAM). Marichuy, visibly emotional, held Osorio's hand as she spoke to her of the woman's pain, a pain that Marichuy recognized as part of her own, a pain that she has similarly felt in visits throughout the country, a pain accompanied by "cries of desperation." These are wounds, she says, that hardly anyone wants to see, hear, much less feel. For that reason, Marichuy stresses, "It is up to us to work together to unmask what is happening." While a woman burned copal to cleanse the area and another blew through a conch shell, Marichuy continued to speak of a wound that will never completely heal, but that can be transformed into a source of strength from which to struggle.

Osorio and Marichuy then began to walk arm in arm, carrying bouquets of flowers, as other CIG members and women from different collectives walked a few steps behind. The photos taken that day capture gazes of solemnity among the tears, of profound determination nourished by the physical reclaiming of a geography marked by death. This first political, solidarity-building act merited its own temporality, one that stretched and extended further beyond the confines established in the event's poster announcement. Those several thousand of us patiently waiting to hear Marichuy continued to wait, until finally, close to sunset, the second event began. Marichuy spoke:

> As members of the National Indigenous Congress we have not stopped paying close attention to the rage and the pain that has been planted here, as is the case of the *compañera* Lesvy Berlin, murdered this very year in Ciudad Universitaria.... We demand truth and punishment to those responsible for her death.... And we tell you that we are and will be here because this pain, this

rage that we have as Indigenous peoples is also for being witness to our dead, our disappeared, our political prisoners detained, for defending what for us is life. We feel rage and pain because thousands of cases of femicide reside in impunity, for the systemic violence that day by day we endure as women in the cities and in rural areas, all of that makes us scream, Ya Basta! (CNI 2017a)

Her speech paused on Ya Basta!—Enough! No more!—a scream that marked the uprising of the EZLN on January 1, 1994. The rebel army understood that NAFTA, which went into effect that same day, meant death to Indigenous peoples, neoliberal policies being the latest expression of capital interests generating elimination. Marichuy repeated Ya Basta! in direct reference to cases of femicide, merely the most extreme of the diverse expressions of violence that confront women daily, regardless of whether they live in the city or in rural areas. By associating Ya Basta! with violence against women, Marichuy recognized the gendered configurations of neoliberalism, along with its free-trade agreements and capitalist interests. In doing so she unfolded new layers of Ya Basta! so as to affirm that justice begins with a determined refusal of gendered violence, a violence fed by the motor of colonial (neo)liberal forces.

Marichuy rests the cry of Ya Basta! on the profound pain released through such an exclamation. It is from that pain that she, as an Indigenous woman, stretches her hand in solidarity to Osorio, a mestiza mother of a femicide victim. In doing so, Marichuy inverts typical expressions of solidarity between women, where those in relative positions of privilege tend to play the role of supporting those whom they see in the eternal category of victim (Mohanty 1984). Here, a women whose community harbors memories of the intergenerational wounds of colonial violence, and who can recognize the pain of Rivera's mother, acts against the isolating impulses of grief to form a bridge and thus seek justice for the pain of others. By extending her hand to Osorio, Marichuy suggests that acts of solidarity across women from different positions can create a counterforce to the expansion of those violences that have historically been concentrated in Indigenous territories.

The refrains of this chapter—gendered violence as welded to ongoing colonial forces, and thus gender justice as responding to colonial wounds—set the foundation for an anticolonial road map of alliances between and among women to counteract a "war against life." Such alliances are fostered by a search for answers to certain open-ended questions: How do we listen to the pain of another, recognizing the particularities of that experience while at the same time drawing bridges between the shared grieving of so many thousands of deaths, of disappearances, and of ecological devastations? What political horizons surface when we center the bodily-territorial ways that violence against Indigenous women is interwoven with violence enacted onto the earth? And from these locations, what does a sense of collective justice look like?

Partial responses to these questions point to a delicate act of alliances that discreetly invite mestiza women to identify with Indigenous women as survivors of decades of genocide, hence weakening the colonialist impulses of dominant feminisms (Chirix García 2015). CIG members extended such an invitation in Neza to an audience of second- and third-generation migrants, whose mainly Indigenous peasant family members had arrived to the urban center in search of employment. Like Marichuy's embrace of Osorio, the event seemed to say, "you too are living the effects of colonial wounds," those very same wounds that—as decolonial thinkers such as Aimé Césaire (2000) emphasize—dehumanize all within the messy colonizer-colonialist matrix. Such profound dehumanization is even more evident now, when such massive bio-destruction affects the life capacities of diverse collectives, including mestizo populations who may not have seen themselves directly affected in decades past.

At the same time, such an invitation requires a collective commitment to critically reflect on how racialized gendered conditions of privilege continue to exist as certain lives are more profoundly devalued than others, despite the growing terrain of the "war against life." For that reason it is a fragile alliance, though also potentially powerful and certainly urgent, given the current state of affairs, when the entire world at last responds to the hushed question, "where does it hurt?" with an insistent, "everywhere" (Warsan Shire, qtd. in Gharib 2016).

References

Cabnal, Lorena. 2010. "Acercamiento a la construcción de la propuesta de pensamento epistémico de las mujeres indígenas feministas comunitárias de Abya Yala." In *Feminismos diversos: El feminismo comunitaria*, edited by ACSUR-Las Segovias, 10–25. Madrid: ACSUR-Las Segovias.

Césaire, Aimé. 2000. *Discourse on Colonialism*. New York: Monthly Review Press.

Chirix García, Emma Delfina. 2015. "¿Colonialismo en el feminismo blanco?" *Comunidad de estúdios maya* (blog). February 6, 2015. http://commaya2012.blogspot.com/2015/02/0-0-1-6-34-glafyra-1-1-39-14.html.

Congreso Nacional Indígena (CNI). 2017a. "Palabra de Marichuy en Ciudad Universitaria en la UNAM." November 29, 2017. https://www.congresonacionalindigena .org/2017/11/29/palabra-marichuy-ciudad-universitaria-la-unam/.

Congreso Nacional Indígena (CNI). 2017b. "Palabra de Marichuy en Neza. Sobre las Mujeres y los feminicidios." November 27, 2017. https://www.congresonacional indigena.org/2017/11/27/palabra-marichuy-neza-las-mujeres-los-feminicidios/.

Congreso Nacional Indígena (CNI). 2017c. "Palabra de vocera Marichuy en el Totonacapan." November 15, 2017. https://www.congresonacionalindigena.org/2017/11/15 /palabra-la-vocera-marichuy-totonacapan/.

Congreso Nacional Indígena (CNI). 2018. "Convocatoria al siguiente paso de la lucha." March 16, 2018. https://www.congresonacionalindigena.org/2018/03/16 /convocatoria-al-siguiente-paso-la-lucha/.

Congreso Nacional Indígena (CNI). n.d. "¿Qué es el CNI?" Accessed October 26, 2020. http://www.congresonacionalindigena.org/que-es-el-cni/.

Cruz Velazquéz, Bettina Lucila. 2018. "Bettina Lucila Cruz Velázquez, Concejala binnizá. Juchitán, Oaxaca." Uploaded January 16, 2018. Video interview, 8:35. *Flores en el desierto*, by Gloria Muñoz Ramírez. Desinformémonos. https://floresenel desierto.desinformemonos.org/videos/bettina.html.

Durán Matute, Inés, and Rocío Moreno, eds. 2018. *Voces del México de abajo: Reflexiones en torno a la propuesta del cig*. Guadalajara: CIESAS.

Forbis, Melissa. 2006. "Autonomy and a Handful of Herbs: Contesting Gender and Ethnic Identities Through Healing." In *Dissident Women: Gender and Cultural Politics in Chiapas*, edited by Shannon Speed, Rosalva Aída Hernández Castillo, and Lynn Stephen, 176–202. Austin: University of Texas Press.

Gharib, Malaka. 2016. "Beyonce's 'Lemonade' Turns a Somali-Brit Poet into a Global Star." *Goats and Soda* (blog), NPR. April 27, 2016. https://www.npr.org/sections /goatsandsoda/2016/04/27/475872852/.

Jurado Mendoza, Fabiola del, Norma Don Juan Pérez, and Coordinadora Nacional de Mujeres Indígenas (CONAMI). 2019. "Emergencia comunitaria de género. Respuesta de las mujeres indígenas a las múltiples violencias y el despojo del territorio." *Ichan Tecolotl*, February 2019. https://ichan.ciesas.edu.mx/puntos -de-encuentro/emergencia-comunitaria-de-genero-respuesta-de-las-mujeres -indigenas-a-las-multiples-violencias-y-el-despojo-del-territorio/.

López Intzin, Juan. 2014. "Racismo." *Juan López Intzin* (blog). October 27, 2014. http://juan-lopez-intzin.blogspot.com.

Mohanty, Chandra. 1984. "Under Western Eyes: Feminist Scholarship and Colonial Discourses." *Boundary 2* 12/13:333–58.

Molina Moreno, Gabriela. 2018. "Gabriela Molina Moreno, Concejala comca'ac. Comunidad Desemboque de los Seris, Sonora." Uploaded January 16, 2018. Video interview, 7:59. *Flores en el desierto*, by Gloria Muñoz Ramírez. Desinformémonos. https://floreseneldesierto.desinformemonos.org/videos/gabriela.html.

Mora, Mariana. 2011. "Producción de conocimientos en el terreno de la autonomía: La investigación como tema de debate político." In *Luchas "muy otras": Zapatismo y autonomía en las comunidades indígenas de Chiapas*, edited by Bruno Baronnet, Mariana Mora Bayo, and Richard Stahler-Sholk, 79–110. Mexico City: CIESAS.

Mora, Mariana. 2017. *Kuxlejal Politics, Indigenous Autonomy, Race and Decolonizing Research in Zapatista Communities*. Austin: University of Texas Press.

Moreno, Rocío. 2018. "Rocío Moreno, Consejala coca. Comunidad de Mezcala, Jalisco." Uploaded January 16, 2018. Video interview, 12:52. *Flores en el desierto*, by Gloria Muñoz Ramírez. Desinformémonos. https://floreseneldesierto.desinfor memonos.org/videos/rocio.html.

Muñoz Ramírez, Gloria. 2018. *Flores en el desierto: Mujeres del Concejo Indígena de Gobierno*. Desinformémonos. Accessed September 10, 2020. https://floresenel desierto.desinformemonos.org/.

Orepeza, Dalri. 2017. "Reciben a Marichuy y comparten las problemáticas en neza." *Desinformémonos, periodismo de abajo*, December 1, 2017. https://desinformemonos .org/reciben-marichuy-comparten-las-problematicas-neza/.

Paredes, Julieta. 2013. *Hilando fino desde el feminismo comunitário*. Mexico City: Cooperativa el rebozo.

Planeta Latino Radio. 2018. "Bettina Cruz en Madrid. Charla sobre las empresas eólicas en el Istmo de Oaxaca." Uploaded April 26, 2018, by Ellos y noostros. YouTube video, 1:53:28. https://m.youtube.com/watch?v=86dOmiOEkP0.

Romero-Hernández, Odilia, Centolia Maldonado Vásquez, Rufino Domínguez-Santos, Maylei Blackwell, and Laura Velasco Ortiz. 2014. "Género, generación y equidad: Los retos del liderazgo indígena binacional entre México y Estados Unidos en la experiencia del Frente Indígena de Organizaciones Binacionales (FIOB)." In *Otros Saberes: Collaborative Research on Indigenous and Afro-Descendant Cultural Politics*, edited by Charles R. Hale and Lynn Stephen, 75–100. Santa Fe, N.Mex.: School for Advanced Research Press.

Salinas Cesáreo, Javier. 2019. "En 2018, 106 feminicidios en Edomex." *La Jornada*, January 27, 2019. https://www.jornada.com.mx/ultimas/2019/01/27/en-2018-106 -feminicidios-en-edomex-6914.html.

Smith, Andrea. 2005. *Conquest: Sexual Violence and American Indian Genocide*. Durham, N.C.: Duke University Press.

Valencia Banda, Myrna Dolores. 2018. "Myrna Dolores Valencia Banda, Concejala yoreme. Comunidad Cohuirimpo, Sonora." Uploaded January 16, 2018. Video interview, 8:42. *Flores en el desierto*, by Gloria Muñoz Ramírez. Desinformémonos. https://floreseneldesierto.desinformemonos.org/videos/myrna.html.

Vázquez Luna, Guadalupe. 2018. "Guadalupe Vázquez Luna, Concejala tsotsil. Comunidad de Acteal, Chiapas." Uploaded January 16, 2018. Video interview, 10:49. *Flores en el desierto*, by Gloria Muñoz Ramírez. Desinformémonos. https://flores eneldesierto.desinformemonos.org/videos/guadalupe.html.

Wolfe, Patrick. 2006. "Settler Colonialism and the Elimination of the Native." *Journal of Genocide Research* 8 (4): 387–409.

CHAPTER 7

Ethical Tribunals and Gendered Violence in Guatemala's Armed Conflict

MORNA MACLEOD

W hile few scholars have framed the violence that occurred during Guatemala's civil war as part of the ongoing project of settler colonialism, the continuity of colonial projects such as re-creating and reifying racial difference to justify land dispossession, committing racialized genocide against Indigenous communities and rape and mutilation of Indigenous women as part of state strategies of counterinsurgency, and providing unequal access to justice for Indigenous peoples suggest that such a framework is appropriate (see Speed 2019). The lens of settler colonialism focuses on different forms of elimination—genocide, forced displacement, assimilation—and erasure of language, rights, and symbolic and material possession and presence (see Wolfe 1999; Veracini 2010; Simpson and Smith 2014). In many ways—and until such recent breakthroughs as the Sepur Zarco trial (2011–16; see chapter 4)—state institutions of justice channeled the violence of settler elimination by blocking access for Indigenous legal claims against the state. Crucially paving the way for the Sepur Zarco trial to take place in the formal justice system were ethical tribunals. These forms of "people's" justice organized by civil society outside of the formal legal system provided experience, language, strategies, and trained witnesses for the possibility of more formal trials. Apart from that, the tribunals also reveal the ongoing struggle for Indigenous women to be heard in their own voices and on their own terms.

This chapter explores two ethical tribunals that condemned gross human rights violations during the Guatemalan armed conflict. At the peak of state counterinsurgency, the Permanent Peoples' Tribunal: Session on Guatemala (PPT-SG), held in Madrid in 1983, was the first of its kind for Central America. Almost thirty years later, the First Tribunal of Consciousness Against Sexual Violence Toward Women took place in Guatemala City in 2010. In the former, the rape of Indigenous women is referred to in various testimonies, and two Indigenous women testified. However, this first ethical tribunal on Guatemala, framed in a counterhegemonic reading of international law, was gender blind. In contrast, the second tribunal, which comprised mainly Maya women testifiers and was based firmly in human rights discourse from a feminist lens, took place during a period of transitional justice, roughly fourteen years after the signing of the peace accords. This second tribunal is a bridge to Sepur Zarco and other trials that followed.

Maya women survivors—or protagonists (Crosby and Lykes 2019)—used tribunals to express in their own voice their lived experiences of brutal state repression, their grievances, and their hopes, as well as the meaningfulness of being heard and recognized. The 1983 PPT-SG did not acknowledge the rape of women, particularly Maya women, during the armed conflict: testifiers spoke, but they were not heard. Sexual violence was rendered invisible, although the women wore it on and in their bodies permanently. It would take another twenty-seven years for sexual violence to be fully recognized in an ethical tribunal, and thirty-three years for it to be legally condemned in 2016 in the Sepur Zarco trial. The chapter traces the changes in context and women's organizing that enabled the "invisible" to become visible and that permitted Indigenous women to become protagonists in the fight against ongoing state projects of Indigenous elimination and assimilation.

My discussion here is based on the 1983 and 2010 tribunals. I first describe the participation of women in ethical tribunals, then analyze these two ethical tribunals and compare them in terms of their recognition of sexual violence and their theoretical and ideological underpinnings, focusing on genocide and connections to theories of settler colonialism and intersectional feminism. After describing my methodological route to exploring both tribunals, I contemplate how we can learn from trauma. A key finding is the tension that exists between the healing potential of testimony given at tribunals and the (secondary) trauma that giving and hearing testimonies can generate. I finish the chapter by highlighting how sexual violence against women has become visible in recent years and assess the opportunities and shortcomings of ethical tribunals as a truth-telling space for Maya women.

Women's Tribunals and Maya Women's Testimonies

The two tribunals I analyze here need to be put into the context of other tribunals that specifically involved the participation of women and violence against women. A pathbreaking International Tribunal on Crimes Against Women was held in Brussels in 1976. Twenty-four years later, in Tokyo, the Violence Against Women in War Network Japan carried out the Women's International War Crimes Tribunal on Japan's Military Sexual Slavery (2000), to break the silence around the widespread use of women from Korea, Indonesia, China, Taiwan, Vietnam, and East Timor as "comfort women" for Japanese soldiers before and during the Second World War. This tribunal of conscience was somewhat different from its predecessors: proceedings were held in Japan, where the violations took place; it was an all-women's tribunal; and it was carried out by grassroots organizers from within the victimized countries, rather than by public intellectuals from abroad. It also highlighted crimes of sexual violence and slavery, which had been routinely disregarded during peace settlements and effectively erased from or ignored in the official records (VAWWN 2002).

Importantly, Yolanda Aguilar, a Guatemalan woman known for her pioneering work on sexual violence during Guatemala's armed conflict, was invited to testify before the 2000 Tokyo tribunal. A few years earlier, Aguilar had helped develop the two vital reports on violence during the Guatemalan Civil War: *Guatemala: Nunca Más* (Guatemala: Never Again; REMHI 1998), and *Guatemala: Memoria del Silencio* (Guatemala: Memory of Silence; CEH 1999). The first of these was the work of the Proyecto Interdiocesano de Recuperación de la Memoria Histórica (REMHI, Recovery of Historical Memory Project), an initiative of the Catholic Archdiocese of Guatemala; the second was the result of a UN truth commission on Guatemala, the Comisión de Esclaracimiento Histórico (CEH, Commission for Historical Clarification). Both initiatives date to 1994; REMHI's specific function was to nurture the upcoming UN truth commission, which would operate between 1997 and 1999. REMHI gathered 5,180 testimonies from victims and survivors, documenting 149 cases of sexual violence. After giving her testimony, Aguilar was invited to be in charge of this issue in REMHI's four-volume report.[1] She then went on to work with the CEH, which documented 9,411 victims of sexual violence in the war, of whom 88.7 percent were Maya women and girls.

The process of testifying for REMHI and CEH was private: staff documented the cases, which then appeared in the final reports. In contrast, testifying in ethical tribunals involves a public performance, whereby a trial is enacted before witnesses. Giving testimony publicly can be liberating or traumatic. When Yolanda gave her testimony in the Tokyo tribunal, she felt frustration with the way that she was pushed to provide testimony about horrible events in a short period of time:

> How is it possible for you to narrate in ten minutes how your brother was killed, your mother shoved about, your house burned; and they'd say "oh no! you've over-extended three minutes, repeat it." It's inhuman. That's the way they were doing it as they had so little time for women from all over the world. Rationally you can understand it, but it isn't human. (pers. comm., July 22, 2014)

While Yolanda found the brief testimonial spaces accorded in the tribunal to be insufficient, other Indigenous women have found their experience on the day of testimony to be strongly shaped by the education, preparation, and accompaniment they receive. Another woman who testified in the 2010 tribunal reveals the level of preparation involved, which was a key part of the Sepur Zarco trial as well:

> I felt calmer after giving my testimony, happy that we were accompanied; alone we wouldn't have dared. First, they trained us how to act in an ethical tribunal, we even did a dramatization: we named a judge, a lawyer, and the rest of us presented what we were going to say. Later they took us to Guatemala City. We also rehearsed there, the day before the trial. (Nentón workshop, July 14, 2014).

---

1. Catholic bishop Monsignor Juan José Gerardi, in charge of REMHI, presented the report in Guatemala City's cathedral on Friday, April 24, 1998; on Sunday, April 26, he was brutally beaten to death. Subsequently, three high-ranking military officers were tried and convicted of his death; a priest was also sentenced for his role as an accomplice to the murder.

By participating in ethical tribunals in situations that make them feel heard and valued, Indigenous women can be part of global civilian initiatives to condemn human rights atrocities, genocide, settler colonialism, and imperialism. They also shame and blame governments and corporations' bad practices. In the case of Guatemala, ethical tribunals have served as rehearsals for subsequent formal trials of genocide and sexual slavery. Indeed, the 2010 First Tribunal of Consciousness Against Sexual Violence Toward Women was a lead-in to the Sepur Zarco trial later in the decade (see Velásquez Nimatuj 2019; Crosby and Lykes 2019; chapter 4 in this volume). One of the fifteen Q'eqchi' women plaintiffs in Sepur Zarco also testified in the 2010 tribunal, and all fifteen participated in a series of preparatory workshops that will be discussed later in this chapter. Most encouraging is that through time, such tribunals have made women survivors—and violence against women— increasingly visible before the world.

Permanent Peoples' Tribunal: Session on Guatemala (1983)

The first highly visible international ethical tribunal on human rights atrocities and genocide in Guatemala was held by the Permanent Peoples' Tribunal in Madrid, January 27–31, 1983. The tribunal looked at evidence going back to the CIA-backed coup that ousted democratically elected president Jacobo Árbenz in 1954, although its main focus was on the massacres, scorched-earth policies, forced disappearances, torture, and killings taking place at the time under General Efraín Ríos Montt. Guatemala had been largely ignored by the international community, and advocacy had been scarce. The PPT-SG was organized by the Comisión de Derechos Humanos de Guatemala (CDHG, Guatemala Human Rights Commission) and the Instituto de Estudios Políticos para América Latina y África (IEPALA, Institute for Political Studies on Latin America and Africa); the latter acted as the tribunal's executive secretary and published the nearly four-hundred-page book on the tribunal a year later (TPP 1984). CDHG co-founder Maricarmen Victory and Carmelo García, both members of IEPALA, played crucial roles in organizing the tribunal (Reyes Prado and Valle 2013), with the support of well-known Guatemalan academics and political activists including Marta Elena Casaús Arzú and Arturo Taracena. European solidarity committees also gave considerable support. Advice was sought from members of the Russell Tribunal and the Lelio Basso Foundation in Rome.

The PPT-SG's jury comprised fifteen public figures (two women and thirteen men), the majority of them well-known academics from Europe, the United States, Latin America, and the Caribbean. The jury also included Mexican bishop Monsignor Sergio Méndez Arceo; writer Eduardo Galeano; the Algerian secretary-general of the International Association of Democratic Journalists, Amar Bentoumi; and two Nobel laureates, George Wald and Adolfo Pérez Esquivel. The honor committee comprised forty-four Guatemalan and European public figures, the only two women being the widows of assassinated Guatemalan politicians Manuel Colom Argueta and Alberto Fuentes Mohr.[2]

The five-day tribunal included twenty-two testifiers (including seven Maya men and two Maya women, Rigoberta Menchú Tum and Carmelita Santos), and fourteen expert reports, three of these presented by women (two foreigners, one Guatemalan, and no Maya). The reports covered a wide range of political and social issues, structural analysis, U.S. intervention, and human rights atrocities in the country. Sexual violence against women was denounced in various testimonies and in two expert reports (by Jesuit priest Ricardo Falla-Sánchez and Justice and Peace Committee coordinator Julia Esquivel).[3] And yet, despite repeated references to rape during the trial, no mention is made of sexual violence against women in the initial list of atrocities nor in the final sentence. This would suggest that sexual violence was so naturalized and underestimated that it was not "worth" indicting or was in fact not legible to most of the people who participated. Embedded and normalized in so many dimensions of social life, public and private, sexual violence was thus rendered invisible.

Denouncing human rights atrocities was the tribunal's central axis, illustrated by Rigoberta Menchú Tum's heartrending account of her mother's slow and torturous death. Menchú first describes how her father, Vicente Menchú, was burned to death in the notorious government-induced fire at the Spanish Embassy on January 31, 1980, after its occupation by a group of

---

2. The jury, which comprised celebrities and public intellectuals, reviewed the testimonies, reports, and other information, and it dictated the sentence at the end of the trial. The honor committee was formed by both Guatemalan and foreign public figures known in Guatemala and abroad.

3. Falla's expert report stated: "The ferocity of the massacres and cannibalism is accompanied by unrestrained sexual violence and a machismo that turns women into animals to gratify the soldiers; afterward, when no longer useful, they are often killed" (TPP 1984, 221).

mainly Indigenous peasants protesting the massacres and asking for support from the Spanish government. Eleven weeks after her father's death, Rigoberta's mother was kidnapped. The following day, the army used her mother's clothes as bait, strewing them on the streets of Uspantán in an effort to trap her children:

> According to the testimony of a cousin, who [also] tortured my mother and even looked after her corpse for four months on the mountainside, my mother was tortured for about twelve days. They changed her Maya dress for a military uniform, they cut her hair, and for twelve days she was cruelly tortured . . . [doctors were brought to resuscitate her], and they began again with the same tortures, they started raping her again. . . . Little by little my mother lost her will to live. When she was again about to die, they took her to a ravine about fifteen minutes away from Uspantán, they dumped her, still alive, among the vegetation. The military guarded her permanently for four months. My mother died slowly, she was eaten by animals, by buzzards, until only the largest bones of her body remained. The military let no one draw near. (TPP 1984, 243)

This heartbreaking account reveals the army's performative actions to publicly teach Maya women a lesson, demonstrating that they can punish and exercise violence on women they deem uncivilized. Not only was Rigoberta's mother repeatedly raped, but her Maya dress was replaced with masculine military attire, and her hair cut in an affront to Indigenous women's dignity (Cumes 2009; De Marinis 2017). One of Rigoberta's cousins participated in her mother's torture and demise, but also provided some kind of closure by reporting her mother's death. The armed conflict provoked family division; many young Indigenous men were forcefully recruited by the army through roundups on market day. Military training dehumanized foot soldiers to prepare them to carry out atrocities, which likely explains how Rigoberta's cousin could treat his aunt like this.

Catechist Carmelita Santos gives another grueling account of sexual violence against women during a massacre:

> In the afternoon they began to rape the women and torture the men. Their cries could be heard from the two surrounding hills. At the end, they [the army] piled the bodies together, poured [liquid from] quart-sized contain-

ers and set them alight. Women, old people, and children were ablaze. One jumped up from the fire, somersaulted and rolled to the ravine. The soldiers, seeing her naked, hooted: her burnt clothing and her rolling were a joke for Ríos Montt's soldiers.... That afternoon alone, 225 women, men, month-old babies, and old people died, burnt to a crisp. (TPP 1984, 280)

By juxtaposing the horror of the event and the soldiers' lack of empathy, the testimony highlights military counterinsurgency attempts to destroy Maya community lives and dignity, always promoting the loss of humanity. But Maya resistance and agency could not be thwarted. Both Menchú and Santos became public figures, continually speaking out against the atrocities taking place in Guatemala. Months after the Tribunal, *I, Rigoberta Menchú* was published (Burgos-Debray and Menchú Tum 1983).

Despite its obscuring of sexual violence, this tribunal had two notable redeeming features. First, as the tribunal was carried out less than a year after the creation of the Unidad Revolucionaria Nacional Guatemalteca (Guatemalan National Revolutionary Unity), a coalition of four revolutionary organizations, it conveyed a refreshing feeling of unity, coordination, and diversity, despite the fact that it had been mainly organized by the CDHG.[4] Second, the testimonies presented at the tribunal came from a broad range of repressed social movements, activist groups, and Indigenous communities: members of the Comité de Unidad Campesina (Committee for Peasant Unity), liberation theology catechists, trade unionists, community radio personalities, Indigenous refugees in Mexico, writers, academics, and relatives of the disappeared. Together they offer a clear insight into the workings of counterinsurgency in successive military regimes, foreign intervention, and the multiple dynamics of social and political resistance. Various Maya people also used the opportunity to talk about Maya culture and cosmovision, and many testimonies refer to the right to rebel against such repressive regimes.[5]

4. According to one interview, the reality behind the scenes was different, with tensions running high among the organizations. This tension was not apparent during the tribunal itself, however, nor in the book. The interviews were carried out mainly by the CDHG, but presented to the Tribunal without specifying this fact.

5. Testimonies gathered during armed conflict are often framed in terms of the right to justice and rebellion, in sharp contrast with testimonies gathered after the signing of peace accords (McAllister 2013). After the signing of the peace accords, testimonies were usually framed in terms of victims and perpetrators.

The tribunal jury condemned torture, killings, and forced disappearance, and it qualified the massacres of indigenous groups as genocide, using the standards adopted by the 1948 UN Convention on the Prevention and Punishment of the Crime of Genocide. It also declared that "the Government of the United States of America is guilty of the aforementioned crimes, given its decisive intervention in Guatemalan affairs, and the Governments of Israel, Argentina, and Chile are guilty of complicity through aid and assistance" (TPP 1984, 400). The jury concluded: "The Tribunal declares that, given the perpetration of the above-mentioned crimes by Guatemala's public powers, the people of Guatemala have the right to exercise all forms of resisting, including armed force, through its representative organizations, against the tyrannical public powers; and the armed force used by the Guatemalan Government to quash resistance is illegitimate" (TPP 1984, 401). This forceful sentence is emblematic of more radical times, sharply contrasting with current neoliberal globalization. But it also exemplifies the way that gendered sexual violence was naturalized and made invisible.

Over the twenty-eight years that separated the two ethical tribunals, Maya women (and Indigenous women more broadly) made great leaps forward in terms of organizing and getting their needs and interests onto national agendas. While the pan-Maya movement emerged at the end of the 1980s, the first show of strength of organized mestiza and Maya women was during the peace accords (1994–96), in the Civil Society Assembly, which ran parallel to—though not binding with—the formal UN–mediated peace negotiations between the government/army and the revolutionary organizations. The vibrancy of the women's and Indigenous peoples "sectors" stood out in comparison to some of the traditional sectors such as trade unions, press, and politicians.

Looking back at the peace accords and advances made for women in the ensuing years, Luz Méndez and Walda Barrios (2010) document achievement in terms of rights obtained, institutions founded (including the Defensoría de la Mujer Indígena, National Office for the Defense of Indigenous Women, established in 1999), and laws passed. These last include Decree no. 97-1996 to prevent, penalize and eradicate domestic violence, and the 2008 law against femicide and other forms of violence against women. The impact of feminist and women's organizing and advocacy, particularly around violence, would be most evident in the next Guatemalan tribunal, which addressed sexual violence directly.

First Tribunal of Consciousness Against Sexual Violence Toward Women (2010)

The dramatic 2010 ethical tribunal on sexual violence and slavery of women during the armed conflict took place in the historic Paraninfo in Guatemala City,[6] with eight hundred persons in the audience (Crosby and Lykes 2019). This event was crucial given that rape as a weapon of war in the thirty-six-year armed conflict was the UN Truth Commission's most underreported human rights violation.[7] The tribunal was organized by an alliance: Unión Nacional de Mujeres Guatemaltecas (UNAMG, National Union of Guatemalan Women), Equipo de Estudios Comunitarios y Acción Psicosocial (ECAP, Community Studies and Psychosocial Action), Mujeres Transformando el Mundo (MTM, Women Transforming the World), Coordinadora Nacional de Viudas de Guatemala (CONAVIGUA, National Coordination of Widows of Guatemala), and the feminist newspaper *La Cuerda*. The tribunal was the culmination of many years of work with women who had survived sexual violence during the armed conflict (Fulchiron, Paz, and López 2009). CONAVIGUA leader Rosalina Tuyuc explains:

> We have systematized many cases of women raped during the internal armed conflict, these remain in silence, in oblivion. The women alone have borne the burden of sadness, the burden of terror, the burden of shame, and the burden of the lack of application of justice. And above all, we have seen that although more than twenty years have passed, the women have undertaken this long journey for these deeds to not remain in impunity. (ECAP 2015)

In a move that highlights the global nature of these tribunals and their travel across continents, women of international renown were appointed as judges. Shihoko Nikawa had previously participated in the 2000 Tokyo tribunal. Teddy Atim came from Nigeria, where sexual violence was rampant in the internal armed conflict. Ex-political prisoner Gladys Canales,

---

6. This auditorium, originally part of the Faculty of Medicine of the Universidad de San Carlos de Guatemala, has hosted important civil society initiatives, the wakes of revolutionary leaders, and the anniversary of the (truncated) Ríos Montt trial on charges of genocide and crimes against humanity.

7. CEH registered 1,465 reports of rape and was only able to verify 285 cases. Women and girls accounted for 99 percent of the cases, and the vast majority (88.7 percent) were Indigenous (CEH 1999). Perhaps the most underreported of all was the rape of men.

came from Peru and was a member of the National Coordination of Women Affected by the Armed Conflict. And the fourth judge, Juana Méndez, is one of the few Maya women in Guatemala to have successfully won a court case for rape.[8]

The tribunal also had fifty witnesses of honor, including Maya and mestiza women, one Maya man, and lawyers, academics and human rights workers from North and South America, Europe, and Japan. The role of the honorary witnesses was mainly to symbolically validate the tribunal and sign the final verdict (Alison Crosby, pers. comm., June 24, 2019). One of the seven expert reports (on culture) was presented by Maya K'iche' anthropologist Irma A. Velásquez Nimatuj, who had previously participated in an ethical tribunal against racism (2002) and has since participated in key court cases against human rights atrocities: the Ríos Montt trial (2014) and Sepur Zarco (see chapter 4). Most testimonies during the tribunal were presented by Maya women. They were dressed in white *huipiles* (blouses), and to ensure their safety, only their silhouettes were projected onto a screen. Maya women also made up a significant part of the public in the crowded hall during the tribunal.

While most testimonies referred to sexual violence during the armed conflict—mainly by the army or, in some cases, by insurgents—the tribunal also aired the recent rape of women as a strategy to criminalize social protest. The following extract of a Maya K'iche' woman's testimony illustrates the women's grievances, as well as the empowering impact of both organizing strategies (on the part of CONAVIGUA) and the training (with ECAP and UNAMG) through which Maya women worked on trauma (Crosby and Lykes, 2011, 2019):

The pain I carry in my soul is what grieves me. So much grief, so much sadness resulting from suffering, I feel this hurts me deeply, it causes me great anguish. I suffer particularly from having been a victim of rape. They [the army] threw me down a ravine, the rocks hurt me . . . the army also raped me. Although I am a long-suffering woman, I know I have my rights and work to demand them. I am here to appeal on behalf of the women

---

8. Juana Méndez was raped by a policeman in 2005. Her case was successfully taken to court by a human rights organization in Guatemala City. In 2008 the policeman was sentenced to twenty years' imprisonment. His sentence was reduced to ten years after an appeal (ACOG-UATE 2011).

who stayed behind, I demand that we, as women, have rights. God knows why I was left alive. I am present here for the women. Thank you for being here and listening to me. This was my voice. (Mendia Azkue and Guzmán Orellana 2012, 40)

Maya women constituted key protagonists in the tribunal: in giving testimony; in being among the witnesses of honor, judges and experts who recognized and condemned sexual violence; and (to a lesser extent) in helping organize the tribunal. They also formed a substantial part of the public, which also included members of civil society organizations, folks from the international community, and some members of state institutions including the judiciary. "The audience was implicated in the testimonies by being called to listen and to know what was being recounted in the testimonies: they were being called to act as witnesses, with its implication of bearing the responsibility of responding to what they heard" (Crosby and Lykes 2019, 79). Being listened to and believed had an immense impact on the testifiers. Angelina, a Maya Chuj tribunal translator, relates:

You could see people's faces [in the audience] when they heard the women talking, they were surprised. I heard commentaries like: "I never imagined that this happened here" . . . as neither they, nor their relatives, had gone through this.[9] The people were listening very attentively, and each time a woman stopped talking, they clapped, even though they could not see their faces, they [applauded] their courage to give their testimony, to share with all of Guatemala so people could know what happened back then. The women said that this was also justice: sharing what they had lived through. "It's true that they're not going to sentence anyone, but other people are finding out what we went through." (pers. comm., July 14, 2014)

Others placed the blame squarely on the Guatemalan state. Maya Alvarado from UNAMG explains: "The aim was to tell Guatemalan society and Guatemala's justice system that it is possible to do right in these cases. This has pedagogical intent that goes beyond symbolic justice. The resolution

---

9. Alison Crosby and M. Brinton Lykes (2019) state that the impact was particularly strong for those women in the audience who had never named the sexual violence they had suffered during the armed conflict.

sentenced the state, inciting it to take charge of many things" (pers. comm., July 11, 2014). Holding the state responsible had a great impact on the Maya survivors. Angelina narrates: "When the women heard that the state was guilty, their faces lit up with smiles. Some, crying, said: 'at last they're listening to us.' One woman said: 'This is a form of justice, because they found the state guilty and not us,' because at the beginning the women felt guilty about what had happened to them, about being raped" (pers. comm. July 14, 2014). This "small act" of justice—blaming the state and not the victims—cannot be underestimated.

Analysis of the Tribunals: Genocide and Settler Colonialism

Both tribunals framed their analysis in terms of state counterinsurgency and genocide. Genocide is referred to thirty-one times in the 2012 Tribunal of Consciousness report. Citing Marta Casaús, Susanne Jonas, and Prudencio García, the report establishes that racism—linked to class—reached its peak during the armed conflict and fueled genocide. The report goes further by claiming that sexual violence also contributed to genocide in Guatemala's internal war. While sexual violence has always existed in contexts of war, the report argues, it was first recognized as a crime against humanity by the UN International Criminal Tribunals for Rwanda and for the former Yugoslavia, in 1998 and 2001, respectively. Before that, sexual violence was regarded as "collateral damage," as in the 1983 PPT-SG. By framing racialized sexual violence in the context of genocide, the 2010 tribunal was able to encompass a broader collective and intersectional analysis. However, the tribunal failed to address the *longue durée* of the structural continuum of violence, referred to in Irma A. Velásquez Nimatuj's expert report (no. 820199) and gathered from the Maya women in workshops organized by Alison Crosby and M. Brinton Lykes (2019).

By framing sexual violence in the context of genocide, the 2010 tribunal positioned itself strategically, and it overcame the false dichotomy between counterinsurgency strategies (e.g., Maya were massacred because they were "revolutionaries") and genocide (e.g., scorched-earth practices and massacres of Indigenous communities happened because they were Maya). Elizabeth Oglesby and Diane M. Nelson (2016, 139) put it succinctly: "The question is not whether the violence was counterinsurgency or genocide; the point is that it was both counterinsurgent and genocidal."

Indigenous intellectuals and their allies have given historical depth to the notion of genocide, linking it to conquest and colonialism. Australian scholar Patrick Wolfe (2006, 388)—while lacking a gendered perspective of genocide—insightfully affirms that "invasion is a structure not an event"; this implies that it is ongoing and includes different moments and forms of genocide and colonialism. Maile Arvin, Eve Tuck, and Angie Morrill (2013, 9) understand genocide as "the still-existing structure of settler colonization and its powerful effects on Indigenous peoples and others." The addition of a gender lens, they say, would enable "new visions of what decolonization might look like for all peoples." The naming of internal colonialism is significant, both because doing so combats processes of silencing and because "authorized voices" for the Latin American left are rarely Indigenous. Indeed, Zapatista women also insisted that the need to combat racism and discrimination was an inherent part of the battle for Indigenous rights and understandings of autonomy (Speed, Hernández Castillo, and Stephen 2006).

Genocide and Gender

Using internal colonialism as a backdrop, we need to look at the theoretical framing and the employment of the term *genocide* in the two ethical tribunals, as well as its relationship (or not) to gendered and sexual violence. The 1983 PPT-SG clearly lacked a gendered perspective in its use of the term, which was related to national liberation struggles against colonialism in Africa and Asia after World War II, as well as to dictatorships in the Southern Cone (Uruguay, Argentina, Chile) and to Central American civil wars in the 1970s and 1980s. The massacre of Indigenous communities in Guatemala is included in this concept of genocide, but it lacks the historical depth suggested by Dian Million (2009), as it refers only to state counterinsurgency during the armed conflict.

Genocide was an essential focus for the PPT-SG, but it was framed in terms of the "people of Guatemala," whereas the 2010 tribunal on sexual violence used the term specifically in relation to Indigenous peoples. The feisty PPT-SG was radical in its critique of state terror and affirmation of the right to insurgency, but it completely obscured—or naturalized—the sexual violence against Maya women and girls. In contrast, the 2010 tribunal was centered on sexual violence from a human rights framework, but it lacked the counterhegemonic radicalism that characterized the PPT-SG, in part because of the constrictions of transitional justice. Maya did not contribute significantly to the framing and carrying out of either tribunal, although they were included in both. This has to do with the kinds of alliances that can be forged. Rita Dhamoon (2015, 32) contends that in building alliances between feminists, power differentials must be taken into account. This work can cause certain anxieties in the project of decolonizing antiracism, as it means facing "how we, as feminists confronting local and global inequities, might benefit from dispossession." She argues that "collective organizing necessitates alliances and coalitions, not only across groups and issues, but also *within* groups, precisely because there are varying forms and degrees of power at play in the margins as well as between various relational centres and peripheries" (33).

Both ethical tribunals, while not organized by Maya, were crucial for making Maya visible. While the 1983 tribunal opened up arenas for Maya men and women's direct advocacy in the international community, the 2010 ethical tribunal was the first opportunity for Maya women's words on sexual violence to be heard and recognized, and it led to legal cases such as Sepur Zarco. However, both tribunals are a far cry from the radical historical approach to genocide with roots in conquest or invasion held by Indigenous intellectuals and allies such as Wolfe (2006).

Finally, neither tribunal report specifically takes an intersectional approach, whereby class, gender, and race or ethnicity "are enmeshed in each other and the particular intersections involved produce specific effects" (Anthias and Yuval-Davis 1983, 63; see also Crenshaw 1991). The PPT-SG's class and anti-imperialist discourse mentions violence toward Indigenous communities but is blind to gender. The Tribunal of Consciousness report refers to gender, racism, and class, but it does not enmesh these and draw out their intersectional specificities vis-à-vis sexual violence (in contrast to the analysis of some of its organizers, like the above-mentioned Maya Alvarado). By focusing solely on sexual violence as a weapon of war, it does not interrogate how the intersection of race and gender shapes women of color's experience of sexual violence and their remedial strategies (Crenshaw 1991, 1242). This lack of intersectionality has to do with the objectives and dynamics of ethical tribunals, forums that legitimately recur to Spivakian strategic essentialism (see Landry and MacLean 1996). Intersectionality follows a different course in the academy, where, "there has been a gradual recognition of the inadequacy of analyzing various social divisions, but especially race and gender, as separate, internally homogeneous, social categories resulting in the marginalization of the specific effects of these, especially on women of colour" (Yuval-Davis 2006, 206). A recognition of the specificities of praxis and theory helps us understand the commonalities and differences between these enterprises.

In contrast to the Tribunal of Consciousness report, Maya women who spoke before the tribunal—as well as some organizers, practitioners, social activists, and scholars involved in the tribunal—have offered rich insights that draw on their understanding of difference, their immersion, and their ongoing contact with Indigenous women (Crosby and Lykes 2012, 2019). Some Maya women mentioned racism in their testimony: "Unfortunately, because we're Indigenous, they don't respect us, they gave the order to kill our communities, our peoples" (Mendia Azkue and Guzmán Orellana 2012, 36). Others illustrated their epistemological understanding of lived trauma through language: "There is great pain in [my] soul . . . who can mend this damage to my heart? It's clear that no one can remove this thorn from my soul. . . . That is why I want to say, in the name of the communities, that this damage should never take place again, it should not be repeated" (Mendia Azkue and Guzmán Orellana 2012, 39). Maya Alvarado discovered that in Mayan languages, "there is no literal translation for rape. . . . When [the women] refer to rape, the word means 'damage to the soul,' no mention at all is made to the body" (pers. comm., July 14, 2014). She reflected on the different ways sexual violence is perceived and evaluated:

> It's a completely different logic. Rita Segato proposes this in her expert report [for Sepur Zarco]. When we talk about sexual violence, we're not talking exclusively about rape; there are a series of elements that concatenate and become sexual violence based on the sexuality of Q'eqchi' women, and this also has a specificity. The women speak with the same pain about rape as they do about having had to wash the soldiers' clothes and cook for them; that is, carry out all the chores assigned to their gender for those who murdered their husbands and sons, and who raped them. So sexual violence is not only the concrete act of rape but includes the sum of all these deeds. (pers. comm., July 14, 2014)

From the Maya Q'eqchi' women, we can glean an intersectional and multidimensional comprehension of sexual violence as both a weapon of war and a part of a *longue durée* of structural and intersectional violence, permeating generations of Maya women, though accentuated by the armed conflict. Some contours of sexual violence are ultimately lost in translation in both the 2010 tribunal and the subsequent Sepur Zarco trial. In the former, this loss is the result of prevailing Western feminist assumptions that exclude collective intersectional analysis and rights; in the latter, it is a matter of a judicial system that seeks "good victims" that can give individuated, fractured, and fragmented testimony, a system that homes in on rape and sexual slavery but omits the epistemological understandings and particular lived experience of Maya women (Crosby and Lykes 2019).

Lessons from Trauma

In 2010, after listening to the ethical tribunal on sexual violence on the Internet, and poring over the powerful tribunal photographs, I decided to work on sexual violence as a weapon of war. However, having become a full-time academic at a public university in Mexico with little support for research and a heavy teaching load, I was facing significant constraints. I had been accustomed, as a practitioner, to spending months of time engaging with the people with whom I was working. In contrast, as an academic who could only come for short stints of time and who had few resources to support travel and time away, I realized that I could not continue to carry out fieldwork in Guatemala in a way that was comfortable for me. As I did not accompany either of the ethical tribunals analyzed in this chapter, I make a side move here to reflect on other direct experiences, to draw out insights that articulate with the tribunals.

In this section, I broaden the focus to include the positionality of accompanier, exploring forms of listening, the impact of secondary trauma, and the need for all involved to find forms of self-care and of emotional and physical healing. Crosby and Lykes (2019) highlight the interrelation between testifying, listening and accompanying. I want to deepen this reflection, taking a dialogic approach to understanding the interconnectedness between survivor-protagonists and those who accompany. Crosby and Lykes (2019) and others warn against the risk of the pornography of violence, where listeners "consume" the suffering of others. This is undeniably an important critique, but we must also consider how the retelling of suffering can be devastating for listeners and accompaniers, and how giving testimony can be either liberatory or traumatic, depending on the existence—or not—of pre-paratory workshops, support networks, and mechanisms to work through trauma. These forms of participation produce different discourses: survivor-protagonists come to understand their own experiences through their contact with mediatory understandings and framings. To achieve this reflection, I weave together personal experiences and those of the two ethical tribunals.

When I first started collaborating with the CDHG in Mexico City in 1983, I was asked to translate. Later, I would also classify testimonies on human rights atrocities. The process of translating invites distance, but classifying testimonies involves making decisions: Was it torture or mutilation? Massacre or summary execution? How can you name, let alone classify, a pregnant Maya woman's having her uterus slashed open and fetus removed? Having to decide, to name and categorize, made me somehow feel complicit. Overcome with grief each time I classified testimonies, I realized that for my own mental health it was time to stop. An Argentinian psychologist (ex-political prisoner who gave therapy to Central American women survivors) explained that the difference was that she was able to process the pain through her therapeutic work, whereas I just "swallowed and swallowed horror." I do not think this form of "consuming grief" was motivated by a parasitical, morbid desire to prey on the pain of others; rather it provoked an intolerable sense of impotence toward injustice. Decades later, some organizations offer self-care and psychosocial services to support both victims and human rights workers, as in the case of the organizing alliance for the 2010 tribunal, which worked with fifty-four Maya women before, during and after the proceedings. Maya organizers and *ajq'ijab'* (spiritual guides) have increasingly introduced ceremonies, invocations, and healing rites into an arena of social organizations and movements. In contrast, others—in a kind of male, militant, stoic approach—have rejected this "feminine" emotional survival strategy. How to be empathetic but maintain a healthy distance continues to be a challenge for many.

My own experience as a "judge" in the 2012 People's Health Tribunal, an ethical tribunal in San Miguel Ixtahuacán to scrutinize the effects of the Canadian mining corporation Goldcorp, was followed by a meeting with the Maya women's group Mujeres Luchadoras por un Nuevo Amanecer (Women Struggling for a New Dawn), created after seven women had received arrest warrants for "meddling" with the company (Macleod 2017; Macleod and Pérez Bámaca 2013; Tribunal Popular 2012). Pleased with the

Health Tribunal, the women were particularly welcoming. My daughter, who had made a radio program of the tribunal, observed how one woman watched me intently for an hour, while her children scratched her, seeking her attention. Finally, she plucked up the courage to speak. For forty-five minutes she gave an agonizing blow-by-blow account of her brother's lynching. She blamed the mining corporation for inciting her neighbors to violence. Feeling impotent, recognizing her acute distress, sensing her falling apart,[10] I could only offer to listen deeply. I did not realize at the time how this detailed lynching account had lodged itself in my body, from where it would explosively emerge, years later, in the form of sobbing. The experience made me mindful of how much secondary trauma we store in our bodies. Maya testifiers—and indeed all testifiers—had to rely on their own forms of coping in the 1983 tribunal, through prayer, revolutionary mystique, or simply a shutting out. In contrast, the 2010 tribunal carefully planned psychosocial healing strategies before, during, and after the event, and in some places started to include Maya spiritual practices. These practices were even more frequent in CONAVIGUA, the Maya widows' organization that co-organized the tribunal.

In 2009, various authors in this current volume organized an event in Mexico City, where Ojibwa Maureen White Eagle presented an anticolonial, antipatriarchal frame for her work to end violence against Native American women. Realizing that her powerful perspective could inspire Maya women, we—together with Pop N'oj—organized a nine-day visit for her to Guatemala that November.[11] We held ten workshops and meetings with Maya women in different regions of Guatemala and the capital. The Maya women resonated deeply with Maureen's historical and epistemological approach, overcoming language barriers.[12] In Guatemala City, a member of Maya women's group Kaqla asked Maureen whether Native Americans understood multiple violence as transmitted from generation to generation. Maureen spoke about historical trauma and intergenerational grief, and the

10. She later received healing sessions with a well-known Maya activist, who herself had undergone persecution and arrest warrants.

11. Pop N'oj was part of Oxfam Australia's Indigenous program in Mesoamerica. When this program closed down in 2005, Pop N'oj became an NGO.

12. In Alta Verapaz, this process involved double acts of interpretation: English–Spanish–Q'eqchi'.

way that unresolved trauma is passed on to future generations.[13] As Million (2009, 70) says, "There is no 'healing' until these wounds are acknowledged and given adequate attention."

In Santiago Atitlán, a young Maya Tz'utujil woman broke down when recounting sexual abuse by an uncle. *Ajq'ij* Virginia Ajxup supported her through energetic rites, but afterward we discussed the need to be more prepared—with herbs and other strategies—when wounds open up while discussing these issues. There were clear differences between the women who came to these encounters and the Maya women who had worked previously on these painful issues, for whom Maureen's four-pronged approach (heart, mind, body, and spirit) was liberating. Women who loosely came together for Maureen's visit were more vulnerable, not having received support such as the ECAP and UNAMG workshops. But the experience on the whole was remarkable: language barriers were overcome by intense connection between Indigenous women and a perspective that created great resonance.

All these experiences and social practices are framed in different kinds of discourse. Maya women—and indeed everyone—appropriate and integrate various perspectives into their own words and forms of testifying. Truth-telling thus depends not only on testifiers' sharing previous experience but also on their learning how to name political repression, personal trauma, and collective wounds. All speech is thus mediated both in its framing and in its hearing. This can entail risks: listeners can leech on or be overwhelmed by others' suffering; learned discourse ("scripts") can exclude testifiers' felt needs.[14] In ethical tribunals—and even more so in official truth commissions and courtrooms—testimony dictates the terms of truth-telling. Discourses of narration are contingent, vary over time, involve women's agency, and can be curtailed or inspired by truth-telling spaces and previous experience.

---

13. "Historical trauma is collective, cumulative wounding [on both] an emotional and psychological level that impacts across a lifetime and through generations, which derives from cataclysmic, massive collective traumatic events, and the unresolved grief impacts both personally and intergenerationally" (Pihama et al. 2014, 251–52; and see Brave Heart and DeBruyn 1998).

14. In a workshop in San Miguel Ixtahuacán where Maya Mam women spoke of the impact of the Goldcorp goldmine on their lives, the learned script in Spanish disappeared when women spoke in Mam. This made me cognizant of the multiple layers of translation that Maya women may face in giving testimony.

Final Reflections

Writing this chapter at the end of the second decade of this millennium, and amid the #MeToo and antifemicide campaigns that have shaken the foundations of patriarchal spaces and institutions, it seems astonishing that sexual violence was illegible to the judges of the 1983 PPT-SG. Although women, some men, and even "authorized voices" such as Jesuit priest Ricardo Falla testified to the rape of Maya women and girls, this testimony fell on deaf ears and was simply rendered invisible.

It would take decades of women's organizing, advances in national and international laws penalizing femicide and violence against women, and recognition of diverse forms of violence as weapons of war in the 1998 Rome Statute of the International Criminal Court to push the issue to the fore. Many women from the alliance, CONAVIGUA, and *La Cuerda* were involved in this struggle for recognition in Guatemala, and the 2010 tribunal was held to redress the invisibilization of sexual violence in spaces of justice. The tribunal became an inspiration for Ixil women to give testimony on sexual violence during the Ríos Montt trial (Oglesby and Nelson 2016), and it served as a testing ground for the Sepur Zarco trial (see Oglesby and Nelson 2016; chapter 4 in this volume).

In this chapter I have also explored how nongovernmental ethical tribunals investigate, publicize, and condemn atrocities and affronts to human dignity, constituting a "weapon of the weak" whereby "individuals speak back to power" (Givoni 2011, 149). As a strategy of the subaltern in the face of immense power imbalances and injustice, and as a form of symbolic political action, ethical tribunals rely on quasi-legal theatrics to enact justice. Their obvious weakness is that they are not legally binding and are usually ignored by the powerful. However, in contexts of extreme impunity, they effectively bypass governments and courts; they are not curtailed by limitations characteristic of legal systems, and in contrast to truth commissions their terms are not dictated by the state or the United Nations. They can express the denunciations of abuse and the aspirations for social justice of grassroots women and men on their own terms and from their own perspectives, though, as we have seen, such narratives are always mediated. Thus, they constitute a mechanism for civil society to *perform* and in some ways even *create* justice, constituting a form of *public shaming* of those responsible for human rights abuses. They not only denounce impunity and the complicity of state justice, but also evoke an alternative paradigm of justice, based on collective action and consciousness. This implies a rethinking of what justice is and how it can be achieved.

Ethical tribunals transcend national borders, mustering solidarity and support from international organizations and movements. Effectiveness of ethical tribunals depends on creativity in catching the public eye. This can be temporary, as in the case of the Permanent Peoples' Tribunal on Guatemala, creating an effective and legitimizing international advocacy tool for several years in the 1980s. The tribunal later sank into oblivion, save for those (in) directly marked by it, mentioned only in passing in academic and practitioner reports, and the sentence in Internet is decontextualized, stripped of greater meanings, for those not "in the know." Online digitized videos would have captured the emotions, solemnity, and performativity permeating the event. In contrast, the 2010 tribunal had far greater alternative and mainstream press, radio, and video coverage. The two tribunals were framed in different readings of genocide: while genocide occluded rape of women in the 1983 tribunal, it served as a backdrop to highlight sexual violence as a weapon of war in 2010, an approach that emphasized the tribunal's political and collective underpinnings. At a larger level, this latter tribunal provided a model, experiences, and strategic learning for Indigenous women and the NGOs who would support them in later formal trials, where the perpetrators of genocide, gendered violence, and sexual slavery were held accountable.

My experience as part of the "jury" in the Health Tribunal made me understand the importance for those testifying of being heard and believed, as well as realizing they are not alone. As such, ethical tribunals provide a space for survivors to exercise agency and to be recognized. This in itself can be a form of reparation, apparent in both tribunals. However, if testifiers—in tribunals or other spaces—have not previously worked on their grief, speaking out can retraumatize, as in the case of the young Maya Tz'utujil woman in Santiago Atitlán. Truth-telling unaccompanied by other forms of healing is not enough, as illustrated by the Maya Mam woman whose brother had been lynched. Few people, like Yolanda Aguilar, process trauma and then leave it behind; this act of release involves the sort of holistic healing that Maureen White Eagle engages in her work with violently abused Native American women. Traumatized testifiers can produce secondary trauma in listeners, but this is not usually the case when those giving testimony have worked on their grief, despite the deep impact their words have on empathetic publics.

Writing about these two tribunals, I have sought to dig up "flashes of memory," as Walter Benjamin ([1940] 2006) would say, to contribute to restoring them to history. The Maya women who participated in these ethical tribunals transcend the category of victims, helping restore or create autonomy in their lives, and agency in their collective well-being.

References

ACOGUATE. 2011. "Trabajando el tema de la violencia contra las mujeres en Guatemala." *En Profundidad* (blog). June 27, 2011. https://acoguate.org/trabajando-el-tema-de-la-violencia-contra-las-mujeres-en-guatemala/.

Anthias, Floya, and Nira Yuval-Davis. 1983. "Contextualizing Feminism: Gender, Ethnic and Class Divisions." *Feminist Review* 15:62–75.

Arvin, Maile, Eve Tuck, Angie Morrill. 2013. "Decolonizing Feminism: Challenging Connections Between Settler Colonialism and Heteropatriarchy." *Feminist Formations* 25 (1): 8–34.

Benjamin, Walter. (1940) 2006. "On the Concept of History." In *Walter Benjamin, Selected Writings*, vol. 4, *1938–1940*, edited by Howard Eiland and Michael W. Jennings, 389–400. Cambridge, Mass.: Harvard University Press.

Brave Heart, María Yellow Horse, and Lemyra M. DeBruyn. 1998. "The American Indian Holocaust: Healing Historical Unresolved Grief." *American Indian and Alaska Native Mental Health Research* 8 (2): 56–78.

Burgos-Debray, Elisabeth, and Rigoberta Menchú Tum. 1983. *Me llamo Rigoberta Menchú y así me nació la conciencia.* Barcelona: Editorial Argos Vergara.

Commission for Historical Clarification (CEH). 1999. *Guatemala Memoria del Silencio.* 12 vols. Guatemala City: CEH.

Crenshaw, Kimberlé Williams. 1991. "Mapping the Margins: Intersectionality, Identity Politics, and Violence Against Women of Color." *Stanford Law Review* 43 (6): 1241–99.

Crosby, Alison, and M. Brinton Lykes. 2011. "Mayan Women Survivors Speak: The Gendered Relations of Truth Telling in Postwar Guatemala." *International Journal of Transitional Justice* 5:456–76.

Crosby, Alison, and M. Brinton Lykes. 2019. *Beyond Repair? Mayan Women's Protagonism in the Aftermath of Genocidal Harm.* New Brunswick, N.J.: Rutgers University Press.

Cumes, Aura. 2009. "'Sufrimos vergüenza': Mujeres k'iche' frente a la justicia comunitaria." *Desacatos* 31:99–114.

De Marinis, Natalia. 2017. "Intersectional Violence: Triqui Women Confront Racism, the State, and Male Leadership." In *Demanding Justice and Security: Indigenous Women and Legal Pluralities in Latin America*, edited by Rachel Sieder, 242–62. New Brunswick, N.J.: Rutgers University Press.

Dhamoon, Rita. 2015. "A Feminist Approach to Decolonizing Anti-Racism: Rethinking Transnationalism, Intersectionality, and Settler Colonialism." *Feral Feminisms* 4:20–37.

Equipo de Estudios Comunitarios y Acción Psicosocial (ECAP). 2015. "Tribunal de Conciencia contra violencia hacia las mujeres durante el Conflicto Armado Guatemala 2010." Uploaded August 5, 2015. YouTube video, 21:01. https://www.you tube.com/watch?v=H1RI0wEQbYw.

Fulchiron, Amandine, Olga Alicia Paz, and Angélica López. 2009. *Tejidos que lleva el alma: Memoria de las mujeres mayas sobrevivientes de violación sexual durante el conflicto armado*. Guatemala City: ECAP and UNAMG.

Givoni, Michal. 2011. "Witnessing/Testimony." *Mafte'akh* 2e:147–69.

Landry, Donna, and Gerald MacLean, eds. 1996. *The Spivak Reader: Selected Works of Gayati Chakravorty Spivak*. New York: Routledge.

Macleod, Morna. 2017. "Ethical Tribunals: Maya Incursions into Symbolic Social Justice." In *In the Balance: Indigeneity, Performance, Globalization*, edited by Helen Gilbert, J. D. Phillipson, and Michelle H. Raheja, 255–72. Liverpool: Liverpool University Press.

Macleod, Morna, and Crisanta Pérez Bámaca. 2013. *Tu'n Tklet Qnan Tx'otx', Q'ix-kojalel, b'ix Tb'anil Qanq'ib'il, En defensa de la Madre Tierra, sentir lo que siente el otro, y el buen vivir. La lucha de Doña Crisanta contra Goldcorp*. Mexico City: CeActl.

McAllister, Carlota. 2013. "Testimonial Truths and Revolutionary Mysteries." In *War by Other Means: Aftermath in Post-Genocide Guatemala*, edited by Carlota McAllister and Diane M. Nelson, 93–115. Durham, N.C.: Duke University Press.

Méndez, Luz, and Walda Barrios. 2010. *Caminos recorridos: Luchas y situación de las mujeres a trece años de los Acuerdos de Paz*. Guatemala City: UNAMG.

Mendia Azkue, Irantzu, and Gloria Guzmán Orellana. 2012. *Ni olvido, ni silencio: Tribunal de Conciencia contra la violencia sexual hacia las mujeres durante el conflicto armado en Guatemala*. Guatemala City: UNAMG.

Million, Dian. 2009. "Felt Theory: An Indigenous Approach to Affect and History." *Wicazo Sa Review* 24 (2): 53–76.

Oglesby, Elizabeth, and Diane M. Nelson. 2016. "Guatemala's Genocide Trial and the Nexus of Racism and Counterinsurgency." *Journal of Genocide Research* 18 (2–3): 133–42.

Pihama, Leonie, Paul Reynolds, Cherryl Smith, John Reid, Linda Tuhiwai Smith, and Rihi Te Nana. 2014. "Positioning Historical Trauma Theory Within Aotearoa New Zealand." *AlterNative* 10 (3): 248–62.

Proyecto Interdiocesano de Recuperación de la Memoria Histórica (REMHI). 1998. *Guatemala Nunca Más*. 4 vols. Guatemala City: Oficina de Derechos Humanos del Arzobispado de Guatemala (ODHAG).

Reyes Prado, Anantonia, and Ruth del Valle. 2013. "Defensa y promoción de los derechos humanos en Guatemala." In *Proceso de paz y contexto internacional*, edited by Virgilio Álvarez Aragón, Carlos Figueroa Ibarra, Arturo Taracena Arriola, Sergio Tischler Visquerra, and Edmundo Urrutia García, 257–335. Vol. 4 of *Guatemala: Historia Reciente (1954–1996)*. Guatemala City: FLACSO.

Simpson, Audra, and Andrea Smith, eds. 2014. *Theorizing Native Studies*. Durham, N.C.: Duke University Press.

Speed, Shannon. 2019. *Incarcerated Stories: Indigenous Women Migrants and Violence in the Settler-Capitalist State*. Chapel Hill: University of North Carolina Press.

Speed, Shannon, Rosalva Aída Hernández Castillo, and Lynn Stephen, eds. 2006. *Dissident Women: Gender and Cultural Politics in Chiapas*. Austin: University of Texas Press.

Tribunal Permanente de los Pueblos (TPP). 1984. *Sesión Guatemala, Madrid, 27–31 de enero de 1983*. Madrid: IEPALA Editorial. Also published in English as *Guatemala, Tyranny on Trial: Permanent Peoples' Tribunal*.

Tribunal Popular Internacional de Salud. 2012. "Health Tribunal: In the Case of Gold Corp Versus Mining-Affected Communities: Verdict." Updated July 15, 2012. https://healthtribunal.org/the-final-verdict/.

Velásquez Nimatuj, Irma Alicia. 2019. *"La justicia nunca estuvo de nuestro lado": Peritaje cultural sobre conflicto armado y violencia sexual en el caso Sepur Zarco, Guatemala*. Bilbao, Spain: Universidad del País Vasco y Hegoa.

Veracini, Lorenzo. 2010. *Settler Colonialism: A Theoretical Overview*. London: Palgrave Macmillan.

Violence Against Women in War Network Japan (VAWWN). 2002. *Women's International War Crimes Tribunal on Japan's Military Sexual Slavery*. The Hague: International Organizing Committee for the Women's International War Crimes Tribunal.

Wolfe, Patrick. 1999. *Settler Colonialism and the Transformation of Anthropology: The Politics and Poetics of an Ethnographic Event*. London: Cassell.

Wolfe, Patrick. 2006. "Settler Colonialism and the Elimination of the Native." *Journal of Genocide Research* 8 (4): 387–409.

Yuval-Davis, Nira. 2006. "Intersectionality and Feminist Politics." *European Journal of Women's Studies* 13 (3): 193–209.

CHAPTER 8

SOVERYEMPTY

narrative DeneNdé poetics
|||| in |||| walled |||| home |||| lands ||||

MARGO TAMEZ

> My body is a place from which to address the whole notion of history and what has happened to us as Aboriginal people.
>
> —Rebecca Belmore, artist statement, *Fringe*

> [There is a need] for more expansive languages with which to grapple with Native experiences of genocide. [Especially] the need for indigenous narrative self-determination, development of decolonial epistemologies and praxes on genocide, and languages for violence that are specifically designed to facilitate dialogue on healing. [For] work [that] not only positions cartography and maps as a particularly useful language for understanding indigenous experiences of genocide, but documents the development of this language, with the intent of supporting and guiding others in creating alternative languages that best fit their nation, community, family, and selves.
>
> —Annita Lucchesi, "-hóhta'hané: Mapping Genocide & Restorative Justice in Native America"

I n this essay, I make room for a decolonial, conceptual space for privileging the introspective understanding that emerges long after a time-specific study, event, or process. Certain introspection is difficult. Certain understanding acquired in working with and alongside Indigenous women confronting sanctioned violence, at times, does not find a place to be registered. This chapter has three sections. In the first, I establish concepts and contexts. I introduce the term *soveryempty*, which I developed in 2016 in a paper delivered at the Clark University symposium "Genocide of Native Americans?" In the second, I share samples of a poetic intertextual form and pictorial language that I developed in 2018–19, motivated by an Indigenous poetics, history, and embodiment course I taught in 2017 aimed at investigating methodologies of difficult knowledge. *Soveryempty* is also informed by new insights on Indigenous trauma expressed in affidavits and testimonies included in the Early Warning / Urgent Action legal procedure utilized to alert the global human rights community of impunity actions in El Calaboz, Lower Rio Grande Valley, Texas. These testimonies were addressed in partnership with Ariel Dulitzky in 2012–13 before the UN Committee on the Elimination of Racial Discrimination. In the third and final section, I share insights on a new generation of Ndé women's resistance, intergenerational and transnational epistemology, and a commitment to embodying dissident knowing in carceral spaces.

1.

Part of the process of knowing with and alongside Indigenous women actively confronting state and organized violence is recognizing the scale of "colonial unknowing," an epistemological orientation that actively negates historical colonial violence and demands that this history be presented in a mode "intelligible" to (comfortable for) settlers (Vimalassery, Pegues, and Goldstein 2016). Indigenous embodied actions of empowerment in knowing things in different ways motivate this response. In this essay, I posit and perform a methodological response for doing and scaffolding difficult knowledge from a walled-in place. On several levels, the concepts shaped within this essay engage work on "colonial unknowing" and disavowal manifesting in both Texas and British Columbia, sites where I am engaged in writing and researching with Indigenous women. In their essay "On Colonial Unknowing," Manu Vimalassery, Juliana Hu Pegues, and Alyosha Goldstein (2016) argue that "the predominant lack of acknowledgement or engagement with the histories and contemporary relations of colonialism—especially with regard to the specificities of Indigenous peoples and colonial entanglements of differential racialization—is not simply a matter of collective amnesia or omission." This essay enacts a form of "refusing and rejecting colonial demands for intelligibility," through an intertextual, critical re-mixing of the archives of "colonial regimes of knowledge/power," which perpetuated hegemonic representation of settler logics and bound these into normalizing specific legible Apache worlds downplaying the carceral. In the walled Ndé world, walls, detention, the carceral, and nonrecognition are fused. To heighten the understanding of this cognitive intractability, I foreground a struggle with hegemonic cultural femininity and negation of the historical experiences of Apache women in the prison and the camp, spaces that underlie the walled-in communities of today. I witness the echoes of historical systems of erasures still deeply embedded in the present: in the Ndé (Lipan Apache) community, and in the way that the Ndé women's use of this knowledge to foster dissident agency and dissident acts constructs a path to an *embrace* of radical subjectivity within contemporary, walled-in gulags. I suggest this is more than revitalization or identity ethnography. Rather, language and beingness are tightly linked to a transgressive agency that emerges through etiological explorations of the beingness of disposability; recognition and embrace of a radicalized identity within a walled-in place energize different solutions formulated by those whose homelands are walled.

Within the context where I work and live, we address the ontology (being) and etiology (questioning the roots) of why developing methodology with intergenerational Indigenous disaster survivors is important. While Ndé peoples don't commonly use the term *colonization*, they refer to its omnipresence as an ongoing catastrophe. Their witnessing of state terror everywhere and all at once magnifies the need for those like me (a poet, historian, and community member) who accompany them in confronting state violence to question structural and systemic colonialism and to voice and enact change. In spaces of our dehumanization, we bear witness to the serious existential issues of human suffering, the beingness of colonization, and the beingness of changing banal structures and confronting those who uphold damage-centered human transactions. As we witness, we know more, we know more deeply, and we contribute to documenting these processes; but we are also co-creating a new structure for remembering and an oral history of being and asking for future generations. We build knowledge on interstitial being and asking about root causes, affect and effect, to support and seek relief for Indigenous relatives who are in pain and in a fight for their dignity. We witness the stories of those we respect, stories that are like digging tools, breaking through the sod of excessive abuses, disrespect, and vile treatment by powerful individuals and groups. We bear witness to continual threatened lives under dire conditions. We recognize in our relationality with those in the carceral state that we also witness a mirroring in pieces and fragments, our deepest self, some of us also intergenerational genocide survivors. On one of my visits with Dovie Thomason (Kiowa/Plains Apache, Lakota), at her home near Carlisle, Pennsylvania, she recounted the way lessons about large-scale violence and catastrophe, imparted to her as a child by her "gramma," were embedded in her being years after.

> One day I was sitting in the arbor with her [gramma]. I been being good. Sometimes the stories were loaded up front, like an inoculation, as you're going on a journey. You know just to keep you safe, vaccinate you before you go, before I went out and realized something might save me from hardship or hurt along the way. (Thomason 2015)

An Apache and Lakota intergenerational genocide survivors' oral history "loaded up front" and "like an inoculation" is, for Dovie, coded language established in one's being conditioned to continual assaults in American society. This may be unintelligible to those who've been privileged to be ignorant, or who choose to ignore causation of Indigenous peoples' distrust, anger, and refusal to forget American genocide. The life-affirming *beingness* of this love act imparts a path for Dovie into voice—as an antigenocide, antiviolence, Indigenous storyteller. It propels her to ask questions *at the root* of her peoples' shatter zone. Linking the Indigenous existential journey of *being here* to the very space of gramma's protective "inoculation," Dovie linked her autobiographical story to root traumas at the Carlisle Indian Industrial School and the intrinsically connected genocides in her Apache Lakota carceral memory.

Colonization in settler societies encodes *difference*; Dovie's "gramma" affirms that intergenerational and recent memory is needed for "inoculating" ourselves with collective embodied knowing and questioning the contours of oppression. In deep commitment to social justice and demilitarization, in our stance against genocide and violence, and through a critical, decolonial, and Indigenous feminist lens, we witness and remember Indigenous women's dehumanization and their need to be heard and seen. Nonetheless, as Indigenous scholars, we are rarely asked to interrogate the ontology and etiology of our witnessing.

Being witness to Ndé women and people walled-in, over twelve years, I've given considerable thought to ontology—beingness—within colossal structures of dehumanization. I get absorbed in matrices of causes, reasons . . . why things are the way things *just* are; how it is that *things are not* functioning; what we need to give more space to, and for. I home in on the causes and the things one thinks because one knows there are causes that cannot be spoken; there are things that don't get spoken after being witnessed. The "colonial demands for intelligibility" are forceful, sometimes requiring the witness to embargo certain kinds of thinking and knowing.

Trauma, suffering, and irreparable harm to Ndé women land protectors was underreported by the U.S. government as it forced land dispossession and displacement of community members, costing them lands, subsistence, and livelihoods. Through militarization and court procedures, the government normalized aggressive militarization as an operation of progress that benefits the economy, stimulating corporate investments. Land theft for profit, a perpetual lock-down, physical separation, and legal limbo inform the existential crisis of being, knowing, and causation, in a walled experienced, 149 months and still going.

The entry-point epigraphs, by Rebecca Belmore and Annita Lucchesi, illuminate ways to understand Indigenous feminist witness, documentation, historiography, and interventions in difficult knowledge. These epigraphs highlight concerns with walls—physical, systemic, oppressive—which weaponize separation and empty human beings deemed unworthy of the authority of being. Refusal catalyzes Indigenous witness to a state of being in a future that, for some, is walled in. I unpack this in the following pages.

Gulag walls have a way of restructuring and invoking the prison camp; they crush, warp, excavate, and dehumanize human spirit and mental state; they assault a (w)holistic sense of beingness in connection with non-walled-in peoples and places. They get built ideologically before they actually get constructed physically. Walls are built fluidly through fastening together, intertextually, dominant colonial discourses of domination and "the enemy." Walled-in Indigenous, intergenerational, genocide-survivor communities contradict the settler-colonial myth that taking land from Indigenous peoples is a predetermined aspect of our past and our present, and that this should be normalized in public memory, not rooted out. Eloisa Tamez, my mother and the Ndé community's most visible land protector, retorted, "they took the land, but they can't take my voice" (Lipan Apache 2013). Indigenous intertextual "voice" and digging at the root to correct official memory are metaphors she deployed for constructing beingness and constructing the cause of beingness in walled-in homelands.

Wall survivors go forward, yet the wall doesn't move, yet somehow the wall must be put out of mind and also discursively put in its place. Walled-in places are storied places. Survivors move back and forth, hardwired into crisis and event. Bearing and sometimes burying scars, distrust, and hostility. Stories want to tell as scissors want to cut. The wall is a large blade. The wall is a seventy-five-mile-long amputation that never heals. The land lacks surgeons who know how to suture its bared nerves, deteriorating cells, clear-cut wounds, and necrotic, infected flesh.

Sovereignty conceals American excisions of Ndé being and Indigenous belonging. Its cutterage of our juridical humanity—Indigenous personhood, rights to recognition—is an emptying, exercised through necropower: a complete, forced occupation, a denial of plural governance with Indigenous peoples, and a legal obstruction to being.[1] In the very space where necropower emptied Ndé for nearly two centuries, the Lower Rio Grande villages, I witnessed an emergence of Ndé women's critical resistances via subversion of settler sovereignty. Many listened, supported, allied, and witnessed this as well. Ndé ideas about how we are different from the American ideal, gendered, cultural Apache shifted as conflict became intractable. We learned that the state has vested interests in maintaining divisions between Apache peoples—on and off reservations, inside and outside Texas. I understood imprisoned Ndé beingness in a very different way than how Apaches see Apache womanhood, a powerful and potent symbol. In the version handed down to me, the Ndé still live in El Calaboz (lit., "the dungeon"), a walled gulag in a heavily militarized bordered region of the continent. Settler military masculinity dominates control over place. I questioned: What's at the root of Ndé women's resistance to settler militarized dispossession in the Lower Rio Grande? Why, in 2007, did Ndé women refuse U.S. dispossession from El Calaboz (the dungeon)?

Ndé walled-in ontology and etiology within carceral place and space shifted my understanding of Ndé crisis and postmemory of gulag beingness. A different language of ordinary power, registering a walled-in knowing of existence, took root. In shared struggle, I witnessed human spirit in and out of checkpoints, enormous gates, inaccessible lands, steel walls, holding

---

1. Since 2010, I've sustained engagement with Achilles Mbembe's (2003) theory of necropower. Key to necropower is the gaining of operational control over the Indigenous space and place, determining who lives and who dies. It involves marginalizing survivors and witnesses *spatially and politically, to the extreme, remote fringes*; diminishing existence to deprived conditions; and harvesting and exploiting survivors, forcing them into an unintelligible identity.

on between a walled world and the nonwalled world. I saw the sanctioned expansion of spatialized *impunity* as American normalcy.

Impunity occurs when a state, in this case the United States, through its own legislation and policy-making, exempts itself (escapes) from accountability, responsibility, punishment, indictment, redress, reparations, or fines of any sort. This involves the obstruction (blocking) of those who attempt to bring the state to justice for human rights violations, and, in these processes, it constitutes a framework of discourses and ideologies, which normalize its denial of victims' rights to redress.

Questions raised by Ndé through me as representative in national and international tribunals have challenged state-sanctioned walled *impunity* as state terror. For example, Ndé land protectors demanded that the state produce evidence about its authority to extinguish Indigenous peoples' historical Crown title to Indigenous lands in Indigenous peoples' possession. Ndé requested that the state produce evidence of extinguishment of Ndé Aboriginal title: a bill of sale, receipt, or other documentation. The state produced none.

In time, as I witnessed elders becoming fluidly communicative in digital platforms, I turned to embodied forms of remembering in/from the *very space* in which indigeneity and Indigenousness were and are *emptied of life*. The purpose was to address communities without access to academic journals and legal court documents, peoples in walled worlds in El Calaboz and beyond: to transmit/witness as an act of curating difficult knowledge. Theirs and mine. Poetry, history, and performance have been tools to voice that which the tribunal process disavowed, such as genocide. This repeated "inoculation" taught me about the importance, yet limitations, of legal briefs, reports, and papers if these are not deployed into the intertextual domain to voice dissent at impunity.

Witnessing, I recognized that neither *Indigenous* sovereignty nor *Native* sovereignty will create or embody relational, respectful, transformative power and autonomy in *Ndé peoples' walled-in homelands*. Rather, they develop a different language of dissent within the carceral, a language of power and oppression from the inside out—as Ndé see land, family, and sky through the gulag.

Sovereignty, for the walled-in, is a root problem within Ndé women's historical context and current condition. Settler juridical dehumanization causes an intractable, everyday acceptance of nonrecognition (nonstatus, in the Canadian context). The uncritical acceptance or enabling of Indigenous nonrecognition, as connected to juridical dehumanization within the wall, conditions the masses to sovereignty. They do not dissent against the master's conditions on those within the wall, as long as their own interests are maintained intact.

Carceral Gulags Through Intertextual Witnessing

The *emptying* of Ndé social and political being, and the reasons for Ndé struggle as dissent, can be located in Ndé narrative, language reclamation, and community stories of post-nineteenth-century carceral existences. At the Lower Rio Grande, these stand in stark contrast to American Apache history.

Memory and postmemory of dehumanization is, for Ndé women, particularly acute; the hegemony of national consumption of Apache identity, distilled by the settler ethnographer H. Henrietta Stockel, works to decontaminate Apacheness of intrinsic ties to Ndé in Texas. This is accomplished through emphasizing Apache gender, culture, physical features, language, and the camp dress within a New Mexico and Arizona settler cultural landscape. The Ndé site of crisis, articulated in settler assemblage, is the very place where Ndé beingness gets disassembled.

The erasure of Ndé from the normalized settler cultural landscapes of Texas has blurred containment and carceral history while foregrounding lucrative oil-, copper-, and uranium-rich Texan industry. The settler disassemblage of Ndé peoples in Texas, distilled down/onto roadside history markers, reveals the settlers' gendered, cultural, and linguistic representation of the past, which stands as a visual and cognitive code for settler physical domination as well as a form of hagiographic masculine sovereignty over Ndé lands, bodies, belonging, and being. El Calaboz, a matrilineal place of Ndé historical carceral knowledge, remained in continuity near the Rio Grande. The El Calaboz community of Ndé, Comanche, and Nahua-descendant families retained memory of sites of blood violence, and retained a village knowledge system, where Ndé women fused the wall's devastation with community oral history and memory archives of violent settler occupations that had garrisoned, imprisoned, and consumed Ndé and relative Indigenous peoples throughout Texas.

The embeddedness of Indigenous oral history and critical Ndé herstory within genocidal occupation was retained differently by Ndé women in the dungeon/El Calaboz, and retaining this identity of a people in a historical dungeon was/is a form of resisting the settler erasure of violence. For Ndé resistance, the "camp" dress is a potent symbol for remembering Apache women's forced assimilation into compulsory womanhood under settler carceral militarism, which normalized and masked settler violence beneath American narratives of progress and expansion. During the wall resistance movement, Ndé anti-carceral discourses stoked my own memory of my grandmother's and great-grandmother's oral herstories of the root origins of the Apache "camp" dress. Ndé women's stories embedded a visual code that confronted us everywhere we traveled in Texas. In reality, compulsory, violent feminization and gendering interlock carceral genocide. Texas is an open-air prison without a parole date for nonrecognized Ndé peoples. Texas settler roadside history embedded in the U.S. wall construction discourses reinforces the layers of settler memory at work in white possession, white sovereignty, and white supremacy, at the root of the wall and nonrecognized Ndé women's "camp" experiences.

I asked: How do Ndé women survivors, undergoing the emptying of beingness, re-create agency to examine roots within our refusal? How are our thoughts and language in walled places a mode of resilience, resistance, and determination to continue thinking, doing, and being human, as well as Ndé?

Immersed in the silencing within impunity, I turned toward digital, cyber networks. Transnational feminist networks introduced me to the work of Egyptian antifascist resistance writer and former prisoner Nawal el Saadawi, who composed powerful memoirs of the carceral on a roll of *toilet paper*, with an eyebrow pencil. Saadawi challenged hegemonic conditioning, and she survived through writing the play *God Resigns in the Summit Meeting*, which "proved so controversial that, . . . her Arabic publishers destroyed it under police duress" (Khaleeli 2010). Saadawi demonstrated the necessity of bearing witness through performance, challenging state-structured and culturally distorted compulsions that inquisitive women should be locked up and silenced. Saadawi's experimentation developed language and thoughts that the state deemed dangerous, unthinkable, punishable. Disposing her to the dungeon/prison subjected her to the space of abjection, the space where she is covered over with something like a de facto cast-iron lid, where the state re-makes her speech and writing as a crime, as unintelligible, while she voices and writes to crystalize the situation of those disposed through state terror normalized.

Annita Lucchesi's (2018, 1) call "for languages for violence that are specifically designed to facilitate dialogue" is a call for communication that can bring together Indigenous survivors of gendered violence, whether they be women, girls, trans, or two spirit. Protective "inoculations" come "in creating alternative languages that best fit their nation, community, family, and selves." This call, and its resonances with Ndé women, supported the exploration of root issues of national and Indigenous erasures (taken up in section 2) within compulsory hegemonic Apache culture. I asked: How are Ndé women's truth, clarification, justice and #LandBack being obstructed?

Rebecca Belmore's artwork *Fringe* (2007) is a significant influence. In reference to it, she stated, "My body is a place from which to address the whole notion of history and what has happened to us as Aboriginal people." Invoking the irreparable violence in settler dispossession and intractable conflict, Belmore redirects us to unlearn the victim-centered stereotypes of Indigenous women. She argues, "She can sustain it. . . . she will get up and go on, but she will carry that mark with her. She will turn her back on the atrocities inflicted upon her body and find resilience in the future." In section 2, I explore this connection.

Examining my own memory archive of crisis as my mother, Eloisa Garcia Tamez, fought off government goons deployed to terrorize her into silence, I turned to Inuit vocalist and musician Lucie Idlout (2003). Her song "E5-770: My Mother's Name" shifted my understanding of an Indigenous woman claiming her carceral lineage. Idlout's raw, vocal bellows, shrieks, and rage directed at the perpetrator, Canada, offered crucial tools.

Linda Tuhiwai Smith (2013, 198–99) posits that "choosing the margins" is crucial to "revisiting the concept of struggle" for Indigenous social justice. Ndé posit radical alterity to hegemonic, Apache identity, shaping dissidence to voice Ndé women's matrilineal, land-based belonging. Ndé will re-story, narrativize, map, envision, and embody our relevant discourses, making this the primary, privileged language within which Ndé struggle for self-determination.

Aromantic Refusal of Enemy Images

Aromantic witness of place and context (identificatory engagement with what the hegemonic rejects) means permitting oneself *to just be*; exercises of being human in the gulag became a commitment to a long-term state of being in relationship to ancestors, damaged and beautiful, in El Calaboz, the dungeon. The dungeon played out on our foremothers' bodies, and it wrote on ours, and it has occupied our minds. Being and still existing is an involved, labor-intensive process of self-recognition and determination to keep moving. Being is not always about dismantling the wall; the compulsion of nonwalled peoples to expect walled peoples to still exist, to keep being, and to also dismantle the wall in the impunity zone without juridical personality, is violent, colonial, and destructive. Escalating U.S. violence in the Ndé walled zone is against the wishes of elder matriarchs. Falling for the tactics of the state to reconstruct Ndé as enemies, increases violence and marginalization in a severely marginalized condition of being deemed a perpetual enemy in nonrecognition. "Enemy images," writes Heidi Burgess (2019), is an embedded logic in being American. "If one is convinced that the other side is bent on one's own destruction, and is less human than one's own group, it is much easier to engage in war, human rights violations, or genocide against the opponent."

Enemy images underscore Indigenous nonrecognition and nonstatus, which are genocidal structures in the United States and Canada. However, *how* Indigenous women are affected by nonrecognition and nonstatus is an issue marginalized in the broader Indigenous struggle for self-determination. Smith (2013, 199) argues, "As a blunt instrument, struggle can also promote actions that simply reinforce hegemony and that have no chance of delivering significant social change."

Acknowledging this, I explore intertextuality for creating important spaces of dialogue and understanding between Ndé women in El Caloboz and Dene and Syilx women in unceded Indigenous territories (interior British Columbia). "Dissident friendships" create, support, nurture, and explore empathy to allow for creative examination of power, history, place, and refusal (Nguyen et al. 2016; Basarudin and Bhattacharya 2016). Dissident friendships that endure often involve lifelong enactments of humility and trial and error in decolonizing violence beyond borders.

These are my observations, from a twelve-year relationship with Ndé women's dissent, along the seventy-mile-long, eighteen-foot-high steel-concrete containment wall and the "blunt instrument" calculated to suppress dissent in El Calaboz.

Indigenous Standpoint

A Ndé research standpoint offers a necessary lens to think with and contribute responsibly to Ndé well-being among a people carrying trauma and a learned distrust. Maggie Walter and Chris Andersen (2013, 86) argue, "How a researcher perceives the world in which his or her research is located is inevitably, but complexly, influenced by the filters and frames of life experiences and social, cultural, economic, and personal identity location. The personal, political, cultural, and the academic become entwined. We are not just researchers; we are *socially located* researchers." I identify as Dene Ndé, although my people are described, anthropologically, as Lipan and Plains Apache. I am an enrolled member of the Lipan Apache Band of Texas. I'm a poet, historian, and educator interested in Indigenous matriarchy, law, land protection, and dispossession, as well as Indigenous women's legal resistances, kinship and radical governance in impunity zones, and disaster and intractable conflict. I do Indigenous documentation to clarify resistance to historical and present-day settler genocide in unceded lands. I use my education as a tool to enhance community support and engage in reciprocity. I am a direct descendant of Rio Grande, Nueces River, Trinity River, Frio River, Guadalupe River, Pecos River land grant and peace treaty landholding peoples of Dene Ndé, Peneteka Comanche, Nahua, Jumano Apache, and Tlaxcalteca parents, grandparents, great-grandparents, and great-great-grandparents (Tamez 2010, 323–26, 592–605). I am directly descended from Catholic Basque and Spanish colonists and settlers who occupied the Middle and Lower Rio Grande Valley, Big Bend, La Junta de los Rios, and the Guadalupe Mountain region. I am active in my parent communities. My band is one of the more than four hundred nonrecognized historically documented Indigenous nations abandoned after the Indian Claims Commission adjourned in 1978 (U.S. Indian Claims 1979, 125). In 2012, the United States estimated that federally nonrecognized tribes numbered approximately four hundred, although Indigenous scholars who specialize in nonrecognition would probably agree that the number is higher (U.S. GAO 2012, 1). My work with Ndé women in Texas, and with Syilx, Secwepemc, and Dene women in unceded territories (British Columbia), is ongoing.

Dispossession Early Warning Urgent Action

Between 2007 and 2009, as the U.S. government forcibly constructed a gulag-style wall, my mother (Eloisa Garcia Tamez) and I collaborated to defend individual and collective Ndé rights to Ndé land and legal title still held in community members' possession.[2] In 2007, we co-founded a community-based organization as two Ndé activist-academics in frontline land protection in El Calaboz, and we called ourselves the Lipan Apache Women Defense (LAW-Defense). Within a few months of establishing the U.S. federal case, we had to promptly shift from a family, land-based physical-spiritual refusal and legal resistance to a solidarity-based political, social, and culturally immersed approach activating a new digital-cyber presence. At the time, I was completing a second poetry collection, and I was in my second year of a doctoral program as a member of an all-Indigenous American studies cohort at Washington State University. There was a tense two-year standoff against the aggressive legal waivers approved by Michael Chertoff (secretary of the U.S. Department of Homeland Security) and deployed to obstruct her case progress. She experienced popular support regionally, nationally, and internationally. With her support team, she worked around the clock every day to protect ancestral land from dispossession. This process involved hearings in federal and international courts and tribunals, and constant defense against hostile media, hate groups, and U.S. legal obstructions. In 2009, while members of our protection and defense team were participating in an academic conference in Albuquerque, New Mexico, the U.S. government seized the land, constructed the wall, and pursued aggressive punitive measures against my mother. I represented the Ndé perspective alongside human rights law defenders, accompanied by Denise Gilman and a team of legal and academic supporters, at the Inter-American Commission on Human Rights (IACHR) of the Organization of American States (OAS). It was at this hearing that I wore a handmade Apache camp dress, symbolizing the history of Ndé women's consciousness in the carceral state. I spoke to foster understanding of the violence of U.S. colonial unknowing, dispossession, and Ndé intergenerational memory of dispossession relative to settler genocide and impunity measures attached to this injustice.

In 2011–12, I had recently relocated to unceded Syilx territory (British Columbia), and human rights legal defender Ariel Dulitzky and I continued to work closely with Ndé community members both on the ground and in

2. Legal title here refers to diverse forms of precolonial, colonial, and modern Indigenous land title (based in treaties, land grants, and land transfers between community members) existing in the Lower Rio Grande in 2007 when the U.S. government began litigation for wall construction. See Tamez (2012).

digital platforms to address the question of why Ndé women refuse dispossession and the wall in El Calaboz. While the answer may seem obvious to many, it was not so to a majority of the law students I cotrained for the case, nor to other experts. With elders and leaders, I energized an in-depth, community-focused documentation process to protect families, knowledge, and lands, and to prepare surviving landholders against individual and community-wide dispossession.

After 2009, dispossessions continued in El Calaboz, directed by the Obama administration. Obama's removal, deportation, and detention policies targeted Indigenous peoples, and his negative legacy upholding U.S. impunity in the walled region, El Calaboz, and related places is felt today. Chertoff expanded his reach into global security, walls, and detention beyond the United States, and his standoff with Ndé women faded from American memory.

In late June 2011, the women from El Calaboz hosted a critical decision-making gathering, focused on Ndé lands, knowledge, and rights, inviting Indigenous and non-Indigenous supporters and witnesses to listen, dialogue, and make collective recommendations about community testimonies to past and current Ndé genocide memory. A memorable dialogue emerged after community members and supporters viewed the documentary film *The Lost Ones* (Rose and Saralegui 2011), privileging Ndé memory of the connection between killing fields in Texas, state-sanctioned child abductions, disappeared peoples, and physical separation of survivors. This is all linked to how certain Ndé are connected to U.S. Indian boarding schools, by way of genocides.

At the conclusion of the gathering, invited participants co-created a declaration of continuing resistance and refusal, demanding recognition and acknowledgment of the illegal dispossession, and return of stolen lands to affected peoples. This declaration called on those of critical consciousness to pressure high-level government officials to investigate intractable conflict between Indigenous peoples and Texas.

The 2011 El Calaboz gathering played a significant role in helping open a different, and necessary, Indigenous truthing space. The clarification of history, as a justice space, formed a type of tribunal by those within walled places who needed to reveal, expose, specify, and determine relevant actions and decisions regarding Ndé women's perspectives. Much of the cultural, social, economic, and political history of the region is not authored by Ndé peoples, or by Ndé women. This is a pattern of deep concern.

Memory Poetics

In the aftermath of the wall construction, I became displaced, unable to find academic employment in the United States. By 2010, I moved to work and live in unceded Syilx territory. There, Syilx and Secwepemc families provided me and family members with hospitality, sanctuary, ceremony, feasts, and kinship. Syilx women shared oral history of ancestral Dene-Lipan-Syilx relationality beyond borders. We forged immutable bonds.

Teaching Ndé feminist epistemology, emerged in the history and poetics of Syilx territory, I found my imagination and creativity energized by Syilx and Dene students. They ignited my interest in my literary roots—oral tradition, oral history, memory, difficult knowledge, song, and dance—and they motivated me to create a pedagogy of Indigenous Ndé memory imagined and enacted through an Indigenous embodiment methodology that I have developed in academic and community settings in Texas, Arizona, Washington, and British Columbia. With a relational structure of Dene-Syilx-Ndé ontology establishing, I structured Dene-Ndé methodology. I investigated long-term disaster cycles, cataclysm, and catastrophic knowing in Ndé story mapping.

Said Another Way

Between 2007 and 2012, Ndé peoples, and specifically Ndé women, resisted U.S. militarized, organized dispossession in El Calaboz, in the unceded Kónítsąįį gokíyąą (Big Water Peoples' Country, Texas-Mexico region). I reclaimed Ndé language into my being as a Ndé activist, poet, and historian. Until 2003, scholarship on Indigenous peoples in/of/from Texas was of marginal consequence to Ndé peoples, who have scarce access to the academy, or its literatures and research across social sciences and humanities.

"soveryempty to me"

Between 2009 and 2012, I experienced significant resistance from high-level state and Indigenous rights experts and organizations on the issue of calling attention to genocide and nonrecognition. They suggested I should "mellow" the message, homogenize the Ndé standpoint and collapse it into "border peoples," collapse Ndé colonial history into "border histories," and reduce

Lipan Apache to a generic/universal U.S.-Mexican history. These assimilative forms of settler cognitive fragility confirmed that the Ndé standpoint on Aboriginal title, Crown title, and treaties, seemingly unintelligible to Indigenous rights experts, was unspeakable knowledge. The attempt to censor Ndé interventions at UN Indigenous forums indicated that minimization, denialism, dehumanization, and obstruction extend into the highest stages of international law.

In 2012, after completing an intervention at the United Nations in Geneva, I returned home for a short visit. I checked in with a community elder and shared my frustrations about the sovereignty maze. She said, "That word, sovereignty, it sounds like *soveryempty*, to me." I thought: *she is truthing.*

Truthing: an act of speaking, telling, writing what is directly observed, and strives to make meaning where there is little reliability upon official and sanctioned facts and definitions of the subject; where difficult knowing and shaping language to knowledge of those deemed subversive is contextualized as not important, not to be bothered about, not normal, to be contained and muffled. Managing the unmanageable truthing is the state's, its subjects', and the corporate dominated state's significant investment in superstructure, substructure, megastructure to suppress irritating anomalies which threaten the dominating groups and minority powers.

FIGURE 1 "truthing|disorder," Margo Tamez.

2. Poetics of Ontology and Etiology

||||SOVERYEMPTY||||

||||the wall is not a wall||||there are holes in the wall||||the wall is a reference to U.S. institutions, systems, and structures||||and emulates each||||that is, the wall||||is a prison, but not a complete prison||||but like all Texas prisons||||it refers back to quashing Indigenous dissent to land theft, abuse, and violence||||and hiding internal genocides|||| ||||capitalism is key||||cheap Indigenous and Black labor||||gas and mineral extraction||||cattle||||barbed wire||||and||||willful mythology||||The wall||||is religion||||but, specifically||||the worship of U.S. dollars||||crucifixion of innocents||||by the

guilty||||Elders said there were other walls before this wall||||Texans and Americans conflate||||domination with progress||||This wall emerged from R&D||||and the academy||||The||||wall||||is a spectrum of war||||from the 1876 Declaration of Taking|||to re-purposed materials from Vietnam||||a spectrum of wars on domestic Indigenous activism||||The wall in El Calaboz||||the dungeon||||links past to present to past||||an American story||||past genocide within||||to current genocides||||Indigenous resistances||||XXXX||||The wall is not beautiful||||the wall is||||XXXX||||a family||||a girl||||a woman||||a man||||a boy||||a school||||a dump site||||a cemetery||||a classroom||||a landfill||||a gang rape||||a laboratory||||a universe||||a bank||||a holiday||||a tourist excursion||||a hobby||||a game||||a trick||||a treat||||a job||||a paycheck||||rent||||debt||||credit||||a date||||a holiday||||a secret||||a murderer||||a victim||||triage||||ER|||a highway||||a labor camp||||a decision||||a promise||||a dead end||||a blur||||a microfocus||||a noun||||a verb||||a subject||||a predicate||||a possessive||||a dispossessive||||a singular||||a plural||||a now||||a then||||an obsession|||| a thing||||alive||||created||||undone||||lived||||disbelieved||||owned||||denied||||known||||unknown||||inherited||||contiguous||||claimed||||acknowledged||||recognized||||dismantled||||smoked|||| sovereignty||||XXXX||||Sovereignty||||XXXX||||so very empty||||SOVERYEMPTY||||woked||||we are woked||||it is soveryempty|||they got nothing for us||||except||||THE DUNGEON||||

||||WALLED||||WAY|||OF||||SEEING||||

SINCE 2009, closely and intimately listening, being with/alongside Ndé
    women, girls, and non-Ndé allies defending and reclaiming earth-
    centered protection as a priority for Ndé sustainability and futures,
my poetry shifted. I noticed forms and thoughts merged different   I
    spent more time home in El Calaboz,
the wall's shadow, forced me   to look through the wall's posts
    to observe happenings on our lands   to the south; forced to see
    land and everyday things in the community that happen   on both
    sides   through
the wall's being and existence.   Seeing lined. Seeing sliced.   Eyes
    adjust and metal posts   imprint onto the brain.   Walled-in seeing
    makes me different.

The wall travels me to places of its emergence story.

I followed seeing and knowing the emerging paradigm where I am
myself. My heightened fractured attention, compartmentalized and
split, elongated form thickly situated by heavier, denser, vertically
steeled cemented staccato. Just the facts.

I wasn't confused. I was walled. Walled new normal. 2007–2012, I counted the wall posts; the
number kept changing. The wall, there all the
time. Denying the wall is mutable. I watched
peoples' bodies curl in, when I brought them to
the wall. Some vomited. Some left meetings in
mid-stride, and drove away fast.

So much steel and cement;   so much weight.
hate (self-hate; group on group hate; gender and sex hate; class
hate; racial hate) was there.

Some showed their ability to climb over and under the
wall (with thought and imagination); some showed
deep humility and wordlessness. That offered relief.

One Indigenous artist showed awe for the wall's shape, function
utility; scale. Others felt anger, repulsion by her objectivity.
She realized   this wasn't the first wall over Ndé.
She had perspective.

Difficult Camp Dress Difficult Testimony

There is risk in speaking difficult knowledge. In testimonies provided to the
IACHR/OAS in 2008, I wore a camp dress, seeking to subvert hegemonic,
temporal, and spatial Apache place, informed by U.S. history's influence on
popular ideas of "Apaches," militarization, prison camps, and reservations
in New Mexico and Arizona. Mobilizing Lower Rio Grande peoples' rivered ways of surviving in Texas, I relinked the camp dress to contemporary
carceral dispossession (figure 2) in Kónítsaįį gokíyąą (Big Water Peoples'
Country), a concept I reclaimed from ethnographic archives and Ndé oral

SOS

Wearing a traditional Apache camp dress, I gave a distress signal to a Ndé audience. The camp dress, with origin in the latter nineteenth century, signifies Apache survivance, cultural endurance, resilience, and continuity. The camp dress is also romanticized by settler ethnographers. When I testified at the IACHR/OAS, the dress took on different meanings. Ndé women refusing the wall, and being walled in, embodied a contemporary understanding of U.S. state-sanctioned violence, through a Lower Rio Grande historical lens. Ndé refusers wearing a camp dress shifted the meaning to El Calaboz, walled. The dress drew the lens to a different Ndé subjectivity; a federally nonrecognized Apache; a Ndé dispossession refuser on an international stage, confronting the U.S. government. The dress fabric signifies low-cost fabric stores in a globalized Walmart military-industrial economy, where working-class Indigenous women purchase fabric for ceremony. This dress emplaces and re-maps Ndé genocide survivors from Aboriginal title lands—*not in reservations*—in *Texas*. I created this to be a labor/work dress to use for working in the bush, cooking, dancing, writing, riding a horse, and enacting decisions. Consumers of the hegemonic Apache woman identity wanted me to do things when I wore this dress, on demand: to know and speak my language; to perform my creation stories and oral traditions; to be stoic; and to be aggressive. Outside of the dress, people wanted me to be a "normal" Spanish-surnamed woman without land-based identity from poor, rural, South Texas. Many rejected my revitalization of Kónítsajį gokíyąą as a system to question power. Some wanted me to speak in Spanish, their language of comfort. One anthropologist regularly suggested that I take "time off" and visit "her" university to learn Spanish. During the walling in of El Calaboz, I had regular intractable conflicts with linguistic imperialism. The critique of "Apache studies" dominated by settlers as a colonizing, hegemonic process—and my understanding of the camp dress's disturbing origin among Ndé women held in nineteenth-century prisoner-of-war camps—is a specter for Ndé in El Calaboz ("the dungeon"). The camp is a continuum.

FIGURE 2 SOS "Testimony at the Inter-American Commission on Human Rights / Organization of American States, October 2008." Still photograph, remixed by Margo Tamez. (Video footage from IAC Hearing on Human Rights; Working Group 2008.)

tradition (Tamez 2016, 2018). Raising questions on walled-in beingness and human rights violations, I brought into relief how U.S. impunity renders the nonrecognized as invisible and violable. In 2019, I modified the camp dress: cut it in strips and wrapped it around my body, documenting my "changing woman" consciousness infused by a decade of violence in the wall's construction and its shadow (figure 7, page 231). Critical poetics is a method to reach within one's survivor identity, confront censorship, and transform my re-made camp dress into an updated version, which is truthing the actual condition of being nonrecognized in a walled impunity zone. The cloth strips are intended to convey a type of physical, mental, and emotional bondage. U.S. juridical dehumanization makes possible a casual acceptance of Indigenous nonrecognition. This condition makes atrocities along the wall possible. The wall normalizes aggression against Indigenous peoples, further diminishing matriarchal decision-making on our lands. By claiming one's actual condition, one can begin to claim, re-dress, and transform one's embodied knowledge. Ndé women's historical knowing and memory is an embedded authority. For the nonrecognized and walled-in, this is a new social justice space beyond impunity and recognition.

I reference oral history and archival collections, how western American textile saturates militarization onto Apache women's bodies; prisons, where camp dresses emerge in American 'Apache studies'; women's experiences—as the camp made normal. Apache women, fetishized, as kind of settler domination porn, symbols of American conquest consumed by ethnographers. This is difficult knowledge.	I am concerned with thingification of Apache women's bodies, sex, gender, and class occurring within carceral spaces— prison and camp; subjugation represented in 'camp dress'; symbolizing, Apache women's assimilation, subjugated legibility of women's governance in a relational kinship territory, in relational kinship decision-making, in relational home land, embodying *gozhoo*.	I couldn't deny the juxtaposition of history and re-dispossession, intractable conflict, low intensity conflict, inflicted on my mother and elders in El Calaboz. Linkages and psychic political inflictions are personal. The situated knowing as a Ndé land title holder, and a witness to dispossession beckons re-emergence of knowing, a return of cataclysms. Asks those who hold truth within them to turn off the mute button.

FIGURE 3 "difficult camp|dress, difficult testimony," Margo Tamez.

FIGURE 4 "ethnographic camp dress, invisible woman, Texas-Mexico border, twenty-first century," Margo Tamez.

||||||| This shame shames us. Speaking and unburying unspeakable thoughts.
||||||| This is circular. Speaking breaks silence.

FIGURE 5 "This shame shames us." Margo Tamez.

Writing lines in after-school detention.
Crime: questioning the narrative.
Where: Texas history class, 7th grade.

We are emptied.
We are emptied.

We are extinct.
We are extinct.

See us run.
See us run.

Run run run.
Run run run.

See us question.
See us question.

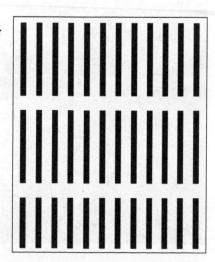

FIGURE 6 Writing lines in after-school detention, Lower Rio Grande Valley, Texas, Margo Tamez.

FIGURE 7. "|Walled-in Affliction|Camp Dress|Distress|SOS|" Margo Tamez.

||||Not here, not there, not anywhere||||

To the nonrecognized, nonrecognition is a long, extended detention without formal procedure. There is no specificity on why you're there and
nowhere.

Who is the warden? When is the release date? How does one appeal?
When . . . ;

A stunted sense of self and being; beingness hijacked;

jumped; managed; masking her numbing she needs to repress rage.

Walled-in beingness is a managed horror; decorated

toxic-tour worthy.

||||Walled in her dreaming. Twin Heroes: Subject |||| Position||||

I've been measuring it. The wall.

I spent nights woken up

immersed in the wall's characteristics. Nobody

officially knows how many pillars make

the wall. Like the nonrecognized,

nobody keeps track of the numbers.

Blurrrrrrrrr.

Each time I go counting, I'm surrounded.

Armed soldiers and armed CBP. I wonder

How many pillars make up the entire wall. I want

To know. I obsessively spend months,

Now years wondering how many damned

Pillars really make up the wall. Knowing

Numbers, in genocide research, is

always emphasized.

FIGURE 8 "Changing Woman|Births Twins|Subject|Position|in|the|Dungeon," Margo Tamez.

translation:

big water house	cut wound illness	grandma laws

FIGURE 9 "In the Dungeon, women are the backbone of language revitalization." Margo Tamez.

||||What a Beautiful Number, after Lucie Idlout||||

"E5-770, my mother's name. E5-770, my mother's name
And what beautiful number
Would I be called by,
born unto, tagged?"
—Lucie Idlout, "E5-770: My Mother's Name"

I inked the case numbers for *Eloisa G. Tamez v. Michael Chertoff, U.S. D.H.S., et al.* (B-08-055) and *Michael Chertoff, U.S. D.H.S., et al.·v. Eloisa G. Tamez* (B-08-351) as testimony of my embodied witnessing from 2007 to 2020, ongoing, in solidarity with all those walled-in without redress, land return, recognition, reparation, or justice. Resistance continues.

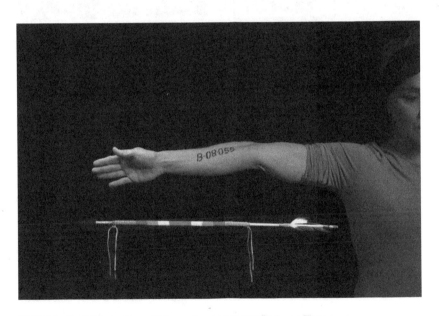

FIGURE 10 "What a beautiful number, B-08-055." Margo Tamez.

What a beautiful number
B-08-055
Eloisa García Tamez'
resistance to Michael Chertoff
(case#) archived.

FIGURE 11 "What a beautiful number, B-08-351." Margo Tamez.

What a beautiful number
B-08-351
Eloisa García Tamez'
dispossession by Michael Chertoff
(case#) archived

3. Conclusion: ||| re-dress, shifting ontology, future beginnings |||

Cedar, a medicine, is a healer.

Cedar provides women and their families with necessary medicine for protecting life during difficult times. Maura Tamez, a Ndé painter and sculptor who graduated from the Okanagan Indian Band's language immersion school, is currently conducting exploratory research on Dene Ndé survival in partnership with Syilx women. In 2015, she received her Isanałesh gotal—painted woman ceremony—mentored by esteemed Mescalero Apache scholar Ines Talamantez, who trained her in the Naííees sacred rite of passage. Visiting Maura in the N'sis'ooloxw Nk'mlpqs village, Ines expressed understanding of connectivity between lands and peoples. Long ago, the ancestors moved within these spaces, and some remained. Ines walked into the mountain with us, drank the clean mountain water, breathed fresh cool air. "I feel honored to be in the place where our ancestors journeyed and carried forward the story of Isanałesh, the girl who survived the flood and traveled on the water to another world, creating the path of pollen," she exclaimed.

Surviving cataclysms, Isanałesh brought knowledge to survive trauma and upheaval, grief, and the suffering that comes with severe physical separation from family and place. In time, she made herself whole again, confronting her changed self and world through her newfound vocabulary in a different and difficult place.

Perhaps that is how intergenerational healing works. Structure, consistency, nurturing, and patience, critical transformation rises and firmly stands ground within the next generation.

Redress will be reframed by the next generation.

Walls fall.

They get dismantled.

Often, humans forget them and neglect remembering why they are there; our memories remain.

With future generations of Indigenous dissidents in mind, in section 2, I used space to shape intertextuality between walls, law, art, and poetry, working to nudge readers out of comfort zones and move them around the page, perhaps forcing a difficult, jarring, and even disturbing spatial and cognitive experience. I sought to make the normal reading and comprehension experience more and more difficult to attain. The repetitive wall building and walled-in intertextual form between the built wall, Indigenous families'

FIGURE 12 "kałdee isdzán" (cedar woman). Maura Tamez. Three-dimensional sculpture, cedar harvested at N'sis'ooloxw (dry creek), Syilx territory, 2018. Private collection. Reproduced by permission from Maura Tamez.

ancestral places, damaged biodiversity, mounds of legal papers and court proceedings, media distortions, silent archives, and institutional silences strongly informed my decision to privilege agency of walled peoples, who know and live differently than nonwalled people. As a Ndé scholar, I refused to scaffold my insights on state violence against Ndé women land protectors, on Ndé women's and peoples' individual and collective losses and devastation. Their testimonies and legal affidavits are in the public record and discussed in articles referenced.

Sometimes, we can barricade ourselves from understanding difficult and complex issues when things are offered to us in the customary, normal way to which we've become accustomed. Early in my mother's legal challenge against Michael Chertoff, she stood on the U.S. federal courthouse steps in Brownsville, Texas, and stated to news reporters, "I'm doing this for my children and grandchildren, as well as your children and grandchildren." Knowing she was speaking to the nation, vis-à-vis journalists pointing mics at her, she understood she was speaking to all Americans following her historical challenge to the U.S. claim to Lipan Apache lands in Texas. Yet, few Americans have utilized the *Tamez v. Chertoff* archives, or integrated a Lipan Apache land protector's Indigenous knowledge on land and law. This is my way of critiquing and contesting the ableist logics in the experience of those who want an easier path to "research" and "study" walled peoples.

This work, thus, is not (auto)ethnographic; that would be a simplistic and inappropriate reading.

It's about a mass experience of being dehumanized, however: that of the able-bodied (those not walled) still needing/wanting the violence to be absorbable to them and on their own terms. Intuiting this settler-colonial "itch" through deep observation, I make the probability of the "itch" being scratched more difficult.

That is, I see the nonwalled settler society as only one of a set of possible subjectivities. They are not the center. From a decolonizing view, it is more important to rip up the page, to gash the normative perception, to unsettle the normalcy of the dominant forms and modes of knowledge translation that tend to erase and distort *the crisis, the disaster, the chaos,* and *the upheaval* within walled-in consciousness. This emerging Indigenous consciousness of walls, prisons, and cages, linked to intergenerational carceral and corporal discipline and impunity, belongs to peoples living the experience in physically walled place, and needs to be delinked from normative borderlands ways of settler thought and consciousness. The conditions of walled-in existence are radically changing, mentally and physically, Indigenous experience in and with spaces of abjection. Indigenous knowing and doing in walled space is worlding a different experience of being, and refusing being iterated as *was*.

Wherever possible, I sought to address the reader's disorientation, weariness, and fatigue. Empathetic to being placed, suddenly, into a different mind and virtual experience, I made every attempt to support the reader in thinking through their feelings of discomfort, without insulting their intelligence. I hope this encouraged readers to be more reflexive about an intuitive human lack of patience with the walled forms and the wall's monotony. I couldn't agree more—the wall is extremely monotonous, dulling, and uncomfortable.

It's true that from within the walled space, you want it to stop. You want it all to end, to get to a point that will make it all make sense, for the repetition to go away.

It won't though. It won't because there isn't a collective will strong enough to make it go away. It is detestable, but people don't want to work together on making the wall go away. There isn't a will to emerge yet, to see that the wall is an expression of their submission to state-sanctioned violence. They want to escape that awful feeling. At that very place, in different ways, and here, I'm saying—*I won't let you.*

Because I care deeply about reader/writer relationships, I brought in traditional forms of analysis, prose, and poetics to explain the approaches being used in each section. I hope these provide tools for further thought on why and how *they are* forms of theorizing power, violence, and the refusals to dispossession utilized by critical Indigenous scholars. We are beginning to write toward different goals, which have been emerging from our frontline rage and irreparable anger and trauma in the last decade.

Finally, through radical indigenization of intertextuality and a casting aside of the book and the page, the body reemerges as the most important surface for inscribing Indigenous numeracy, statistics, law, and horror. Writers learn by writing the body.

Future generations will require different examples for expanding their collective consciousness and understanding of beingness and for finding the roots of how things happen and get so damaged.

Interdisciplinary, creative-critical methodologies are needed for challenging compulsory and regulatory modes of doing. They open up imagination as one of the last free spaces for enacting and embodying refusal and being.

I prioritized these embodiments in order to dismantle the very boundaries being re-formed to contain Indigenous minds, bodies, families, rights, and spirits. Demands for intelligibility, while important, also require that we examine the terms of those through the lens of knowing how ableist bodies in nonwalled places want things a certain way. This is an important part of the beingness of witness, at least in my understanding of walled-in peoples' experiences in El Calaboz. Nonwalled ableism strikes a deeply discordant tone. Resistance to compulsory obedience, in the current Covid-19 era, an en masse dystopia of imposed physical distance, separation, and house arrest, re-instills in some the demand to be unharnessed and de-contained. Indigenous communities who endure enforced and unending carceral containment and separation vis-à-vis walled dispossession will create new truthing languages and forms to witness anti-Indigenous racism, discrimination, and human rights violations. We must invent new ways to document an impunity space of violence, which is denied by the state, which officially doesn't document what it does to federally nonrecognized tribes in Indigenous lands never relinquished nor ceded.

References

Basarudin, Azza, and Himika Bhattacharya. 2016. "Meditations on Friendship: Politics of Feminist Solidarity in Ethnography." In *Dissident Friendships: Feminism, Imperialism, and Transnational Solidarity*, edited by Elora Halim Chowdhury and Liz Philipose, 43–70. Champaign: University of Illinois Press.

Belmore, Rebecca. 2007. *Fringe*. Artwork. *Rebecca Belmore* (artist's website). Accessed September 15, 2020. https://www.rebeccabelmore.com/fringe/.

Burgess, Heidi. 2019. "Enemy Images." *Beyond Intractability*, edited by Guy Burgess and Heidi Burgess. Conflict Information Consortium, University of Colorado, Boulder. Posted October 2003, revised December 2019. https://www.beyondintractability.org/essay/enemy_image.

Idlout, Lucie. 2003. *E5-770: My Mother's Name*. Heart Wreck Records, AR 601122. CD.

Khaleeli, Homa. 2010. "Nawal El Saadawi: Egypt's Radical Feminist." *Guardian*, April 15, 2010. https://www.theguardian.com/lifeandstyle/2010/apr/15/nawal-el-saadawi-egyptian-feminist.

Lipan Apache Women Defense. 2013. "Eloisa García Tamez goes back to federal court against the United States." *Lipan Apache Women Defense* (blog). April 27, 2013. https://lipancommunitydefense.wordpress.com/2013/04/27/eloisa-garcia-tamez-goes-back-to-federal-court-against-the-united-states/.

Lucchesi, Annita. 2018. "-hóhta'hané: Mapping Genocide & Restorative Justice in Native America." *Proceedings of the International Cartographic Association* 1 (71). https://doi.org/10.5194/ica-proc-1-71-2018.

Mbembe, Achille. 2003. "Necropolitics." Translated by Libby Meintjes. *Public Culture* 15 (1): 11–40.

Nguyen, Nicole, A. Wendy Nastasi, Angie Mejia, Anya Stanger, Meredith Madden, and Chandra Talpade Mohanty. 2016. "Epistemic Friendships: Collective Knowledge-Making Through Transnational Feminist Praxis." In *Dissident Friendships: Feminism, Imperialism, and Transnational Solidarity*, edited by Elora Halim Chowdhury and Liz Philipose, 11–42. Champaign: University of Illinois Press.

Rose, Susan, and Manuel Saralegui. 2011. *The Lost Ones: Long Journey Home*. Montana CINE International Film Festival. Documentary film, 42 min.

Smith, Linda Tuhiwai. 2013. *Decolonizing Methodologies: Research and Indigenous Peoples*. 2nd ed. Dunedin, New Zealand: Otago University Press.

Tamez, Margo. 2010. "Returning Lipan Apache Women's Laws, Lands, & Power in El Calaboz Ranchería, Texas-Mexico Border." PhD diss., Washington State University.

Tamez, Margo. 2012. "Kónitsąąíí gokíyaa Ndé: Big Water Peoples' Homeland—A Shadow of Self-Determination in a Bifurcated Traditional Territory." Paper presented at the UN Seminar "Strengthening Partnerships Between States and Indigenous Peoples," Geneva, July 16–17, 2012.

Tamez, Margo. 2016. "Indigenous Women's Rivered Refusals in El Calaboz." *Diálogo* 19 (1): 7–21.

Tamez, Margo. 2018. "Margo Tamez on Indigenous Resistance to the U.S.-Mexico Border Wall." Interview. In *Speaking of Indigenous Politics: Conversations with Activists, Scholars, and Tribal Leaders*, by J. Kēhaulani Kauanui, 293–311. Minneapolis: University of Minnesota Press.

Thomason, Dovie. 2015. "My Name is Dovie." Indigenous oral autobiography performance. University of Manitoba. January 22, 2015. Vimeo video, 32:46. https://vimeo.com/193972360.

U.S. Government Accountability Office (GAO). 2012. *Indian Issues: Federal Funding for Non-Federally Recognizes Tribes*. Report to the Honorable Dan Boren, House of Representatives. GAO-12-348. Washington, D.C.: GAO.

U.S. Indian Claims Commission. 1979. *United States Indian Claims Commission, August 13, 1946, September 30, 1978: Final Report*. Washington, D.C.: Government Printing Office.

Vimalassery, Manu, Juliana Hu Pegues, and Alyosha Goldstein. 2016. "On Colonial Unknowing." *Theory and Event* 19 (4). https://muse.jhu.edu/article/633283.

Walter, Maggie, and Chris Andersen. *Indigenous Statistics: A Quantitative Research Methodology*. London: Routledge, 2013.

Working Group on Human Rights and the Border Wall. 2008. "Video of the Working Group on Human Rights and the Border Wall Hearing Before the IAC." University of Texas School of Law. October 2008. Texas ScholarWorks. http://hdl.handle.net/2152/15720.

Indigenous Women and Violence in the Time of Coronavirus

LYNN STEPHEN AND SHANNON SPEED

A s final revisions to this manuscript were completed, we had already entered a new historical moment from that in which the manuscript was drafted. The onset of the coronavirus pandemic has dramatically changed and will continue to change the world. While, in this book, we focused on the harsh structural conditions in which Indigenous women are subject to multiple violences and the multiple ways they seek justice, even those terrible conditions seem favorable in comparison to today. The historic moment of pandemic we are living in as we write this epilogue has both laid bare already existing structural inequalities of all kinds and heightened them even further. Here, we want to consider how the structure of settler logics and their particular intersectional gendered impact in this pandemic have important power effects in this moment and beyond. We also want to suggest the importance of Indigenous women's intergenerational and transnational knowledge, and a commitment to holding space for that knowledge in multiple carceral spaces experienced by Indigenous women inside and outside of their bodies.

"The Deadliest Pandemic": Silence and Gendered Violence at Home

As many countries have been under strict stay-at-home orders, Indigenous women trying to flee violence, as well as those that already have—the displaced, the deported, and those sitting in detention centers or awaiting asylum hearings in the United States—have seen their vulnerability sky-rocket. Indigenous and other women who experience violence in Mexico, in Guatemala, or in the United States—whether at home, at work, in public, or in their communities—have nowhere to which to flee. All three countries have been under curfew orders and stay-at-home decrees, and many shelters for women fleeing gendered violence, particularly in Guatemala, have been shut down. While complaints filed about violence against women are up in some countries, in Guatemala they fell by 75.46 percent during the first two weeks of the quarantine (Gámez 2020). This is not because violence has decreased, but because women have been silenced.

Claudia Hernández, executive director of Fundación Sobrevivientes (Survivors Foundation), and Giovanna Lemus, executive coordinator of the Grupo Guatemalteco de Mujeres (Group of Guatemalan Women), both stated to the press in April 2020 that their shelters were closed.[1] "We are not going to take in anyone . . . while we are going through the forty days of quarantine to assure that the persons who we take in are not infected with COVID-19," reported Lemus (Gámez 2020). In places with no shelters and few to no social services, the pandemic has made things even worse. Women who might not have gone to the police but who would have normally gone to family members, neighbors, local NGOs, or even church groups for support are now not able to do so. They have to stay at home.

In Mexico, almost one thousand women were murdered in the first three months of 2020, leading advocates to warn that the country is seeing a rise in gendered violence due to the coronavirus lockdown and raising fears that more women might die as a result of violence than of COVID-19 during the pandemic (Oppenheim 2020). This, in a country where the femicide rate had already more than doubled in the previous five years, and in which it is estimated that seven of ten femicide victims are killed in their own homes. The stay-at-home orders leave women trapped with violent perpetrators, leaving little route for escape. Economic stress adds to the dynamics of vio-lence, creating a dangerous scenario for women. The Red Nacional de Refu-gios (National Network of Shelters)—a network of almost seventy refuges

---

1. Fundación Sobrevivientes administers a shelter in Guatemala City for adult victims of violence, and the Grupo Guatemalteco de Mujeres oversees seven *centros de apoyo integral para mujeres sobrevivientes de violencia* (centers of integral support for women survivors of violence) across the southern part of Guatemala.

across Mexico for women who have suffered violence—reported that calls in March and April 2020 were up more than 80 percent (Oppenheim 2020). Between April and May, reports put the rise in emergency calls to Mexico's shelters at 60 percent (Prusa, García Nice, and Soledad 2020; Franco 2020). As one politician framed it, "The deadliest pandemic for women in our country, more than the coronavirus, is feminicidal violence" (Martha Tagle, Citizens' Movement Party, cited in Oppenheim 2020). The UN Office for Coordination of Humanitarian Affairs echoed this sentiment, saying, "for many women living through the coronavirus pandemic in Latin America, the greater health risk might be staying home" (Prusa, García Nice, and Soledad 2020).

In summer 2019, co-author Lynn Stephen worked collaboratively to carry out focus groups with Indigenous women in Guatemala on their strategies when confronted with gendered violence. Her collaborators included political scientist Erin Beck of the University of Oregon; Magdalena Ordoñez, Mam, regional delegate for the Defensoría de la Mujer Indígena (DEMI, National Office for the Defense of Indigenous Women) in Huehuetenango; Miriam Hernandez, Aguacateca, social worker at DEMI; Odilia Jimenez, Mam, of the Asociación de Mujeres Rio Isquizal (Women's Association of Rio Izquizal) in San Sebastián, Huehuetango; and Julia and Argelia (both Mam who didn't want their last names used) of the Fraternidad de Presbiteriales Mayas (Maya Presbyterian Fraternity), centered in Xela. These collaborators organize and support women's groups in dozens of rural Indigenous communities in the departments of Huehuetenango and Quetzaltenango. Working with them, we held five one-time focus group conversations of between five and eight women on experiences with police, local judges, the formal justice system, barriers to accessing these systems, and the systems of support they use when confronted with different types of violence. Most of the women we had conversations with were Mam, but one group also included Aguacateco women from Aguacatán, Huehuetenango.

Indigenous women from the focus groups who shared that they would not go to police, local officials, or local justices of the peace to report gendered violence—often because of terrible past experiences—nevertheless said that they would seek out help with a local NGO, church, friends, or relatives. For example, Lucretia shared what a local female justice of the peace told her when she wanted to receive a restraining order against her husband, who had beaten her so badly that he injured her leg:

And the judge said: "reconcile, this is an opportunity." She saw where I was beaten, but she said, you have an opportunity to reconcile. My husband started to make stuff up that wasn't true, but the judge believed him. That how things ended up in the local court. Then my husband just got used to hitting me, to hurting me, to treating me terrible. Then a friend of mine said to me, "you need to go to a place where they support Indigenous women."

Following this incident, Lucretia went from her community to the regional city of Huehuetenango, where she saw an Indigenous psychologist at the local branch of DEMI and also had access to an Indigenous social worker who supported her. Had Lucretia faced this situation in 2020, under lockdown orders, she would not have been able to leave her house, let alone make the trip to the regional capital. In a focus group outside of Xela, women shared how despite the existence of police and official courts, they most often went to fellow church members for support and advice, sometimes in their own communities, but also in the regional capital.

In the context of the pandemic, shelter-in-place orders and strictly enforced curfews cut off these forms of support and access to assistance. In Guatemala, as elsewhere, the ordinary, everyday obstacles to formal and informal mechanisms of support and justice for survivors of gendered violence are even more sharply amplified. Lucrecia de Cáceres, secretary for women in the Guatemalan attorney general's office, reported in the press, "We see women with fractured noses, injured arms, bloody heads, and we have between five and six rapes that were reported." Despite the decrease in reported violence, Cáceres noted, "we are worried, because it is not possible that violence has decreased so drastically and violence doesn't exist, but on the contrary, it is the silence of many women in their homes" (Cuevas 2020). If a government official like Cáceres is acknowledging women's silence and inability to access justice, find protection, and report violence, then we can imagine the entrenched terror women face on a daily basis.

Immigration and Asylum in the COVID Era

On April 20, 2020, U.S. president Donald Trump tweeted about a new executive order: "In light of the attack from the Invisible Enemy, as well as the need to protect the jobs of our GREAT American Citizens, I will be signing an Executive Order to temporarily suspend immigration into the United States!" (@realDonaldTrump). This tweet brings together several anti-immigrant narratives that have been circulating for decades in the United States, binding them to disease. "The Invisible Enemy" directly refers to COVID-19, but as a metaphor it also evokes terrorism and terrorists. It was used to exclude Central American migrants in the 1970s and 1980s, applied against people from the Middle East and other areas of the world after 9/11, and broadly expanded by Trump in his travel ban of 2018, which was upheld by the U.S. Supreme Court. The invisible enemy metaphor also serves Trump's continued criminalization of all categories of migrants and immigrants. The reference to "GREAT American Citizens" clearly evokes whiteness, leaning on historical white supremacy, and pandering to the president's political base. By claiming to suspend all immigration to the United States, he is trying to fulfill a long-held settler fantasy that in fact has come close to reality.

Some women we wrote about in this book were asylum seekers. Over the past year, access to asylum in the United States has been effectively shut down through a combination of policies including the Migrant Protection Protocols or "Remain in Mexico," which proclaimed Mexico to be a "safe second country," fast tracking deportations in remote immigration courts, incarcerating families and children, and closing the border and denying access to asylum seekers. According to an April 2020 article in the *Washington Post,* "During the past few weeks of the coronavirus crisis, U.S. border authorities have expelled 10,000 border crossers in an average of just a little more than an hour and a half each, which has effectively emptied out U.S. Border Patrol holding facilities of detainees" (Miroff, Darsey, and Armus 2020). And the United States, with by far the largest number of COVID-19 cases and deaths as of fall 2000, has been steadily deporting Mexican and Central American detainees. According to the Guatemalan government, dozens of deportees who were flown back to Guatemala from the United States in late March and April tested positive for COVID-19 (Dickerson and Semple 2020). The majority of these refugees are Indigenous.

As of May 1, 2020, the United States had 246,608 Guatemala immigration cases pending, primarily for asylum (TRAC 2020). Guatemala has the largest number of pending immigration cases in the United States. The suspension of asylum hearings means that many Indigenous Guatemalans in the United States seeking asylum are now living suspended lives—often lacking a source of income and facing total uncertainty about when their cases will be heard. While until recently immigration courts were rushing through the cases of recent arrivals, particularly those in detention, the pandemic's arrival in the United States temporarily closed many U.S. immigration courts. Only immigration courts adjacent to detention centers are fully open—which excludes most immigration courts. The vast majority of immigration courts not located in or next to detention centers were only open for the filing of cases. According to the U.S. Executive Office for Immigration Review in mid-April, "All non-detained hearings scheduled through May 15, 2020, have been postponed" (U.S. Department of Justice 2020a). As of October 15, 2020, hearings in non-detained cases at courts without an announced date were postponed through October 30, 2020. Some immigration courts remained closed in October 2020, except for filing and detained hearings, creating a further backlog (U.S. Department of Justice 2020b).

A majority of backlogged cases involve people not in detention, thus many Indigenous migrants seeking asylum who are already in the United States face an uncertain future. For Indigenous women awaiting their asylum hearings in the States, the uncertainty of the pandemic is further magnified by the precarity of their legal status and inability to work. This can render them dependent on abusers for economic survival. Many confront this uncertainty in crowded living situations, with multiple families sharing apartments and houses and facing food scarcity together. Fear of deportation continues as many cohabitate with undocumented family members. Further, shelter-in-place orders leave migrant women in the United States, like women in Mexico and Guatemala, trapped with abusers. They may be even less likely to make a call for help if their Spanish is limited, or if they fear deportation.

New Forms of Caging During COVID

Co-author Shannon Speed (2019, 71–72) has written elsewhere about how incarceration in many ways characterizes the lives of Indigenous women at home and in migration. In making this case, she draws on the work of Kelly Lytle Hernandez (2017) about the human caging of immigrants, what Hernandez positions as part of the settler drive to revoke the right of racialized outsiders to be within the invaded territory, and its contemporary form in relation to the neoliberal mandate for privatization (of prisons and many other institutions). Long before the pandemic, women were caged by their inability to report violence or gain redress for it; by criminalization due to their race, class, and gender; and by forced migrations in which they are held captive in immigrant "safe" houses, cartel kidnapping quarters, trailer trucks, border camps, or detention centers. They are trapped by their deportability once in the United States. Their lives are so multiply constrained by various forces that they are, simply stated, not free.

The pandemic has increased this carceral dynamic, as women experiencing intrafamilial violence on stay-at-home orders are trapped with their partners, women in prisons are trapped with the virus, and women in migration are subject to even more draconian policies than before the pandemic. State-induced quarantines, curfews (in Guatemala), and shelter-in-place orders result in prison at home, imprisonment in the body and in the mind. The violence of prolonged incarceration is paralleled by what can happen in homes where Indigenous women cannot leave, cannot access any kind of assistance, and may be severely constrained not only by male perpetrators in their home, but also by local police and authorities. If they do flee, these women are often locked inside of tractor trailers on their journey through Mexico, or tightly controlled in the trucks and buses that are the transportation system to the border. Some are kidnapped and detained by organized crime groups in Mexico or on the border. Once they reach the border, most are detained and put into detention in U.S. Immigration and Customs Enforcement (ICE) facilities. If released into the United States, they are shacked with ankle bracelet monitors, extending the carceral experience of Indigenous women refugees to all spaces in their life with this public brand of deportability. Pandemic-inspired policies such as the suspension of immigration to the United States and the Remain in Mexico policy either leave women trapped in the United States in a permanent state of surveilled deportability due to suspended asylum hearings, or trapped in Mexico, by no stretch of the imagination a "safe second country."

As some contributors to this volume have discussed, Indigenous women are frequently criminalized due to their race, class, and gender, both at home and in migration. Incarceration in the COVID era brings heightened danger and injustice. For Indigenous women who are imprisoned, being detained with the virus can be fatal. In Mexico, Leo Zavaleta—Me'phaa poet, member of the Colectiva Editorial Hermanas de la Sombra (Shadow Editorial Collective; see chapter 2), torture survivor, and leader who was unjustly incarcerated—had her health continually weakened through the conditions in prison, just like so many imprisoned women do. She left us on May 9, 2020, due to COVID-19, exacerbated by her underlying conditions. She was not alone. COVID outbreaks in prisons and immigration detention centers pose a real threat to the lives of those they hold captive.

In short, the spaces of literal and embodied incarceration have exponentially multiplied in the pandemic, caging Indigenous women in new and insidious ways. The words and spirit of Zavaleta are with us, as are those of the many incarcerated Indigenous women in the world who continue to resist and create new knowledge despite different forms of caging.

Final Thoughts

When we began this book, the authors shared a collective concern with the heightened states of violence the women we work with were experiencing. With the book, we sought to explore that violence, considering how women worked toward justice, how they achieved it, or how they were variously structurally constrained from doing so. We wanted to consider how settler-capitalist state structures repeatedly subjected Indigenous women to intersectional violence. We also wanted to consider our own place in this picture, as activist scholars with profound political and personal commitments to those with whom we worked. We wanted to reflect, for a future generation of scholars, on the various contradictions, constraints, and embodied effects of such work and the possibilities for new ways of conceptualizing and practicing embodied, activist research. As suggested by Margo Tamez in this volume (chapter 8), "creative-critical methodologies are needed for challenging compulsory and regulatory modes of doing. They open up imagination as one of the last free spaces for enacting and embodying refusal and being."

The coronavirus pandemic has, nearly everywhere, laid bare the vast inequities and injustices of the current state of settler capitalism. For Indigenous women, already intersectionally subject to some of the worst conditions of settler capitalism, violence and caging are more heightened than ever, and justice more elusive. Yet, Indigenous women continue to persevere and build survival strategies—evidence of strength, resilience, and creativity. Indigenous peoples have survived centuries of settler-generated pandemics and settler-capitalist caging. They have fought for centuries to retain lifeways that are distinct. It is our hope, as we close this book, that beyond the pandemic, our countries will look to Indigenous people for the knowledge that is needed to move beyond settler capitalism, potentially saving our planet and our species in the process. In the meantime, we wish Indigenous women everywhere success in their fight for justice and an end the violence that cages them.

References

Cuevas, Douglas. 2020. "Cuarentena: Mujeres escapan de la violencia en plena crisis por el coronavirus." *Prensa Libre*, April 14, 2020. https://www.prensalibre.com /guatemala/comunitario/mujeres-escapan-de-la-violencia-en-plena-crisis-del -coronavirus/.

Dickerson, Kaitlin, and Kirk Semple. 2020. "U.S. Deported Thousands amid COVID-19 Outbreak. Some Proved to Be Sick." *New York Times*, April 18, 2020. https://www .nytimes.com/2020/04/18/us/deportations-coronavirus-guatemala.html.

Franco, Marina E. 2020. "La violencia contra las mujeres en México se agrava ante el COVID-19." *Noticias Telemundo*, April 7, 2020.

Gámez, Natalia. 2020. "Cuarentena: Aunque la padezcan, menos mujeres denuncia violencia." *Con Criterio*, April 6, 2020. http://concriterio.gt/cuarentena-aunque -la-padezcan-menos-mujeres-denuncian-violencia/.

Hernández, Kelly Lytle. 2017. *City of Inmates: Conquest, Rebellion, and the Rise of Human Caging in Los Angeles, 1771–1965*. Chapel Hill: University of North Carolina Press.

Miroff, Nick, Josh Dawsey, and Teo Armus. 2020. "Trump Administration Working Out Details of Suspending Immigration During Coronavirus Crisis, Plans to Close Off the United States to a New Extreme." *Washington Post*, April 21, 2020. https:// www.washingtonpost.com/immigration/coronavirus-trump-immigration/2020 /04/21/a2a465aa-837a-11ea-9728-c74380d9d410_story.html.

Oppenheim, Maya. 2020. "Mexico Sees Almost 1,000 Women Murdered in Three Months as Domestic Abuse Concerns Rise amid Coronavirus." *Independent*, April 28, 2020. https://www.independent.co.uk/news/world/americas/mexico-coronavirus -domestic-violence-women-murder-femicide-lockdown-a9488321.html.

Prusa, Anya, Beatriz García Nice, and Olivia Soledad. 2020. "Pandemic of Violence: Protecting Women During COVID-19." *Weekly Asado* (blog), Wilson Center. May 15, 2020. https://www.wilsoncenter.org/blog-post/pandemic-violence -protecting-women-during-covid-19.

Speed, Shannon. 2019. *Incarcerated Stories: Indigenous Women Migrants and Violence in the Settler-Capitalist State*. Chapel Hill: University of North Carolina Press.

TRAC Immigration. 2020. Immigration Court Backlog Tool. Syracuse University. Data updated May 1, 2020. https://trac.syr.edu/phptools/immigration/court _backlog/.

U.S. Department of Justice. 2020a. Executive Office for Immigration Review. "EOIR Operational Status During the Coronavirus Pandemic." Accessed April 15, 2020. https://www.justice.gov/eoir/eoir-operational-status-during-coronavirus -pandemic. Removed from website as of October 1, 2020.

U.S. Department of Justice. 2020b. "EOIR Operational Status. Find Immigration Courts Operational Status." Accessed October 16, 2020. https://www.justice.gov /eoir-operational-status.

CONTRIBUTORS

R. Aída Hernández Castillo was born in Ensenada, Baja California, and earned her doctorate in anthropology from Stanford University in 1996. She is professor and senior researcher at the Center for Research and Advanced Studies in Social Anthropology (CIESAS) in Mexico City. She began working as a journalist for a Central American press agency when she was eighteen years old. Since her undergraduate years, she has combined her academic work with media projects in radio, video, and journalism. Her academic work promotes Indigenous and women's rights in Latin America. She has done fieldwork in Indigenous communities in the Mexican states of Chiapas, Guerrero, and Morelos, and she has also worked with Guatemalan refugees and with African immigrants in southern Spain. She has published twenty-two books including, most recently, *Multiple InJustices: Indigenous Women, Law, and Political Struggle in Latin America*, and her academic work has been translated into English, French, Portuguese, and Japanese. She received the LASA/Oxfam America Martin Diskin Memorial Lectureship in 2003 for her activist research, and she held the Simón Bolívar Chair in Latin American Studies from the University of Cambridge in 2013–14.

Morna Macleod is a researcher and professor in the social science postgraduate program at the Autonomous State University of Morelos (UAEM), Mexico. She has a master's degree and a doctorate in Latin American studies from the National Autonomous University of Mexico (UNAM). She was a human rights worker in the late 1970s and early 1980s, first with Chile (from London) and then with Guatemala (from Mexico). She worked in Oxfam (UK and Australia) and was also an independent consultant based in Mexico for over a decade. Some of her recent publications include the co-edited volumes *Resisting Violence: Emotional Communities in Latin America* (with Natalia De Marinis) and *América latina: Entre el autoritarismo y la democratización, 1930–2012* (co-edited with Marta Casaús Arzú), as well as the solo-authored books *Ri Ajxokon ri Amaq'i' Chi Iximulew: Organizaciones revolucionarias, indianistas y pueblos indígenas en el conflicto armado—Análisis y debate* and *Nietas del Fuego, Creadoras del Alba. Luchas político-culturales de mujeres mayas.* She is currently working on multiple violence in Mexico and particularly in Morelos.

Mariana Mora has a doctorate in social anthropology from the University of Texas at Austin and a master's degree in Latin American studies from Stanford University. She is currently based at the Center for Research and Advanced Studies in Social Anthropology (CIESAS) in Mexico City and was previously an associate professor in the Department of Anthropology at Tulane University. Her research has centered on Indigenous autonomy, the critical use of rights, and the current context of violence in Mexico. She is the author of *Kuxlejal Politics: Indigenous Autonomy, Race, and Decolonizing Research in Zapatista Communities* and co-editor of *Luchas "muy otras": Zapatismo y autonomía en las comunidades indígenas de Chiapas*, and she has additional publications in both English and Spanish. Her teaching areas include social movements, state formation, violence, race and racialization, human rights, Indigenous and Afro-descended people in Latin America, decolonial activist research methods, testimonies and ethnography, and feminist anthropology.

María Teresa Sierra is a senior research professor at the Center for Research and Advanced Studies in Social Anthropology (CIESAS) in Mexico City. She is member of Mexico's National Research System (SNI 3) and the Mexican Academy of Sciences. She received a doctorate in sociology from the University of Paris VIII. Her areas of research include legal and political anthropology; gender, violence, and human rights; identity politics; and cultural diversity. She founded the Latin American Network of Legal Anthropology and was president of its Sixth Congress, held in Mexico. Her publications include the monographs *Discurso, cultura y poder* and *"Haciendo justicia." Interlegalidad, derecho y género en regiones indígenas*, as well as the co-edited volumes *El Estado y los indígenas en tiempos del PAN: Neoindigenismo, legalidad e identidad* (with R. Aída Hernández Castillo and Sarela Paz), *Justicia y diversidad en América Latina: Pueblos indígenas ante la globalización* (with Victoria Chenaut, Magdalena Gómez, and Héctor Ortiz), *Justicias indígenas y Estado: Violencias contemporáneas* (with R. Aída Hernández Castillo and Rachel Sieder), and *Pueblos indígenas y Estado en México, la disputa por la justicia y el derecho* (with Santiago Bastos).

Shannon Speed is a tribal citizen of the Chickasaw Nation of Oklahoma. She is director of the American Indian Studies Center (AISC) and professor of gender studies and anthropology at the University of California, Los Angeles. She has worked for the last two decades in Mexico and in the United States on issues of Indigenous autonomy, sovereignty, gender, neoliberalism, violence, migration, social justice, and activist research. She has published six monographs and edited volumes, including, most recently, *Incarcerated Stories: Indigenous Women Migrants and Violence in the Settler-Capitalist State*. Earlier works include the monograph *Rights in Rebellion: Indigenous Struggle and Human Rights in Chiapas*, as well as the co-edited volumes *Gobernar (en) la diversidad: Experiencias indígenas desde América Latina* (with Xochitl Leyva Solano and Araceli Burguete), *Human Rights in the Maya Region: Global Politics, Cultural Contentions, and Moral Engagements* (with Pedro Pitarch and Xochitl Leyva Solano), and *Dissident Women: Gender and Cultural Politics in Chiapas* (with R. Aída Hernández Castillo and Lynn Stephen). Dr. Speed served as the president of the Native American and Indigenous Studies Association (NAISA) from 2018 to 2020. She was born and raised in Los Angeles.

Lynn Stephen is Philip H. Knight Chair and Distinguished Professor of Anthropology at the University of Oregon, where she is also a participating faculty member in Indigenous, race, and ethnic studies (IRES), Latin American studies, and women's, gender, and sexuality studies. She founded the Center for Latino/a and Latin American Studies (CLLAS) and served as director for nine years (2007–16). In 2018–19, she served as president of the Latin American Studies Association (LASA), with 12,000 members in up to ninety countries. Her scholarly work centers on the impact of globalization, migration, nationalism, and the politics of culture on Indigenous communities in the Americas. She engages political economy, ethnohistory, and ethnography to create a hemispheric lens on major challenges faced by Indigenous peoples (out-migration, tourism, economic development, and low-intensity war) and their creative responses to these challenges. Her work highlights Indigenous epistemologies and their theoretical and methodological relevance to advancing our knowledge of human-environmental connectivity. She has also produced groundbreaking analyses on gender, economic development, and migration; globalization and social movements; indigenous autonomy; and, through her concept of the transborder, the history of Latinx communities spread across multiple borders. She has a strong commitment to collaborative research projects that produce findings accessible to the wider public, and her work includes films such as *Sad Happiness: Cinthya's Transborder Journey* and websites such as the digital companion site for her book *We Are the Face of Oaxaca: Testimony and Social Movements* (also published in Spanish as *Somas la Cara de Oaxaca*). Stephen has written over ninety scholarly articles and authored or edited fourteen books, including *Otros Saberes: Collaborative Research on Indigenous and Afro-Descendant Cultural Politics* (co-edited with Charles R. Hale) and *Transborder Lives: Indigenous Oaxacans in Mexico, California, and Oregon.*

Margo Tamez (Dene Ndé; Lipan Apache Band of Texas) is an associate professor in Indigenous studies at the University of British Columbia, Okanagan. She holds a PhD in American studies from Washington State University, an MFA in poetry from Arizona State University, and two BAs from the University of Texas at Austin: one in art history and the other in archaeological studies. Her creative writing, scholarship, and advocacy bring together Indigenous epistemologies, place-based participatory methodologies (encompassing southern and southwest Texas and the Rio Grande River Valley), Indigenous poetics, gender and women's studies, revitalization, oral tradition, visual sovereignty, genocide studies, and Indigenous recognition. Born and raised in the Ndé Kónitsąąíí Gokíyaa (Big Water Peoples' Country/Texas), she is the author of *Alleys and Allies, Naked Wanting,* and *Raven Eye.* Her books in progress include a historical monograph, "We Remained: Transhistorical Genocide, Belonging, Memory and Knowing in Ndé Kónitsąąíígokíyaa, Big Water Country"; a new volume of poetry, "Father | Genocide: New and Selected Work, 2007–2017"; and an edited volume,

"Gathering Together We Decide: Indigenous Peoples, Dispossession Memories, and Resistance Methodologies, 2007–2017."

Irma A. Velásquez Nimatuj is a journalist, social anthropologist, and international spokeswoman. She has been at the forefront of struggles for respect for Indigenous cultures. She was executive director of the Mecanismo de Apoyo a Pueblos Indígenas Oxlajuj Tzikin (Support Mechanism for Indigenous Peoples) from 2005 to 2013. She is the first Maya K'iche' woman to earn a doctorate in social anthropology, and she initiated the court case that made racial discrimination illegal in Guatemala. She has won numerous academic fellowships and awards for her journalism. She was a member of the Latin American Consulting Group of Indigenous Leaders for UNICEF and participates in the UN through the Permanent Forum on Indigenous Issues. She also served as adviser on Indigenous issues for the Americas and the Caribbean Regional Office of UN Women (2014–15). She is the author of *Pueblos indígenas, estado y lucha por tierra en Guatemala* and *La pequeña burguesía indígena comercial de Guatemala: Desigualdades de clase, raza y género*. She writes a weekly newspaper column in *El Periódico de Guatemala*, and through both her political and academic efforts she seeks to create viable and realistic ways to foster equality for Indigenous people and a truly democratic and participatory democracy in Guatemala.

INDEX

Afro-descent peoples, 80, 113, 150, 158, 160, 175, 177, 254; Afro-Brazilian feminist scholars, 45; Afro-Mexican peoples, 169, 170, 171, 175

Aguilar, Yolanda, 186–87, 205; time limitations in public tribunals, 187

American Civil Liberties Union (ACLU), 129

American Correctional Association (ACA), 62, 63–64, 65

anthropology: activist research methodology, 133–6; and colonial past, 31, 33; anthropological research, 95; challenge of avoiding victimization, 34; colonial logics of anthropological knowledge production, 165; complexities in anthropological research, 29, 32; decolonization of, 32; personal challenges in conducting the research, 121; potential of producing a pornography of violence, 34, 200; tensions in, 33. *See also* collaboration

Aranguren Romero, Juan Pablo, 66; contradictions in social research, 66

Asamblea de Pueblos Indígenas del Istmo de Tehuantepec en Defensa de la Tierra y el Territorio (Assembly of Indigenous Peoples of the Tehuantepec Isthmus in Defense of Land and Territory), 173

assimilationist projects, 4, 11, 36, 150, 170n6, 184, 185, 217. *See also* settler colonialism/states

Asociación de Comadronas del Area Mam (Mam Area Association of Midwives), 136

Asociación de Mujeres Río Isquizal (Río Isquizal Women's Association), 136

Atlacholoaya Social Readaptation Center (Morelos, Mexico), 50–64; arbitrary detentions, 55; Life Histories workshop, 50, 52, 53, 54, 55; methodology, 51; racial and class hierarchies in, 52; torture, 55. *See also* criminalization; prisonalization

Ayotzinapa (Guerrero), 9; disappearance of forty-three students in, 9, 81

Beatty, Andrew, 29n2, 37–38

Beck, Erin, 135, 137, 245

Behar, Ruth, 28; emotion, social commitment, and political engagement, 28; personal and intellectual understanding, 28

Muñoz Cabrera, Patricia, 75, 78, 92n8, 96; violence against Indigenous women (VAW), 96

narco-economies, 47, 54, 161n2, 172, 174–78; increasing power of organized crime organizations, 132; narco-state interests, 157, 169, 170, 175; narco-state terror, 171. *See also* capitalism
national security: and displacement of Indigenous human rights issues, 8; discourse, 8; Indigenous dispossession, 4; state apparatuses, 9. *See also* capitalism; settler colonialism/states
National Coordination of Widow of Guatemala (CONAVIGUA), 16, 193, 194, 202, 204
National Union of Guatemalan Women (UNAMG), 16, 100, 193, 194, 195, 203
Necropower, 214, 214n1
Neoliberalism, 131, 180; and multicriminalism, 9, 132; and multiculturalism, 8. *See also* capitalism
Nichols, Robert, 49, 49n6; carceral system, 49
Nicolás Ruiz (Chiapas, Mexico), 33

Obama, Barack H.: policies of removal, deportation, and detention, 222
Operation Streamline, 13
Organization of American States (OAS), 12, 221, 225

Permanent People's Tribunal (1983, *Tribunal Permanente de los Pueblos*), 16, 105, 185, 188–92, 205; collective and intersectional framing, 196; conclusion of jury, 192; does not address the structural continuum of violence ,196; gender blind, 185; genocide noted, 196; linking of racism, class, and genocide, 196; sexual violence naturalized and rendered invisible, 185, 189, 192. *See also* First Tribunal of Consciousness Against Sexual Violence Toward Women (2010)
Plácido, Apolonia (Na'savi), 77, 87–89; the aggrieved, 87–88; intimidating threats against, 88; extortion phone call from *Los Rojos*, 89; fear for her security, 89; challenge to male authority in CRAC-PC, 94
Policía Comunitaria (Community Police; Guerrero, Mexico), 74–76, 79, 80–81, 82–85, 93, 94; debate on priority of security over justice, 93; declining influence, 88; internal fragmentation, 81; internal gender dynamics, 93; struggles for autonomy, 76. *See also promotoras de justicia; Coordinadora Regional de Autoridades Comunitarias*
Positionality, 36, 39, 126, 134, 162, 165, 200; importance of the politics of location, 133
Primer Encuentro Internacional, Politico, Artístico, Deportivo y Cultural de Mujeres que Luchan (First International Political, Artistic, Sport, and Cultural Meeting of Women who Struggle), 158; inversion of gender roles, 159
prisonization/detention, 43, 48; and political anatomy, 43; and war on drugs, 43; carceral system, 49; community in prison, 50, 67; and cultures of death, 62; as violent form of acculturation, 43; carceral gulags, 216–18; incarceration of Indigenous women, 43–73; prison as colonial enclave, 43–73; prisoners of statistics, 47; prisonization defined, 43n2; settler carceral militarism, 217; Texas as an open-air prison, 217. *See also* Atlacholoaya Social Readapatation Center; *Colectiva Editorial de la Sombra*; criminalization; violence; war on drugs (Mexico)

system, 120; settler-colonial myth,
213; settler-colonial neoliberal state,
132; settler-colonial political economy,
132; settler-generated pandemics, 250;
settler juridical dehumanization, 215.
See also capitalism; violence
Sharp, Ellen Jane, 144–46; local security
committees as vigilantes, 145. *See also*
Burrell, Jennifer
Sieder, Rachel, ix, 9, 16, 50n7–8, 75, 78,
131, 145–46; power of the counterinsurgency state, 145
Simpson, Audra, 11, 184
Slavery, 4, 16, 120; sexual and domestic
slavery, 16, 100–102, 107, 110, 116, 120,
122, 186, 188, 193, 200, 205. *See also*
labor exploitation
social justice, 4, 20, 31, 34, 67, 204, 212,
218, 228. *See also* justice
soveryempty, 209–41. *See also* Tamez,
Margo; Tamez, Eloisa García
state as a *patron*, the, 167
stolen generations (Indigenous boarding
schools), 36
Sudbury, Julia, 47; U.S. prisons as global
model, 47. *See also* criminalization of
Indigenous peoples; prisonization
Suzack, Cherul, 10

Tamez, Eloisa García (Lipan Apache), 213,
218, 220, 235, 236; *Tamez v. Chertoff*,
235, 239; *Chertoff v. Tamez*, 235. *See
also* Tamez, Margo
Tehuacán (Mexican carbonated water),
55, 55n11; used in torture (*tehuacanazo*), 55n11
Tepoztlán (Morelos, Mexico), 7, 8, 9, 171
Texans United for Families, 33
Theidon, Kimberly, 10
time of "pure suffering" (*mosojantel/bal-
dio*), the, 166. *See also* settler colonial-
ism/states; violence

Trump, Donald J., 14, 35, 129, 130, 148,
149, 246, 247; criminalization of
migrants by, 247. *See also* Remain in
Mexico policy

unauthorized entry: first unauthorized
entry, misdemeanor, 13; felony entry,
13
U.N. Convention on the Prevention and
Punishment of the Crime of Genocide, 192. *See also* femicide; genocide;
violence
Under the Guamuchil's Shadow (documentary), 59
*Unión Nacional de Mujeres Guatemalte-
cas* (UNAMG, National Union of
Guatemalan Women), 100, 193

victimization of Indigenous peoples,
particularly women, 4, 11. *See also*
criminalization; femicide; genocide;
violence
violence: accumulated gendered violence, 144–46; and accumulation
of harm, 90; and assimilation, 150;
and capitalist depravations, 27; and
collective pain, 40, 166; and collective
repression, 17; and femicide, 81; and
health, 78; and insecurities, 93; and
inseparability of public and private
forms, 126, 130, 132; and inseparability
of state and nonstate actors, 126, 130,
132; and production of pain, trauma,
and fear, 9; as being "dragged in", 90,
91, 93; as collective harm, 16; brutal-
ization, 29; by male soldiers against
women, 81; collective vulnerability, 36;
complexity in understanding "violence against women", 20; continuum
of, 76, 77; criminalization, 43; death,
17; destruction of property, 17, 78;
different forms of elimination, 184;